Islamic Thought

'*Islamic Thought*' is ideal for anyone who wants to understand more about Muslim beliefs and the Islamic faith.' *Oliver Leaman, University of Kentucky, USA*

Islamic Thought is a fresh and contemporary introduction to the philosophies and doctrines of Islam. Abdullah Saeed, a distinguished Muslim scholar, traces the development of religious knowledge in Islam, from the pre-modern to the modern period. The book focuses on Muslim thought, as well as the development, production and transmission of religious knowledge, and the trends, schools and movements which have contributed to the production of this knowledge.

Key topics in Islamic culture are explored, including the development of the Islamic intellectual tradition, the two foundation texts, the Qur'an and hadith, legal thought, theological thought, mystical thought, Islamic art, philosophical thought, political thought, and renewal, reform and rethinking today. In the face of changes in Islamic law, and the influence of Western societies, as well as developments in gender rights, human rights and globalization, and in reaction to contemporary social and political events, Muslim beliefs are changing and adapting. Through this rich and varied discussion, Saeed presents a fascinating depiction of one of the world's major living religions.

Islamic Thought is essential reading for students beginning the study of Islam but will also interest anyone seeking to learn more about one of the world's great religions.

Abdullah Saeed is the Sultan of Oman Professor of Arab and Islamic Studies, and the Director of the Centre for the Study of Contemporary Islam at the University of Melbourne, Australia. He has written widely on Islam and contemporary Muslim issues and is the author and editor of a number of books, including *Interpreting the Qur'an* (2006), *Approaches to the Qur'an in Contemporary Indonesia* (editor, 2005), *Freedom of Religion, Apostasy and Islam* (co-author 2004), *Islam and Political Legitimacy* (co-editor 2004), *Islam in Australia* (2003) and *Islamic Banking and Interest* (1996).

Islamic Thought

An introduction

Abdullah Saeed

LONDON AND NEW YORK

First published 2006
by Routledge
2 Park Square, Milton Park, Abingdon, Oxon OX14 4RN

Simultaneously published in the USA and Canada
by Routledge
270 Madison Ave, New York, NY 10016

Reprinted 2007

Routledge is an imprint of the Taylor & Francis Group, an informa business

Typeset in Sabon by Keystroke, 28 High Street, Tettenhall, Wolverhampton
Printed and bound in Great Britain by Antony Rowe Ltd, Chippenham, Wiltshire

British Library Cataloguing in Publication Data
A catalogue record for this book is available from the British Library

Library of Congress Cataloging in Publication Data
A catalog record for this book has been requested

ISBN 10: 0–415–36408–6 (hbk)
ISBN 10: 0–415–36409–4 (pbk)
ISBN 10: 0–203–01524–X (ebk)

ISBN 13: 978–0–415–36408–9 (hbk)
ISBN 13: 978–0–415–36409–6 (pbk)
ISBN 13: 978–0–203–01524–7 (ebk)

Contents

Introduction

This book is primarily aimed at undergraduate students in courses connected with Islam, Muslim societies, Islamic thought and religious studies as well as a general readership. It should be seen as an introduction to Islamic thought. It does not focus on one single aspect of thought; instead, it deals with a range of areas of Islamic thought from the foundation texts to law, theology, philosophy, politics, art and mysticism as well as key trends of Islamic thought in both the pre-modern and modern periods. This book is not a history of Islam, Islamic culture or Islamic civilization. Its primary focus is on Muslim doctrines, the development, production and transmission of religious knowledge, and the key trends, schools and movements that have contributed to the production of this knowledge.

Islam, like any other religion, is much more than just doctrines and religious knowledge. But understanding the doctrinal and religious knowledge background will help the reader understand other aspects, such as institutions specific to Islam, how Islam was lived in the past and how its adherents practise it in the present.

Because of the way the book is structured, it was always difficult to avoid some repetition. Instead of eliminating such minor repetitions completely, I decided to leave them as they are. Since areas of Islamic thought are connected to each other, any attempt to draw a line between one area and another, for instance between the Qur'an and law, would ultimately fail. Similarly because for each area of Islamic thought covered in the book I have provided in each chapter an overview of the development of the area, from the earliest times of Islam to the modern period, the last two chapters might seem somewhat unnecessary. However, I believe that the last two chapters in fact help us to understand modern developments in Islamic thought in general and to contextualize many debates associated with Islamic thought today.

In dealing with the topics covered I have tried my best to remain as neutral as possible, making comments as fairly as possible in order to represent the complexities associated with the issues covered. But such neutrality is often difficult as I am bound to bring into the book how I see the world. My biases therefore creep into the text on a number of issues. Despite the book's shortcomings, I do hope this book will be an accessible guide to the extremely rich and diverse tradition of Islamic thought.

I have tried to make the ideas presented as accessible as I could, avoiding unfamiliar language as far as possible. Where such terms are used I have tried to provide the translation or the meaning of the term. At the end, I have also provided a glossary for easy reference and a bibliography. Where relevant, timelines, brief explanation of concepts and summaries of key points and texts are provided in text boxes, particularly in the earlier chapters.

Transliteration

For transliteration of Arabic terms, given this book is primarily meant for non-specialists, I have adopted a simple system. I have avoided the use of macrons (for example ū, ī or ā) or dots below certain letters. I have also avoided the use of the symbol ' for *'ayn* at the beginning of a word but used it where that occurs in the middle (for instance *shari'a*). Similarly, where the *hamza* occurs at the beginning of a word, I have avoided using the symbol ' but where it occurs in the middle, I have generally used it (for instance, Qur'an). The *h* indicating a *ta' marbuta* is also dropped throughout the book.

Dates

Where the text refers to dates, in general, I have provided two dates as follows: 1/622. The first date '1' refers to the year in the Islamic calendar and the second '622' refers to the year in Common Era (CE). For the twentieth century, I have given not the Islamic dates but CE only (for example, 1930). In order to make clear when a person lived, for the key people mentioned in the book, I have provided the year of death, for example: Muhammad (d. 11/632).

Chapter outline

Chapter 1 forms the basic context for the remainder of the book. It examines the fundamental teachings of the Prophet Muhammad, the development of religious knowledge and the social and political contexts that shaped the Islamic intellectual tradition. It depicts the key centres of learning with particular reference to higher education institutions and the patrons and scholars who founded them and fostered their development.

Chapter 2 explores the first primary foundation text, the Qur'an. In particular it addresses issues such as the Qur'an as revelation or text; a brief overview of the history of the text; approaches to understanding the Qur'an and its interpretation; and the centrality of the Qur'an in Muslim life and practice.

Chapter 3 examines the development of the concept of Sunna (the normative behaviour of the Prophet Muhammad); approaches to the documentation and understanding of Sunna (in hadith); the centrality of the hadith in Muslim life and practice; and modern debates on the authenticity of hadith and Muslim responses.

Chapter 4 explores the notions of *shari'a* and *fiqh*. It also examines how law is 'constructed' in the juristic schools, highlighting some of the key principles of jurisprudence (*usul al-fiqh*). It includes sections on Islamic law in the colonial period, on the debate on law, shari'a and Islamization, and on the reform of law today.

Chapter 5 is devoted to Islamic theology (*kalam*) and its place within the Islamic intellectual tradition. It discusses theological trends and their central ideas as well as the decline of early groups such as the Mu'tazilis and the gradual increase in the influence of the Ash'aris, moving on to modern developments.

Chapter 6 approaches Sufism historically by tracing the origins and development of Sufism and explaining the Sufi path. It includes key Sufi orders and their characteristics, and concludes by looking at Sufism today.

Chapter 7 provides an introduction to some key aspects of Islamic artistic expression and the debates on what is considered Islamic art and what is acceptable or not islamically.

Chapter 8 traces the Muslim interest in philosophy and the lively context in which this interest arose and developed. This chapter includes some key philosophical contributions by Muslim philosophers, both classical and modern.

Chapter 9 deals with Muslim political thought. It includes the early Khariji, Sunni and Shi'i theories of the imamate and the caliphate, and summarizes the concepts of governance and statecraft of several thinkers. Included in the chapter are also some important contemporary debates on concepts such as state and citizenship among Muslims.

Chapter 10 is about renewal and reform in Islam and Muslim modernism. The chapter describes key Islamic trends or movements that appeared from the eighteenth to the twentieth centuries.

The Epilogue summarizes several key trends in Islamic thought today. It focuses on six broad trends which seem to be the most dominant.

Acknowledgements

I would like to thank a number of colleagues, friends and others for contributing significantly to the development and writing of this book. In particular I would like to thank Rachel Woodlock, who assisted me in the research for the book as well as reading the draft manuscript very thoroughly and polishing it; and Andy Fuller, Redha Ameur, Imran Lum, Anisa Buckley and Eeqbal Hassim, who assisted me in the research for the book and contributed significantly to it. Any errors, omissions and problems in the book are of course mine.

I thank Lesley Riddle for her encouragement to write the book, Andrew Rippin for his comments on the first draft, Gemma Dunn for editorial support, Donna Williams for her critical reading of the book and John Banks for copyediting the book. I also thank my wife, Rasheeda, and my son, Isaam, for their wonderful support throughout the project.

Chapter 1

Transmission of religious knowledge and Islamic thought

This chapter introduces the basic teachings of Islam and how its body of knowledge has been transmitted from the earliest Muslims. The main topics addressed are the essential teachings of the Prophet Muhammad and the inception and growth of Islamic educational institutions.[1]

Muhammad's life: key events

570: Birth of Muhammad in Mecca as an orphan

576: Muhammad's mother dies

595: Muhammad marries Khadija

610: Muhammad receives his first revelation from God

615: Because of the persecution of his followers by Meccans, Muhammad asks his followers to flee to Abyssinia (which was ruled by a Christian king)

619: Khadija, the Prophet's wife, dies

622: Muhammad and his followers migrate to Medina. Beginning of Islamic calendar

624: First battle between Muslims in Medina and their opponents of Mecca in which the Meccans were defeated (Battle of Badr)

632: Muhammad dies

The emergence of Islam was deeply connected to the history of its birthplace. In the early seventh century of the Common Era (CE), Mecca was a rather marginal town outside the influence of the two powerful empires of the time: the largely Christian Byzantine Empire and the predominantly Zoroastrian Sassanid Empire, both situated to the north of Arabia.

The people of Mecca mostly belonged to the Quraysh tribe. As there was no ruler or formal state structures, the town was governed through a consultative process administered by the elders and chiefs. Economically, life in Mecca and its surrounding regions was difficult. The land was generally arid and there was no agriculture. Many Meccans relied on trade and the movement of goods using transport by camel (caravans) for their livelihood. Education was limited to the basic skills necessary for survival, such as the use of armaments (swords and arrows) and the riding of camels and horses. Only a few people were literate, but that did not prevent the Meccans from having a particular love of their language, Arabic. Poetry and poets were revered, and expression in beautiful language was considered the pinnacle of intellectual activity. According to traditional accounts, several famous poems were displayed in important places like the Ka'ba, a cube-shaped building in Mecca that served as a major point of pilgrimage for the pre-Islamic Arabs and for Muslims as well later.

Mecca

Mecca is the holiest city for Muslims. It is where the Ka'ba (a cubical building surrounded today by the Sacred Mosque) is, and it is towards the Ka'ba that Muslims turn every day, at least five times a day in their prayers. Muslims believe that the Ka'ba was built by the Prophet Abraham and his son Ishmael as a place of worship of the One God and a site of pilgrimage. The beginning of Mecca, according to Muslim belief, therefore goes back to the time of Abraham. According to tradition, it is through the lineage of Ishmael that the Prophet Muhammad comes. It was because of pilgrimage by Arabs and being a trading post that Mecca became a town of significance from around the fifth century CE.

Muhammad, the Prophet of Islam, was born in Mecca in approximately 570 CE. His father Abd Allah died before he was born and his mother Amina died during his early childhood, leaving the young boy an orphan to be cared for by relatives. In his twenties, he married Khadija, a wealthy widow, with whom he had several children. He worked in his wife's business and lived an unremarkable life until the age of forty. Unlike other Meccans, Muhammad liked to spend time apart for reflection and meditation, often in a cave outside Mecca. Muslim tradition holds that during one of these retreats he experienced his first 'revelation' from God, in approximately 610 CE.

Initially, he was not sure what to make of the experience of receiving revelation (divine messages in the Arabic language). After his initial doubts passed, however, he began to receive further divine messages. Muhammad began teaching them to his close friends and family and, after some time, to the wider Meccan community. His original message was that Meccans should accept that there is only one God, the creator and sustainer of everything, who had sent Muhammad as a messenger. These early revelations also emphasized that the Meccan people needed to care for the needy and disadvantaged. The Meccans believed in the existence of a higher god and a number of lesser gods, many of which were placed in the sanctuary Ka'ba. For them the idea of believing only in 'one god' which Muhammad was preaching was unacceptable.

Six pillars of faith: essential beliefs of a Muslim

- Belief in God (Allah)
- Belief in the angels
- Belief in the revealed books
- Belief in the messengers (prophets)
- Belief in the resurrection and the events of the Day of Judgement
- Belief in the predestination of all things and events (qada) and God's decree

Five pillars of Islam: essential practices of a Muslim

- To testify that none has the right to be worshipped but God (Allah) and Muhammad is God's messenger
- To offer the five compulsory prayers (salat)
- To pay the obligatory charity (zakat)
- To perform pilgrimage to Mecca (hajj)
- To fast during the month of Ramadan

Most Meccans were sceptical of Muhammad's claims and refused to accept his teachings. However, a number of Muhammad's relatives and close friends and some of the marginalized inhabitants of Mecca accepted his call and followed him. At the same time as some were coming to accept his teachings, opposition grew, and those with vested power interests in Mecca, who felt challenged by Muhammad's social justice tied to radical monotheism, began to put obstacles in his way. They punished his followers, particularly slaves and women. Gradually, the persecution in Mecca intensified. As a result,

Muhammad instructed his small group of followers to flee the town and seek the protection of the Negus, the Christian ruler of Abyssinia (in modern-day Ethiopia). These Muslims, whose number was approximately eighty, left for Abyssinia secretly and in small groups in 615 CE. It was under the protection of the Negus that the first Muslim migrant community was able to practise its religion freely. Despite the efforts of the Meccan leaders to have the Muslims forcibly returned to Mecca, the Negus refused to comply, and gave the Muslims permission to live and practise their new religion freely under his protection.

The Islamic calendar

The Islamic calendar is a lunar calendar. It contains 12 months (some of 29 days and others 30 days) that are based on the motion of the moon. This book and other works on Islam often give dates in the style 1/622. This means Year 1 of the Islamic calendar is equivalent to Year 622 in the Gregorian calendar (which is based on the motion of the sun). The Islamic year is therefore shorter than the Gregorian year, so that there is no exact equivalence between Islamic and Gregorian year numbering, and in successive years, Islamic months and festivals occur at different dates in the Gregorian calendar. Today, many Muslims use the Islamic calendar for religious purposes but for civil purposes they often use the Gregorian calendar. Some Western books use the style AH (Anno Hegirae) for Islamic dates.

Muhammad continued to preach to the people of Mecca and others nearby without much success. However, he managed to win over to his teachings a large number of people from Yathrib, a town to the north of Mecca. These new converts promised to protect and support the Prophet if he were to leave Mecca and migrate to Yathrib, which came to be known as Medina, from a phrase meaning 'city of the Prophet'. In 622 CE (the date at which the Islamic calendar, also called '*hijri* calendar', begins), Muhammad migrated to Medina, where he was joined by many of his Meccan followers. The Meccan and Medinan Muslims together formed the Muslim community, away from the persecution of Meccans. Medina thus became the base for Islam and it was from there that Islam began to spread widely throughout Arabia. By the time he died in 11/632, the Prophet had established a 'state' based in Medina and much of Arabia was under the control of the Muslims of Medina. At the time of the Prophet's death, Muslim tradition holds, his followers numbered over one hundred thousand.

The expansion of Muslim rule in the first century of Islam

632: Prophet Muhammad dies; a large part of Arabia is under Muslim control or allied with Muslims

633: Muslims begin conquest of Iraq

634: Muslims begin conquest of Syria

637: Fall of Sassanid (Persian) empire to Muslims

638: Fall of Jerusalem to Muslims

642: Fall of Alexandria (Egypt) to Muslims

705: Muslims control Central Asia

711: Muslims begin conquest of Spain

732: Christians (Franks) withstand the advance of Muslims into France.

Early transmission of religious knowledge

Muslim religious knowledge was first imparted via the Qur'an (the divine messages the Prophet received and which were put together in the form of a book shortly after the death of the Prophet) and its interpretations. It seems to have been common for the Prophet to expound the meaning of verses of the Qur'an to his immediate followers, who were known as 'Companions' (sahaba).[2] His interpretation of the Qur'an was ad hoc and depended entirely on circumstances. His practice seems to have been simply to recite to those present what he had received as revelation, and to give an interpretation only when his followers did not understand.

One of the early difficulties for the Companions was to comprehend some of the terms and expressions in the Qur'an. A second difficulty for the Companions was in understanding some of the historical references in the Qur'an. Interest in such references, particularly to stories of the earlier prophets (such as Noah, Abraham and Moses) and nations of the past, increased further when younger Companions began to elaborate on the Qur'an after the death of Prophet Muhammad. Some Companions approached local Jews and Christians – known as 'people of the Book' (ahl al-kitab)[3] – and asked them about pre-Islamic events and stories. A number of Jewish converts to Islam, such as Abd Allah b. Sallam (d. 43/663), actively passed on biblical knowledge to the Companions. In the post-prophetic period, several Companions engaged in this on a much greater scale with converts to Islam from the 'people of the Book'.

The growing body of hadith – traditions about the sayings and activities of Prophet Muhammad – also attracted the interest of the Companions and the following generation of Muslims, known as the 'Successors' (*tabi'un*).[4] This interest in hadith led in the first/seventh and second/eighth centuries to the emergence of a group of 'hadith collectors'. These people travelled from town to town in search of hadith and with them knowledge of Islam spread widely. In this process, the texts and narrators of hadith were identified and finally recorded in writing in the first three centuries after the death of the Prophet.

Political and religious tensions and the emergence of key trends

Key early Muslim trends

Kharijis: those who rebelled against the fourth caliph Ali and remained hostile to the Umayyads

Shi'a (or *Shi'is*): sided with Ali and elevated him and the family of the Prophet

Qadaris: believed in human freedom

Jabris: believed in predestination (opposite of Qadaris)

Murji'is: those who believed that it is not up to human beings to determine the fate of Muslims who commit grave sins; their judgement is left to God

Mu'tazilis: intellectual descendants of Qadaris; believed in human freedom and adopted a particularly strict version of monotheism

Sunnis: mainstream Muslims who followed the path of Sunna and accepted a middle ground between the Qadaris and the Jabris on human freedom as well as between the Shi'a and the Kharijis

Sufis: emphasized the spiritual dimension of Islam.

The first thirty years after the death of the Prophet (11–41/632–661) was a period of social and political tension within the body politic of the Muslim community. Problems among Muslims were not simply about political leadership but also about what and who represented religious authority. Some Muslims wanted to remain faithful to the letter and spirit of the religion and avoid debilitating disputes in the community by remaining politically neutral. Others took sides, which escalated into arguments over who was or was not a true Muslim. In fact, binaries of this nature were among the earliest questions posed in Muslim theological discourses in the first century of Islamic history, and many were to become key questions of Islamic theology.

Community upheaval continued in the Umayyad period (41–132/661–750). Several groups with diverse theological or religio-political orientations emerged. Among these were the Kharijis (*khawarij*), the Shi'a, the Qadaris (*qadariyya*), the Mu'tazilis (*mu'tazila*), the Jabris (*jabriyya*) and the Murji'is (*murji'a*).

Kharijis

The Kharijis, the earliest of these groups, emerged even before the establishment of the Umayyad rule in 41/661. They began in the aftermath of the Battle of Siffin in 37/657, which had brought the fourth caliph, Ali b. Abi Talib (d. 40/661), into war with the Syrian governor Mu'awiya b. Abi Sufyan (d. 60/680).[5] The Kharijis believed that by engaging in war against one another and by committing grave sins, Muslims on both sides of this war became apostates or unbelievers. The Kharijis also believed that any Muslim, regardless of ethnic background or social status, could become the political leader of the Muslims simply on the basis of their religious virtue and refusal to compromise.[6] They also believed that Muslims should rebel against any unjust ruler. They initiated heated debates on notions of 'Muslim', 'believer', 'disbeliever' and 'idolater'.

Shi'a

The Shi'a, whose name is drawn from *shi'at* Ali (partisans of Ali), believed that in political succession the family of the Prophet should be given priority over any other Muslim. They argued that Ali, the Prophet's cousin and son-in-law, should have been his immediate political successor. All political leadership of the community should thus have remained within the Prophet's family. From this basic position the Shi'a developed a distinctive theological system over the first three centuries of Islam.

Murji'is

Apart from the Kharijis and the Shi'a, other trends of thought emerged during the first and second centuries of Islam. Some of these were refinements of positions adopted by earlier groups on theological or religio-political matters. The Murji'is opposed the Khariji view that anyone who commits a major sin is an unbeliever.[7] The Murji'is were not a distinct group, but rather a broad intellectual trend, which attracted a large number of Muslims. The Murji'is held that a person's belief should be judged not on their actions but on their words. Only by committing the sin of idolatry (*shirk*) did a Muslim cease to be a believer. *Shirk* meant 'associating other beings (or deities) with God'.[8]

The Murji'i position attempted to minimize division within the community. It also kept within the fold of Islam the Companions who were engaged in early military confrontations with one another. The Murji'i position also protected a range of early Muslim groups from being excluded from the fold of religion as it enabled Kharijis, Shi'a and Umayyads all to be defined as believers; it was God alone who would determine their fate on the Day of Judgement.[9]

Jabris

Closely related to the Murji'is in the Umayyad period were the Jabris. According to the Jabris, human beings do not have control over their actions, as they are all predetermined by God. Some Umayyads used religion and religious ideas to justify their decisions on political matters and to legitimize their rule, and supported the views of the Jabris and the Murji'is. This is not surprising, as a number of Umayyad rulers committed heinous crimes including the wanton killing of Muslim subjects. According to the Khariji view, these rulers should have been ousted as unbelievers and unsuitable rulers of the Muslim community. However, in the Jabri view these rulers could not be labelled unbelievers as God had predetermined their actions and so their legitimacy remained relatively untarnished. Thus, in conjunction with their doctrine of predetermination, the Jabris argued that the crimes of the Umayyads were in a sense 'sanctioned' by God.

Qadaris

It is in this context that the Qadaris, who challenged the Jabris and the Umayyads, emerged. The Qadaris believed that God does not pre-ordain what people do: human beings are free and can choose between right and wrong. This conflicted with the interests of the Umayyad rulers. The Qadari position implied that it was possible to challenge and even change the status quo. This radical view, particularly if supported by the Khariji militancy, according to which anyone who committed a major sin was an unbeliever, posed a potentially powerful threat to the Umayyad political elite.

Mu'tazilis

An important development was the rise of the Mu'tazilis, who accepted some of the Qadari views on human freedom. They agreed with some Khariji views, although they modified the definition of 'true believer' and the status of those who commit grave sins. The Mu'tazilis also aimed at preserving the strict monotheism of Islam by emphasizing the uniqueness of God. As part of this, they believed, for example, that the Qur'an (which is considered to be the speech of God) was 'created' by God. For them, if Muslims believe that the Qur'an is the speech of God and therefore co-eternal with God, it will compromise the monotheism the Qur'an and the Prophet taught. Mu'tazili ideas were, in a sense, an extension of earlier theological developments and quite moderate in comparison with some earlier views. However, a number of their ideas – in particular the created status of the Qur'an – led to controversy that has left its mark on the collective psyche of Muslims to the present day.

Sunnis

It was in this theological and religio-political context that Sunnism developed between the first/seventh and the third/ninth centuries, when early debates gave way to a synthesis of sorts. Certain positions adopted by all of the groups referred to above were refined and developed into what may be called the 'mainstream' outlook adopted by the majority of Muslims. This mainstream came to be known as 'people of the Sunna' (*ahl al-sunna* or those who follow the path of the Prophet), or Sunni Islam, which accepted a set of theological creeds[10] and schools of religious law.[11] Coupled with this was the consolidation of a number of scholastic disciplines, including interpretation of the Qur'an, collection of hadith, the principles of jurisprudence and the recording of early Islamic history. Given that Sunnism reflected the position of the majority of Muslims, it came to be seen as 'orthodoxy'.

Sufis

Sufism, or Islamic mysticism, also emerged in the second/eighth century and gradually developed into Sufi orders throughout the Muslim regions. Unlike the other groups, Sufis tended to be more accommodating and inclusive:

> Because Sufis cared only for the heart's inner disposition, they were not conformists who required that true Muslims should everywhere submit to the same outward modes. They tolerated local differences, even between Christianity and Islam.[12]

Other Muslims wanted to differentiate themselves from non-Muslims in order to demonstrate superiority in the authenticity and truth of what they professed. Sufis accommodated diversity and drew in elements from other religious traditions. This, with their popular influence and esoteric views on religion, ensured that they remained the target of non-Sufi scholars. The result was often persecution and even the execution of some leading Sufis.

In this theological fluidity, elements of intolerance among Muslims developed and grew. Sunnis and Shi'as exchanged accusations of extremism and even heresy, and Sufis were labelled deviant by their opponents. Charges and counter-charges of heresy, apostasy and even disbelief (*kufr*) continued in several guises into the modern period, with varying degrees of intensity.

Growth and dissemination of Islamic knowledge

The beginning of Islamic knowledge is rooted in the Qur'an and the traditions of the Prophet. However, Muslims came into contact with a range of civilizations as a result of the spread of Islam in the seventh century CE, and inherited forms of knowledge from philosophy to natural sciences, leading to what some scholars refer to as 'Islamic sciences'. Muslims inherited such knowledge from Persians, Egyptians, Greeks, Indians and even Chinese. In turn Muslims added to them and enriched them and transmitted them to others, including Europeans. Although this book does not deal with all aspects of 'Islamic sciences', it will be useful to show how some Muslim thinkers classified various forms of knowledge. The following is an outline of the classification of knowledge by the Muslim philosopher al-Farabi (d. 339/950):

- Science of Language (with seven sub-divisions)
- Logic (divided into eight parts)
- Mathematical Sciences (including Arithmetic, Geometry, Optics, Astronomy, Music, Weights, and Ingenious Devices)
- Physics or Natural Science (divided into eight parts)
- Metaphysics (divided into three parts)
- Political Science, Jurisprudence and Dialectical Theology[13]

Another famous classification is that of the theologian al-Ghazali (d. 505/1111). He divided sciences into 'religious' and 'intellectual':

1. Religious sciences:

   Science of fundamental principles

   - Science of divine unity
   - Science of prophethood
   - Science of eschatology
   - Science of sources of religious knowledge (such as the Qur'an, Sunna and Consensus as well as Arabic linguistic sciences)

   Science of branches or derived principles

   - Science of people's obligations to God (religious rites and worship)
   - Science of people's obligations to society (transactions and contractual obligations)
   - Science of obligations to one's own soul (moral qualities)

2. Intellectual sciences:

- Mathematics
- Logic
- Physics or the natural sciences
- Sciences of beings beyond nature, or metaphysics (such as ontology, knowledge of divine essence, attributes and activities; knowledge of simple substances like angelic substances; knowledge of the subtle world; science of prophecy).[14]

Although these areas of knowledge were of interest to Muslim scholars throughout much of Islamic history, my interest in this book does not go beyond key areas of what al-Ghazali calls 'religious sciences', as these are most closely associated with the term 'Islamic thought'.

The range of disciplines that accompanied the emergence of distinct schools of thought in the Qur'an and hadith studies, law, theology, philosophy, science and Arabic linguistics and literature saw the development of educational institutions to disseminate teaching and research. By the fifth/eleventh century, the madrasas (seminary, college, Islamic education institution) were emerging as institutions of Islamic learning. The scholars of religion (ulama) became the transmitters of formal Islamic knowledge, and formed an international elite in all parts of the Muslim world. The ulama saw the transmission of knowledge as their foremost duty, given the dangers inherent in the change or loss of authentic teachings with the passage of time. The further each generation moved from the time of the Prophet, the greater the chance of losing the truth. The main task of the ulama was to preserve, transmit and defend religious law – the shari'a – as well as to provide legal decisions and judgements to the populace. They also performed a wide range of other functions, such as administering mosques, schools and orphanages, and serving as diplomats and courtiers.[15]

During the fifth/eleventh and sixth/twelfth centuries, madrasas were established in Iraq and Syria. By the end of the sixth/twelfth century, at least thirty madrasas existed in Damascus and Cairo.[16] Over time, a network of such madrasas spread throughout the length and breadth of the Muslim world.[17] Al-Azhar, the most famous seminary, was founded in Cairo in 361/972 by the Fatimids (297–567/909–1171), a North African Ismaili Shi'i dynasty. It later became a Sunni institution, and the greatest traditional Islamic seminary in the Sunni world.

In the madrasas as well as in other study circles, scholars taught legal and theological subjects, in addition to medicine, literature, mathematics, natural sciences, and philosophy.[18] In some madrasas, certain controversial fields such as theology, logic and philosophy were avoided but were accepted in others. The growth and development of the madrasa system continued and achieved its greatest period during the Ottoman empire. According to Rahman:

From the organizational point of view, the *madrasa* system reached its highest point in the Ottoman Empire where *madrasas* were systematically instituted, endowed and maintained . . . with remarkable administrative skill and efficiency. The ulama were organized in a hierarchy and became almost a caste in the Ottoman society. These traditional seats of learning are still functioning all over the Muslim world outside Turkey.[19]

In madrasas, common texts were often used across regions and became canons for the schools of law. For example, the ulama in Timbuktu (in modern day Mali) used the same books as their counterparts in Morocco and Egypt; the openness to rational sciences on the part of some Sunni and Shi'i Muslims also led to commonality of texts among their ulama.[20]

The ulama used a system of certification called the *ijaza* (licence). Traditionally, licences were given by an individual scholar (as opposed to a *licentia* granted by a university) which enabled his or her students to pass on a body of knowledge received from that scholar.[21] There were several types of ijazas, which were often verbal rather than written. 'What was granted was as much an emblem of a bond to a shaykh [teacher] as a certificate with a fixed value in social relations.'[22]

While the ulama flourished in cities and areas of state power, Sufis reached all parts of the Muslim world, particularly remote areas where kinship and tribal organization were paramount. From the third/ninth century, disciples gathered around certain Sufi shaykhs to follow their 'way' (*tariqa*) – their method for travelling towards direct experiential knowledge of God, sometimes congregating in Sufi hospices. The central ritual of the tariqa was the shaykh's *dhikr* (his or her particular form of devotion for remembering God).

The disciples of Sufi shaykhs were central to the transmission of mystical knowledge and became part of the shaykh's chain of spiritual transmission (*silsila*). Following their initiation, disciples swore an oath of allegiance, received a special cloak, and were taught a special protective prayer. When they completed their training, they received a certificate showing the chain of transmission of spiritual knowledge, from the Prophet to their particular shaykh. From around the seventh/thirteenth century, Sufi groups began to establish specific orders, which differed in their rituals and practices for remembering God. These Sufi orders were pivotal in transmitting mystical knowledge throughout the Muslim world. The great tolerance and flexibility of Sufis has helped them build bridges between Islam and other religious traditions. Also, Sufis played a key role in spreading Islam to remote regions. The firm establishment of Islam in central Asia, Sind and Bengal was due to the Sufis, who also travelled to North Africa, Anatolia and the Balkans.[23]

Ulama in the modern period

During the pre-modern period (before the mid-nineteenth century CE), the social status and position of the ulama, as transmitters of religious knowledge, were based on their multiple roles as scholars, judges and jurists and other key functions in society. As administrators of charitable endowments, they often had substantial economic independence. The ulama controlled the training of students, basing this on a model in which religious disciplines were given priority. The influence of religion in all aspects of life in the society thus confirmed the social role of the ulama. By contrast, in the modern period, the nation state has appropriated many of the key functions that were previously the prerogative of the ulama, often curtailing their power in the process, with varying degrees of success.

Part of this marginalization of the ulama is of their own making. Today, educational curricula for Islamic disciplines in religious seminaries (and increasingly in Islamic 'universities') in many cases do not seem to prepare ulama to deal effectively with modernity, let alone the educational needs of a modern society. Their studies are often regarded as outdated. Consequently, for many Muslims the degrees they confer enjoy little prestige. Those who enrol in Islamic studies in Muslim societies are often seen as people without access to, or the ability to undertake, more 'impressive' disciplines, such as medicine, engineering and the sciences. Those undertaking religious studies may not have had the opportunity to go to a school where they could study modern disciplines. Their only form of education may have been that of the traditional madrasa, where only 'religious' education was available. Such disadvantaged students accessing the free, inadequate education in a traditional madrasa often move on to another marginalized institution, the religious seminary. This prepares them to be religious functionaries who lead the prayers in mosques and teach Qur'an classes. The fortunate ones may find a job in the bureaucracy of a department of religious affairs (to become part of the 'official ulama'). Irrespective of career prospects, many of these ulama are seen to be ill-equipped to deal with the more complex issues of modern life.

In modern nation states where Islamic law is implemented, such as Saudi Arabia and Iran, the 'official' ulama enjoy a relatively important role. However, in countries where the legal system has been secularized or heavily modified, that role is limited and their importance is minimal. The primary role given to ulama in the legal systems of most modern Muslim nation states is administering family law, which is still enforced (at least in part) in such states. Matters such as marriage, divorce, inheritance and, in some cases, child custody fall within the scope of family law. Some Muslim states, for instance Malaysia, have adopted a system of shari'a courts whose jurisdiction is strictly defined as falling within the area of family law. Besides this, the ulama also administer so-called 'Islamic affairs'. This covers mosque management, imams, celebration of important religious festivals, some religious education in schools and the issuing of fatwas requested by the state. The gradual increase in islamization witnessed in the late twentieth and early twenty-first centuries may again increase the role and importance of the ulama.[24]

Chapter 2

The Qur'an
The primary foundation text

This chapter[1] provides an overview of issues surrounding the Qur'an, the central text of Islam. For Muslims, the Qur'an is the literal word of God received verbatim by the Prophet Muhammad in his native Arabic tongue,[2] who passed it on to his followers. It is the most sacred of religious texts for Muslims. The Qur'an is the foundation of Islam and the primary source of guidance for Muslims in all aspects of life, whether spiritual, legal, moral, political, economic or social.

It was during one of his cave retreats that Muhammad experienced his first revelation, in 610 CE. Muhammad reportedly heard a voice instructing him to 'read'. Three times the voice repeated its command, with Muhammad replying 'I cannot read'. Finally, the voice said:

> Read, in the name of your Lord who created: created the human being of clotted blood. Read, for your Lord is most generous, the one who taught the use of the pen, taught the human being what he did not know.[3]

According to Muslim tradition, these verses were the first of many revelations that Prophet Muhammad received over the twenty-two years of his prophetic mission (610–632 CE). In the Qur'an as we have it today, the verses are the first five verses of the ninety-sixth chapter, commonly known as 'The Clot' or 'Read!'

The Qur'an as revelation

The Arabic term *wahy* means revelation or inspiration. In its more technical sense, wahy is that which God communicates to His prophets and messengers. It can also mean the scripture revealed to particular prophets, such as the Torah given to Moses, the Gospel of Jesus and the Qur'an sent to Muhammad.

Many verses in the Qur'an have a direct bearing on the concept of wahy, whether that received by Prophet Muhammad or by other prophetic figures such as Abraham. The Qur'an uses the word wahy and its variants on a number of occasions spanning both the Meccan (610–22 CE) and Medinan (622–32 CE) periods. The terms are used often in the sense of conveying a message from God to both human beings and other creatures, indicating that wahy is not limited to a relationship between God and His prophets alone. In fact, there are several forms of wahy as inspiration mentioned in the Qur'an: to inanimate objects;[4] to animals;[5] to human beings in general, such as the mother of Moses;[6] to prophets in particular, such as Jesus;[7] and to angels.[8]

The Qur'an gives some explanation of the way in which revelation comes from God to human beings: 'It is not appropriate for a human being that God should speak to him but by inspiration, or from behind a veil, or by sending a messenger to reveal, by divine permission, what is God's will.'[9] The most immediate mode of communication comes directly from God to the person intended, without voice or messenger. The person who receives it 'understands' the message and that it is from God. The second method, 'from behind a veil', means that God speaks to a person through a liminal medium such as a vision or a dream. The best example of this is when God spoke to Moses 'from behind' the burning bush.[10] The third method, 'by sending a messenger' (understood to be an angel), is considered the surest and clearest form of revelation, if the least direct. Many Muslim theologians believe this was the most common form of revelatory experience the Prophet had in receiving the Qur'an. For them, the angel brought the word of God to the Prophet verbatim, without any alteration or change, in a language the Prophet understood, his native Arabic tongue.[11]

As to any human element in the production of the Qur'an, the text itself stresses that the Prophet was required only to receive the sacred text and that he had no authority to change it.[12] The Qur'an strongly denies that it is the speech or ideas of the Prophet or, indeed, of any other person.[13] It also asserts that the Arabic revelation came directly from God to protect it from human-induced errors or inaccuracies. The Qur'an declares, 'Do they not consider the Qur'an – were it from other than God, they would have found much contradiction in it.'[14] The angel was entrusted with a direct message in Arabic, not simply with meanings and ideas. It was intended to be immediately comprehensible to ordinary people. The Qur'an says: 'This is a revelation from the Lord of all worlds: the faithful spirit [the angel] brought it down to your heart, that you may be a herald in clear Arabic speech.'[15]

For the Prophet, the revelations he received were undoubtedly real, even though he could explain the modality of both the revelation and the experience only in metaphorical terms. For example, a hadith records that the Prophet described receiving revelation as like the 'ringing of a bell'.[16] Despite being unable to give a precise description of the experience, the Prophet was firm in his view that the context of revelation was objective, not subjective. His experiences as reported in hadith of seeing the intermediary (the angel), at times hearing the angelic voice and comprehending what was said, all indicate the objective reality of the content of the revelation for him.[17]

The mainstream Muslim view of revelation asserts that the *language* of revelation is an essential aspect of its divine content. The words of the Qur'an are equivalent to the verbal revelation the Prophet himself received. When the Qur'an says that God says, speaks or commands, these terms are to be taken literally by Muslims. Via the intermediary, the Prophet receives this Arabic communication and transmits it verbatim to his followers, who in turn do the same for the generations succeeding them. The Qur'an is thus considered a faithful transmission of a verbally revealed message in its original format.

For Muslims, the Qur'an was and is primarily an oral and aural experience. The Arabs of seventh-century CE Hijaz (in Arabia) were, on the whole, an 'unlettered' people who had received no previous scripture or guidance. Nevertheless, the art of poetry and its recitation was highly prized in Arabic culture. When Muhammad began communicating verses of the Qur'an, it had a compelling effect on his audience. Even today, the experience of reciting the Qur'an is pervasive in Muslim cultures:

> The sound of Qur'anic recitation can move people to tears, from Umar, the powerful second Caliph of Islam, to the average farmer, villager, or townsman of today, including those who may not be particularly observant or religious in temperament.[18]

Despite its oral and aural nature, several verses indicate that, even during the lifetime of the Prophet, the Qur'an was envisioned as a scripture or book like earlier scriptures given to prophets before Muhammad.[19] The Qur'an uses the word *kitab* (book) to refer to itself dozens of times in various contexts. Even though the text was compiled into book format only after the death of the Prophet, clearly the Qur'an considered itself to be scripture: 'Recite what has been revealed to you of the Book of your Lord. No one can change the words of God';[20] and 'We have sent down a Book to you, wherein is your reminder.'[21]

In the modern period, a number of Muslim scholars have attempted to rethink the commonly accepted theory of revelation in Islamic theology. The Pakistani-American scholar Fazlur Rahman (d. 1988) believed that early Muslim theologians did not have the intellectual capacity to confront the issue of the close relationship between the Prophet and the Qur'an.[22] Rahman felt it was important to emphasize the role of the Prophet in the matrix of revelation, i.e. the close connection between the Qur'an as word of God, the Prophet and his mission, and the socio-historical context in which the Qur'an was revealed. However, Rahman did not argue that the Qur'an was the word of the Prophet; his concern was the lack of emphasis, in the widely accepted view of revelation, on the close relationship between the Qur'an and the socio-historical context of the revelation.[23] This relationship, if emphasized, would allow Muslim scholars to reinterpret some sections of the Qur'an in the light of contemporary realities and challenges, in his view.

The compilation of the Qur'an

The concept of the Qur'an as a book or scripture was well established before the Prophet's death in 11/632.[24] Being from an oral culture, the Prophet and a large number of his followers had retained the Qur'an by memory. Some had written down verses on various materials. However, it was not put together or compiled into a single volume at that stage. Immediately after the death of the Prophet, a number of his Companions began to think about 'collecting' all the parts of the Qur'an into one volume to safeguard it against corruption and distortion. According to Muslim tradition, those entrusted with the task were a committee of senior Companions who were among those most closely associated with the Qur'an during the time of the Prophet. It was completed during the reign of the third successor to the Prophet, his son-in-law Uthman b. Affan (d. 35/656).

A tradition of the Prophet records that the Qur'an was revealed to him in seven 'modes' (understood to be seven dialects of Arabic or ways of reading). Although the precise details of the modes are not known, there is some indication in the hadith that the Prophet permitted some flexibility in the Companions' recitation of certain words or verses of the Qur'an. Based on this flexibility, there existed some variations to the way in which certain words of the Qur'an were recited.

At the time of the death of the Prophet, several Companions possessed personal collections of some chapters and verses that differed slightly from what was collected and authenticated under the direction of Uthman. Critics may question whether the collected material that now exists as Qur'anic text represents the totality of what was revealed to the Prophet. For Muslims, the 'codex' (mushaf) of Uthman is the historical, authentic codification of the Qur'anic revelation. Any material excluded by the Companions from the final codified text was not considered part of the Qur'an. As a result, Muslims do not question seriously the authenticity and reliability of the compilation.

The structure of the Qur'an

The Qur'an is roughly the length of the Christian New Testament. It is divided into 114 chapters (sura) of varying length. The first chapter, known as 'The Opening' (al-Fatiha), is very short. It resembles a prayer and comprises seven verses (aya), including the opening invocation. It is the most recited chapter from the Qur'an, as Muslims recite it several times a day as part of their ritual prayers. Throughout the world, most Muslims would be able to recite that particular chapter in the original Arabic. It reads:

> In the name of God, the Benevolent, the Merciful. Praise be to God, Lord of the universe, the Benevolent, the Merciful, Ruler of the Day of Requital. It is You we serve, to You we turn for help. Show us the straight path, the path of those You have favoured, not of those who are objects of anger, nor of those who wander astray.[25]

The second chapter, called 'The Cow' (al-Baqara), is the longest in the Qur'an and comprises 286 verses. The chapters that follow generally become shorter and shorter up to the last, 'The People' (al-Nas), which is one of the shortest in the Qur'an.

Except for the ninth chapter, every chapter begins with the invocation 'In the name of God, the Benevolent, the Merciful' (bismillah al-rahman al-rahim). Many Muslims believe that this phrase constitutes the first verse of each chapter. Others argue that it is not really part of the text of the Qur'an (except where it occurs within the chapter rather than heading it, for example, in the thirtieth verse of the twenty-seventh chapter), but is simply an invocation used to begin a task. The reasoning is that, since Muslims are instructed to begin all praiseworthy tasks by invoking the name of God, and the recitation of the Qur'an is one of the noblest acts a Muslim can perform, it is important to say this phrase before beginning recitation.

For those beginning the study of the Qur'an, topics in the Islamic scripture can appear haphazard. Within long chapters, verses often jump from one subject to another, and often it can be difficult to see links between the topics. Furthermore, content is not chronologically ordered. Muslims believe that the Qur'anic text is arranged in the present format based on the Prophet's instructions. While short chapters were more likely revealed as units, individual verses of many medium and longer chapters may have come at very different times during the twenty-two-year prophetic mission. It is important to note that chapters from the beginning of the Qur'an are not necessarily from early in the Prophet's mission. The earliest revelations are actually at the end of the Qur'anic text as we have it today.

Three tools from traditional Islamic scholarship can provide clues to the timeline of the text. First there is literature describing the occasions of revelation; the events and issues in the Prophet's life marking the reception of a Qur'anic verse or verses, such as after the Battle of Badr (2/624). Unfortunately, only a small percentage of Qur'anic verses have occasions of revelation recorded for them, and even then there are often contradictory accounts in the literature, which makes the dating of large parts of the Qur'an difficult.

Next, there are lists of verses that are referred to as 'abrogated' or 'abrogating'. The 'abrogated' verses are legal verses whose rulings are nullified by other verses (abrogating verses). Most Sunni authorities hold that the Qur'an and Sunna contain verses and teachings that were replaced with different instructions later in the prophetic mission. Some of the abrogated verses still appear in the Qur'an, although their rulings are no longer in force, such as the command to give charity before approaching the Prophet for a private audience.[26] Also, there are some rulings in Islamic law that continue to exist, such as the punishment of stoning for married adulterers, despite the fact that the verses of the Qur'an once reportedly used to support such rulings are no longer extant. However, the issue of abrogation is controversial. There is no consensus on which verses are abrogating or abrogated, and Shi'i scholars (as well as a small number of Sunni authorities) do not fully accept the classical theory of abrogation.

Last, there are lists of Meccan and Medinan chapters. Scholars of the Qur'an drew up lists to divide the chapters into those revealed before the flight of the Prophet to Medina (marking the beginning of the Islamic calendar) and called 'Meccan', and those given afterwards, called 'Medinan'. Most of the chapters from the Meccan period deal with matters such as depicting God as the creator and sustainer of all that exists, how human beings should be grateful to God and how they should relate to Him. The early chapters also often address social justice issues, including the treatment of the poor and disadvantaged. They state that God has bestowed many favours on the people of Mecca and the surrounding regions. The following is an example of one of the earliest Meccan chapters, in which the Prophet is reminded of God's goodwill towards him and which contains an exhortation to help the disadvantaged:

> By the morning, bright, and the night when it is calm, your Lord has not left you [Muhammad], and is not incensed: hereafter will be better for you than what was before; your Lord will surely give to you, and you will be content. Did God not find you orphaned and give shelter? And God found you wandering and gave guidance. And God found you needy and gave sufficiency. So do not oppress the orphan, and do not rebuff the seeker. And tell of the kindness of your Lord.[27]

The Medinan chapters often deal with issues related to community organization, rule and judgement, war and peace and inter-religious relations.

One difficulty in approaching the Qur'an lies in its grammatical structure and its use of multiple pronouns in reference to God. The speaker of the Qur'an, which Muslims believe is none other than God, uses the first person singular: 'and *I* only created sprites and humans for them to serve *Me*';[28] but more often than not the first person plural predominates: '*We* will surely test you with something of fear and hunger'.[29] At times, God is even referred to in the second person: 'It is *You* we serve, to *You* we turn for help',[30] as well as in the third person: '*It* is God, unique'.[31]

The major themes of the Qur'an

The Qur'an deals with many themes but one overarching theme stands out: the relationship of the one God to human beings. All other themes revolve around this central theme.

One God

The Qur'an affirms a monotheistic conception of God. For the polytheists of the Prophet's era, lesser gods functioned as intermediaries between the higher god (*al-ilah* or *allah* 'the God') and themselves. The Qur'an, however, rejected the idea that there are many gods in addition to a higher god. There is only one God, referred to as Allah or by His attributes such as 'the Merciful', 'the Compassionate', 'the Creator', 'the Sustainer', 'the Everlasting', 'the First', 'the Last', 'the Omnipotent', 'the Dispenser of Rewards', 'the Just', 'the Reckoner', or 'the Wise'. Muslim tradition holds that God possesses innumerable names, ninety-nine of which are known. These names, lists of which were compiled from the Qur'anic text, are used widely by Muslims to refer to God.

Spiritual beings

The Qur'an acknowledges there are beings belonging to the spiritual realm, beings beyond our immediate human experience, such as angels. The Qur'an often mentions angels, some of whom have specific functions, such as bringing revelation to prophets or forewarning death. In fact, one of the six 'pillars' of faith in Islam is the belief in angels. The Qur'an says:

> The messenger [Muhammad] believes in what has been sent down to him from his Lord, and so do the believers. Every one believes in God and God's angels, and God's scriptures and God's messengers.[32]

Below angels, who are obedient to God, are other spiritual beings called the *jinn* (sprites). Jinn are believed to be imperceptible beings, created of smokeless fire, which may or may not be obedient to God. There are many references to jinn in the Qur'an, and sometimes they appear paired with human beings. For example, the Qur'an says: 'Even if humans and sprites all gathered together to produce something like this Qur'an, they could not produce anything like it, even if they helped each other.'[33]

Satan as the symbol of evil

The Qur'anic symbol of disobedience to God is the Satan, the archetype of which is also known by the proper name Iblis. Iblis is a creature described in the Qur'an as *jinn* in origin but who somehow came to be associated with angels.[34] In the story of creation, God informed the angels that He wanted to create a human being called Adam. Some of the angels protested that this being would create havoc on earth and shed blood. God rejected their protestations, created Adam and taught him the names of all things, after which He asked the angels to bow down to him. All the angels obeyed God; however, Iblis objected to God's command and argued that he, Iblis, was superior to Adam on account of being created from fire, while Adam was a creature of clay.[35] Iblis was condemned for rebelling against God, but also given a temporary reprieve until the Day of Judgement, at which time he, and those who follow his misguidance, will be punished for their rebellion. Thus, in the Qur'an, the forces of good are represented by God and the forces of evil by Satan.

Creation of human beings and God's guidance through prophets

The creation of human beings is described in various passages: the creation of a single soul and its mate, from whom countless human beings have sprung;[36] the nature of human existence and the cycle of reproduction;[37] and the story of the primordial Adam and his wife (known in tradition as Hawwa or Eve). Both Adam and Eve, according to the Qur'an, were tempted by Satan, removed from the 'Garden', forgiven by God and sent to the mundane world in order to fulfil their divinely appointed destinies.[38] Part of God's promise to Adam and his wife is that their descendents would be sent prophets and messengers with guidance from God.

Names of prophets mentioned in the Qur'an

Adam	Harun (Aaron)
Idris (Enoch)	Da'ud (David)
Nuh (Noah)	Sulayman (Solomon)
Hud (Heber)	Zulkifl (probably Ezekiel)
Salih (Shelah)	Al-Yasa' (Elisha)
Lut (Lot)	Ayyub (Job)
Ibrahim (Abraham)	Yunus (Jonah)
Isma'il (Ishmael)	Zakariyya (Zechariah)
Ishaq (Isaac)	Yahya (John)
Ya'qub (Jacob)	Ilyas (Elijah)
Yusuf (Joseph)	Isa (Jesus)
Shu'ayb (probably Jethro)	Muhammad
Musa (Moses)	

According to Muslim tradition, these prophetic figures number in the hundreds of thousands. However, only twenty-five are mentioned by name in the Qur'an. They include familiar biblical figures such as Adam, Noah, Abraham, Isaac, Jacob, Joseph, Moses, Zechariah, David, Solomon and Jesus. All taught the basic message of belief in the one God, Creator and Sustainer of the universe, and that human beings should recognize this and lead an ethical and moral life.

Attitude to other religions

The Qur'an has a somewhat ambivalent attitude towards the recipients of previous revelations, whom it calls 'people of the Book'. This term refers to those who received divine scriptures, for instance, Jews and Christians. At times it appears harshly critical of the failure of older religious communities (such as the Jews and Christians) to accept the prophethood of Muhammad, and the new guidance given by God.[39] At other times, it affirms the righteous among other faiths: 'The Muslims and the Jews, and the Sabians and the Christians, any who believe in God and the last day and do good will not be in fear and they will not grieve.'[40] The Qur'an censures religious exclusion,[41] but also acknowledges a purpose in the diversity of religions.[42]

Life after death

Those who follow God's path will enter Paradise (*janna*) and those who follow Satan's path will enter Hell (*jahannam*). The life to come is not transient, but everlasting. Descriptions of both Paradise and Hell are included in many chapters, particularly the Meccan ones.

The Qur'an on Paradise

And their [believers'] recompense shall be Paradise, and silken garments, because they were patient. Reclining on raised thrones, they will see there neither the excessive heat of the sun, nor the excessive cold. The shade will be close upon them, and bunches of fruit will hang low within their reach. Vessels of silver and cups of crystal will be passed around amongst them, crystal-clear, made of silver. They will determine the measure of them according to their wishes. They will be given a cup [of wine of paradise] mixed with *zanjabil*, and a fountain called *Salsabil*. And around them will [serve] youths of perpetual [freshness]. If you see them, you would think they are scattered pearls.

When you look there [in Paradise] you will see a delight [that cannot be imagined], and a great dominion. Their garments will be of fine green silk and gold embroidery. They will be adorned with bracelets of silver, and their Lord will give them a pure drink. (Qur'an 76: 12–21)

The Qur'an as a source of law

An important theme of the Qur'an is legal guidance, and related matters, about how the Muslim community should conduct itself. This includes how to worship God through prayer; fasting and pilgrimage; marriage and divorce; the restriction of polygyny; the regulation of slavery; spending money to help the poor and needy; relations between the sexes; children and custody; prohibition of gambling and alcohol; punishment for crimes such as theft, murder, adultery and slander; war and peace; commercial transactions; and inheritance. It also covers moral injunctions such as truthfulness, moderation in behaviour, justice, fairness, forgiveness, honesty, kindness to one's parents, generosity, and the keeping of promises.

Despite their importance, legal injunctions must be placed in perspective. The number of legal verses in the Qur'an ranges from two hundred to five hundred, depending on the definition of the term 'legal'. This is a relatively small portion of the entire text of the Qur'an, which contains approximately 6,300 verses.

How to understand and interpret the Qur'an

Muslim scholars have developed a great number of Qur'anic exegetical (critical explanation) works over the past fourteen hundred years. Some of these rely heavily on the Qur'an and the explanations of the Prophet; others draw on additional sources to expound the meanings of the Qur'an. Some have produced mystical, linguistic, literary, philosophical, theological or legal exegetical works. In the modern period, a rich array of exegetical works has been produced.

The Qur'an is, for Muslims, the revealed word of God. Hence, the exegesis of the Qur'an (tafsir) has emerged as one of the most revered disciplines in Islam. Given that the life of the early Muslims revolved around the Qur'an, one of their earliest concerns was to understand the message of the sacred text.

The beginnings of Qur'anic exegesis (tafsir)

A rudimentary exegetical tradition began during the Prophet Muhammad's time. The Qur'an says that one of the functions of the Prophet was to explain the Qur'an. There is debate among Muslims as to whether the Prophet ever provided explanations for the whole Qur'an. Those who say he did rely on the Qur'anic verse 'And We revealed to you the Reminder [the Qur'an], that you might clarify to people what had been revealed to them, and that they might reflect'.[43]

Little of the Prophet's own exegesis of the Qur'an is recorded, and much of this exists only in the form of what we may call 'practical exegesis', which refers to the Prophet's putting into practice Qur'anic instructions, and which is collected in the hadith. Because of his legacy of actions and deeds, we should see the time of the Prophet as the richest period of exegetical activity through practice.

Even though the Prophet had hundreds of followers (Companions) closely connected with him at the time of his death, only a few reportedly contributed directly to Qur'anic exegesis. They included the first four caliphs, Abu Bakr (d. 13/634), Umar (d. 24/644), Uthman (d. 35/656) and Ali (d. 40/661), as well as A'isha (d. 58/678), one of the Prophet's wives. Other Companions included Abd Allah ibn Mas'ud, who settled in Iraq, Ubay ibn Ka'b in Medina, Abd Allah ibn Abbas in Mecca, and Zayd ibn Thabit in Medina. Of these, the most celebrated is Abd Allah ibn Abbas, who reportedly had a large number of students in Mecca and is known as the 'Interpreter of the Qur'an'. The *tafsir* tradition that developed during the course of the first/ seventh and second/eighth centuries traced its material and inspiration to these teachers.

The Companions who engaged in exegesis had several sources for understanding and interpreting the Qur'an: parts of the Qur'anic text itself that explained other parts; information received from the Prophet, both oral and established practice; and their own understanding of what the Qur'anic text meant. They were also familiar with the language of the Qur'an, the context of the revelation, the Prophet's ways of thinking, and the norms, values and customs of the Arabs, all of which gave them a unique basis for making sense of the Qur'anic text within the overall framework of the emerging 'established practice' of the community. The need for interpretation increased with the second generation of Muslims, known as 'Successors' (*tabi'un*), who were a more diverse group.

Islam expands and diversifies

Diverse groups, traditions and new converts to Islam emerged as Muslims conquered lands and grew in influence. During the first/seventh century, the domain of Islam expanded dramatically to include all of Arabia and a large part of the Middle East and North Africa, lands previously under the Sassanid and Byzantine empires. The Companions were flexible in relating the Qur'an and their experiences with the Prophet to the newly emerging conditions. In this, they appear to have relied on key objectives of the Qur'anic message, such as 'establishing justice'. An instance of this development is the second caliph Umar's rationale for not distributing the lands (in present-day Iraq) that were conquered during his caliphate (13–24/634–44). Unlike the Prophet, Umar refused to distribute the land as booty to warriors who conquered Iraq, arguing that the relevant Qur'anic verses on the distribution of booty in general did not favour such a division of land. In his view, the land should be retained as public property from which the whole community would benefit, not just the warriors. In his interpretation of the relevant Qur'anic texts, he was relying on the general Qur'anic principle of 'justice' and the need to share wealth with the wider community.

Also during the first/seventh century, influences from both the Jewish and Christian traditions (later called *isra'iliyyat*) began to enter the discourse of Qur'anic exegesis via converts to Islam from those traditions. These converts found an eager audience in scholars, storytellers and popular preachers who wanted to fill in details that were often only alluded to in the Qur'anic narratives, such as about Joseph, Moses and Jesus.

Qur'anic exegesis moves from oral to written transmission

There is debate in the literature on Qur'anic scholarship as to whether Qur'anic exegesis was written down in the first/seventh century. While Muslim tradition holds that some written works existed from the mid first/seventh century, the evidence of recent research indicates that they began to emerge at least by the early part of the second/eighth century.[44] The earliest exegesis (going back to the time of the Prophet and the Companions) was transmitted generally orally. Ibn Khaldun (d. 808/1406) suggests that the explanations of the Qur'an 'continued to be transmitted among the early Muslims until knowledge became organized in scholarly disciplines and systematic scholarly works began to be written. At that time, most of these explanations were committed to writing'.[45] The exegetical writings from this early period, where they exist, are not necessarily complete commentaries; rather, they should be seen as the beginning of the documentation of teachings related to Qur'anic exegesis.

It was perhaps natural for Qur'anic exegesis to begin with brief explanatory comments on specific words or phrases of the Qur'an that appeared unclear, difficult or ambiguous. Much of the very early exegesis falls into this category. An example is by Mujahid ibn Jabr (d. 104/722), who belongs to the Meccan tradition of tafsir. Another form of early tafsir was related to the community's interest in legal and ritual matters. Given that a number of Qur'anic verses deal with law and ritual, this must have been an important part of the

Prophet's explanatory task. An example of this early form of exegesis is by Muqatil ibn Sulayman (d. 150/767). In his *Interpretation of Five Hundred Verses (Tafsir khams mi'at aya)* he dealt with several legal topics: prayer, almsgiving, fasting and pilgrimage, marriage and contracts, and punishments related to theft, adultery and alcohol.[46] Towards the end of the second/eighth century exegetical works began to cover the entire Qur'an, from beginning to end. Perhaps the most important figure in this type of exegesis is al-Tabari (d. 310/923).

At this point, two different approaches to exegesis became crystallized – that which emphasized 'tradition' (tradition-based exegesis, *tafsir bi al-ma'thur*) and that which focused on 'reason' (reason-based exegesis, *tafsir bi al-ra'y*). In Sunni Islam, tradition-based exegesis is the most authoritative form of exegesis because it is based on one of the most important sources of religious authority: the Prophet and his Companions who were able to elaborate on the meaning of the Qur'an on the basis of the Prophet's instructions (hadith). Even exegesis by Successors (the second generation of Muslims) is considered as deriving its authority from the Prophet himself, either directly or indirectly.

Some Muslims considered reason-based exegesis unacceptable, because, in their view, the Qur'an prohibited it.[47] It is said that the Prophet Muhammad prohibited reason-based exegesis on the authority of the hadith: 'Whoever explains the Qur'an without knowledge let him take his place in Hell.'[48] There are also reports that the Companions were afraid to interpret the Qur'an on the basis of reason.

Distinct trends and schools emerge

The third/ninth century saw the maturing of distinct schools or trends within Islam, following heated debates among Muslims on religio-political, legal and theological issues. While the seed of many of these trends lay in the mid first/seventh century, it took one to two centuries for them to take form. We cannot talk about Sunni, Shi'i or Khariji exegesis in the first/seventh century, but we can use those terms in the third/ninth century. The vast majority of Muslims (mainstream in terms of numbers) came to be known as Sunnis. The other main groups were Kharijis and Shi'a, who were further subdivided into Zaydis, Twelvers (or Imamis) and Ismailis. There were also the Sufis (mystics), the theologians, and the jurists who usually belonged to one of the three key groups.

Sunnism developed in the course of the first/seventh to the third/ninth centuries. Early debates on religio-political and theological issues ranged from who can become an imam (caliph or ruler), freewill versus predestination, God's attributes, the definition of 'believer' or 'unbeliever', to the status of those who commit grave sins. In the third/ninth and fourth/tenth centuries, Sunnism accepted a set of creeds and legal schools (*madhhab*). With this came the consolidation of Islamic disciplines that provided the intellectual basis for Sunnism: Qur'anic exegesis (tafsir), hadith, fiqh and early Islamic history. Given that it reflected the position of the majority of Muslims, Sunnism also came to be considered the 'orthodoxy'.

Tabari's exegetical work represents the most important early Sunni exegesis. He was born in Tabaristan in Persia and studied the Qur'an, hadith, jurisprudence, history, grammar, lexicography and poetry. While Tabari's writings are vast and varied, our interest is primarily in his multi-volume exegetical work (popularly known as *Tafsir of Tabari*). Tabari brought together in this massive work much of the tafsir-related material of his time. He commented on each verse of the Qur'an from beginning to end, brought together hadith and other reports attributed to early authorities in relation to each verse, provided grammatical and linguistic analyses, noted system-ically the various meanings of each text attributed to early authorities and finally offered his own interpretation and the reasons for choosing that inter-pretation. Tabari's *Tafsir* is usually identified with the exegesis based on tradition, although in some respects it can be associated with exegesis based on reason as well. From the time of Tabari, a large number of multi-volume exegetical works emerged that fall into the broad category of Sunni exegesis.

Key characteristics of Sunni exegesis include, for instance: emphasis on literal interpretation of the Qur'an wherever possible, strongly justified by linguistic evidence; reliance on tradition in explaining the text; use of reason within limits; rejection of esoteric meanings as unjustifiable speculation; respect for the Companions of the Prophet collectively as the most important source of religious authority after the Prophet; acceptance of a set of theological positions on God's attributes, religious doctrines, prophecy and revelation, the definition of a 'believer' (Muslim), and sources of authority in law; and rejection of positions held by rationalist theologians known as Mu'tazilis.

The Shi'a, the second most important religio-political group of Muslims, are subdivided into a number of groups. An important difference between the Shi'i and Sunni Muslims relates to the Shi'i doctrine of the imam and their respective views of the Companions.

The Imamis (also known as Twelvers) are the largest subgroup among the Shi'a. The early Imamis criticized the mode of compilation of the Qur'anic text during the caliphate of Uthman. They accused the compilers of omitting and adding verses. However, many later Imami scholars toned down the criticism and said that the existing Qur'anic text did not contain falsifica-tions.[49] For Imamis, the Shi'i imams are divinely inspired and endowed with a special knowledge. The imam should also be nominated as heir by his predecessor.[50] Thus, Ali was the first imam designated by the Prophet himself, and any who befriended him are considered friends of the Shi'a, but any who opposed him are seen as enemies, an example of an enemy being the Prophet's wife A'isha, because of her political opposition to Ali. Imamis were also heavily influenced theologically by the rationalist Mu'tazilis. Moreover, Imamis believed in differences between the 'inner' and 'outer' meanings of the Qur'an. This allowed them to read into the Qur'an a range of theological and religio-political views. Among the key Imami scholars of Qur'anic exegesis are al-Tusi (d. 460/1067), and al-Tabarsi (d. 548/1153).

Many other trends of exegesis existed and continued to develop. Despite this dynamic intellectual development, the vibrancy, creativity and innovation that existed in exegesis began to wane from around the seventh/thirteenth century.

The Spanish philosopher Ibn Rushd (d. 595/1198) on allegorical interpretation of the Qur'an as a resolution of apparent contradictions

Now since this religion is true and summons to the study which leads to the knowledge of the Truth, we the Muslim community know definitively that demonstrative study [that is, philosophy] does not lead to (conclusions) conflicting with what Scripture has given us; for truth does not oppose truth but accords with it and bears witness to it. This being so whenever demonstrative study leads to any manner of knowledge about any being, that being is inevitably either unmentioned or mentioned in Scripture. If it is unmentioned, there is no contradiction, and it is the same case as an act whose category is unmentioned so that the [Muslim] lawyer has to infer it by reasoning from Scripture. If Scripture does speak about it, the apparent meaning of the words inevitably either accords or conflicts with the conclusions of (philosophical) demonstration about it. If this apparent meaning accords, there is no conflict. If it conflicts, there is a call for allegorical interpretation. The meaning of 'allegorical interpretation' is: the extension of the significance of an expression from real to metaphorical significance, without forsaking therein the standard metaphorical practices of Arabic, such as calling a thing by the name of something resembling it or a cause or a consequence or accompaniment of it, or other such things as are enumerated in accounts of the kinds of metaphorical speech.[51]

Qur'anic exegesis in the modern age

In the modern period, that is, from the mid nineteenth century, Qur'anic exegesis was rekindled and further developed. A modernist exegesis developed because many Muslims, particularly of a non-traditionalist orientation, sought to redefine their understanding of the Qur'an in the light of modernity. This was exemplified in scholars such as Sayyid Ahmad Khan (d. 1898) of India and Muhammad Abduh (d. 1905) of Egypt. Both stressed the importance of moving away from imitation of the past towards a responsive approach compatible with modern life. The Qur'an could guide Muslims towards becoming part of the modern world. Both scholars had an affinity with rationalist thinkers in early Islam, such as the Mu'tazilis and saw the need for interpretation of the Qur'an with a scientific worldview in mind.[52]

An example of this new approach was Muhammad Abduh's analysis of polygamy. The problem he confronted was whether men should continue to be allowed four wives in an era of greater gender equality and in the light of changed social, political and economic conditions. Abduh's solution was to reinterpret relevant phrases in the Qur'an. Abduh argued that, by Qur'anic logic, a man may be married to only one woman because permission to marry more than one is conditional upon 'justice'. According to Abduh, monogamy was the ideal and just form of marriage, as multiple wives might not receive equal access to their husband, and they (and their children) might receive less financial support. Therefore, Abduh argued, it was necessary to accept changes in interpretation in line with changed circumstances.[53]

Another distinctly modern approach involves examining the Qur'an in the light of modern science (called scientific exegesis). Scientific exegesis can be understood in two ways. First is the approach taken by the Egyptian Tantawi Jawhari (d. 1940), who wrote an encyclopaedic work of scientific exegesis. Although referred to as a 'tafsir', it is not a tafsir in the strict classical sense, but an encyclopaedia that enables Muslims to link the text of the Qur'an to a modern scientific worldview. The second use of scientific exegesis is to highlight the so-called 'scientific miraculous nature of the Qur'an'. This method is apologetic and attempts to demonstrate that modern scientific achievements were foreseen in the Qur'an fourteen centuries ago.[54]

Another significant trend has been socio-political exegesis. The foremost proponent of this was Sayyid Qutb (d. 1966), who wrote his *In the Shadow of the Qur'an* (*Fi Zilal al-Qur'an*) essentially to provide a new perspective on the relevance of the Qur'an to today's Muslims. He has an uncompromising commitment to his view of Islam. His portrayal of many of the institutions of modern society as akin to pre-Islamic institutions (*jahiliyya*), that is, un-Islamic, has ensured him an important place among those whose primary aim is to establish Islam as the dominant socio-political force in Muslim societies. Qutb's work, an example of a tafsir of a personal reflective nature, is somewhat divorced from standard exegetical tradition in its more free-floating ideas. It draws on the modern world and its challenges, and refuses to follow dogmatically early approaches to tafsir. This perhaps explains its wide acceptability among younger Muslims. In many ways, it is among the most inspiring and powerful tafsir in the contemporary world for young Muslims influenced by the ideas of the best-known 'political Islamist' movement, the Muslim Brotherhood.[55]

A controversial and challenging manner of studying the Qur'an has arisen from a literary perspective. The Egyptian literary critic Taha Husayn (d. 1973) generated a controversy in Egypt when he argued for analysing the Qur'an as a literary text and suggested that the biblical stories mentioned in the Qur'an may not necessarily be historical.

In the mid twentieth century, another popular approach emerged called thematic exegesis. This approach emphasizes the unity of the Qur'anic text over the interpretation of verses in isolation. Verse-by-verse interpretation is seen as distorting the Qur'anic message, and as not giving sufficient emphasis to related verses on a particular theme across the Qur'an. This form of exegesis goes back to the ideas developed by Amin al-Khuli of Egypt (d. 1967), who emphasized that it is more beneficial to interpret the Qur'an by focusing on specific themes. In this way, one can explore in depth such concepts as 'justice' and 'unity of God' by looking at all aspects of the concept as dealt with in the Qur'an in different chapters. Practitioners argue that this approach can be useful today in dealing with contemporary questions such as women's rights, human rights and ethical problems. Thematic exegesis has become very popular and influential in many parts of the Muslim world, including Egypt and Indonesia.[56]

Muslim feminism brings cultural politics into exegetical scholarship. Several Muslim feminist interpretations have recently argued that it is important to reread the Qur'an because the 'male-oriented' readings of early and modern scholars and theologians are biased against women. Historical injustices against women have therefore been perpetuated through sexist interpretations. Feminist scholars have argued that the Qur'anic rules and values concerning women must be understood in the light of the socio-historical context of the revelation and its interpretation, and then adjusted to accord women a more central role.[57]

The literature on Qur'anic exegesis in the modern period shows that there is a strong desire on the part of Muslims, scholars and laity alike, to find the relevance of the Qur'an for contemporary issues without compromising its core beliefs and practices. This is seen as particularly urgent in relation to the Qur'an's ethico-legal content. There are, broadly speaking, three trends among those who believe that the ethico-legal content of the Qur'an is relevant to Muslims in the modern period: textualists, semi-textualists and contextualists.[58]

The textualists seek to maintain the exegesis of the Qur'an as handed down by tradition and argue for a strict following of the text (as well as the 'authorized' interpretations within the tradition, whether Sunni or Shi'i). The semi-textualists essentially follow the textualists, but attempt to present the Qur'anic ethico-legal content in modern garb. They do not ask fundamental questions about the relationship of the ethico-legal content to the socio-historical context of the Qur'an. Among supporters of this approach are the Muslim Brotherhood and Jamaat-i-Islami.[59] In contrast, the contextualists emphasize both the socio-historical context of the Qur'an and its subsequent interpretation. They argue for understanding the ethico-legal content in the light of the political, social, historical, religious and economic contexts in which this content was revealed, understood, interpreted and applied. They ask for a high degree of freedom for the modern Muslim scholar in arriving at what is mutable (changeable) and immutable (unchangeable) in the ethico-legal content. Contextualists are led by the work of scholars such as Fazlur Rahman. They represent an important step in relating the Qur'anic text to the contemporary needs of Muslim societies. Rahman relies heavily on understanding the historical context of the revelation at the macro level, and then relating it to a particular need of the modern period. In this, he draws on the idea of the 'prophetic spirit' or, in other words, how the Prophet might act were he living today.[60]

The exegesis of the Qur'an has a long, complicated and contested history. Therefore, it is vital to be aware of the broad influences and trends that impact on scholarly understandings of the Qur'an and bear these in mind when attempting to understand the Qur'an and its place within the Muslim faith and the believer's daily life. For those who do not read Arabic, a first step in understanding the Qur'an is to use a translation with a commentary in the form of extensive footnotes, for example Muhammad Asad's *The Message of the Qur'an*[61] or A. Yusuf Ali's *The Meaning of the Holy Qur'an*.[62] Abu'l Ala Mawdudi's *Towards Understanding the Qur'an*[63] is also a popular modern commentary.

Chapter 3

The Sunna of the Prophet

The most important source of authority for Muslims, after the Qur'an, is the normative behaviour of the Prophet Muhammad (known as Sunna). Sunna is literally 'the trodden path' and originally meant the customary law and practices prevalent in Arabia during the pre-Islamic era. For Muslims, however, it came to represent the normative behaviour of the Prophet. This Sunna is documented in hadith. Originally, the term hadith simply meant 'new' and was used in reference to a story or a report.[1] Later, it came to refer to information about the Prophet Muhammad, such as his sayings and deeds and descriptions of his person, as reported by the Companions.

Before Muhammad ibn Idris al-Shafi'i (d. 204/819), after whom the influential Shafi'i school of law was named, a distinction was often made between Sunna and hadith. The Sunna was seen as the normative behaviour of the Prophet supported by generally agreed-upon practice of the Muslim community which in turn was based on the practice of the Prophet and the earliest Muslims. The focus was on 'normative practice'. This practice may or may not be supported by a particular hadith. What this means is that where there is a particular practice followed by the community and there is also a hadith to support that practice, the reliability of the hadith is strengthened. Similarly, where there is a hadith but no supporting practice, questions could be raised about the reliability of the hadith. A clear distinction therefore needed to be made between 'Sunna' and 'hadith' at the time. However, in the post-Shafi'i period – in large part due to his arguments – Sunna came to be equated with hadith. For Shafi'i, any authentic hadith was Sunna, whether or not there was a common practice in the community to back that hadith.

In both classical and modern times, however, arguments have been raised against equating the Sunna with the canons of hadith. Groups such as the Kharijis and the Mu'tazilis in the classical period (and certain modernists today) accepted the validity of the Sunna as the normative practice of the Prophet, but objected to the formulation of Sunna in hadith terms.[2]

Anatomy of a hadith

A hadith has two parts: (1) a chain of transmitters (*isnad*), which lists the names of the authorities who transmitted the particular hadith; and (2) a text (*matn*) which is the content of the hadith.[3]

Chain of transmitters:

> Yahya related to me from Malik from Hisham ibn Urwa from his father from A'isha, the wife of the Prophet [may Allah bless him and grant him peace].

Text:

> . . . that al-Harith ibn Hisham asked the Messenger of Allah [may Allah bless him and grant him peace], 'How does the revelation come to you?' and the Messenger of Allah [may Allah bless him and grant him peace] said, 'Sometimes it comes to me like the ringing of a bell, and that is the hardest for me, and when it leaves me I remember what has been said. And sometimes the angel appears to me in the likeness of a man and talks to me and I remember what he says.' A'isha added, 'I saw it [revelation] coming down on him on an intensely cold day, and when it had left him his forehead was dripping with sweat.'[4]

Hadith *qudsi*

While hadith usually refers to traditions reporting the sayings and deeds of the Prophet Muhammad, some hadith belong to a special subset called hadith *qudsi* (sacred hadith). This is where the content of the hadith deals with something that God has said or revealed, but couched in the words of the Prophet. They differ from the verses of the Qur'an, in that the latter are considered the actual words of God, not of the Prophet. A hadith qudsi, for example, cannot be recited in the obligatory prayer in place of verses of the Qur'an.[5] An example of a hadith qudsi is:

> On the authority of Anas [may Allah be pleased with him], who said: I heard the Messenger of Allah [may the blessings and peace of Allah be upon him] say: 'Allah the Almighty said: "O child of Adam, so long as you call upon Me and ask of Me, I shall forgive you for what you have done, and I shall not mind. O child of Adam, were your sins to reach the clouds of the sky and were you then to ask forgiveness of Me, I would forgive you. O child of Adam, were you to come to Me with sins nearly as great as the earth and were you then to face Me, ascribing no partner to Me, I would bring you forgiveness nearly as great as it [i.e. the earth]".'[6]

Hadith: the standard Muslim view

Preservation and collection

Many Muslims believe that preservation of hadith began during the time of the Prophet. This was not in the form of written documents, but through memorization, a method familiar to the Arabs of the time, whose culture was largely an oral one and through which the common knowledge of the society was preserved. It is generally accepted that transmission of hadith began to occur during the Prophet's time when those of his followers who witnessed a particular instruction conveyed it to others who were not present.[7] Such a practice was to be expected given the importance of the role of the Prophet in the first Muslim community. Among those who were well known for their transmission of a large number of hadith was the Prophet's wife A'isha bint Abu Bakr (d. 58/678), who had the opportunity to observe him most closely. She even criticized other Muslims if she felt they were transmitting hadith incorrectly, and acted as a judge for determining the veracity of a report.[8]

After the death of the Prophet, reports about his judgements, opinions and practice must have played an important role in the decision-making in the first Muslim community, at least in areas where the Prophet had expressed views that were commonly known. During the Prophet's lifetime, many of his followers sought his opinion on a wide variety of matters, following the dictates of the Qur'an: 'Believers . . . obey the messenger [Muhammad]',[9] and 'You have an excellent example in the messenger of God'.[10] After his passing, it is understandable that his Companions would wish to pass on such information to new Muslims enlarging the Muslim community.

Reports suggest that in transmission of hadith some Companions asked others to provide evidence for the truth of what was being transmitted, but not necessarily on a systematic basis. Several Companions were active in transmitting hadith in their teachings, for example Ubay ibn Ka'b (d. circa 35/656), Abd Allah ibn Mas'ud (d. 32/652), Abd Allah ibn Abbas (d. 68/687), Ali ibn Abi Talib (d. 40/661) and, as previously mentioned, A'isha. Following the Prophet's death, writing down of hadith was not seen as important. It was the Umayyad caliph Umar ibn Abd al-Aziz (d. 101/720)[11] who is credited with being the first to organize the collation and recording of collections of hadith.[12]

As the Prophet's Companions and their successors moved away from Medina and Mecca, spreading out across the ever-widening Muslim caliphate (empire), more and more students of hadith began to emerge and travel in search of hadith knowledge. Furthermore, sectarian strife and the establishment of the first dynastic caliphate (Umayyads in 41/661) gave some urgency to acquiring knowledge from authentic sources.[13] Mecca, Medina, Yemen, Iraq and Syria became major centres of hadith collection and gradually written collections became indispensable. Among the first collections, probably works of a legal character, were those of Ibn Jurayj (d. 157/774), al-Awza'i (d. 159/775), and Sufyan al-Thawri (d. 161/777); however, none is extant.[14] Among the earliest surviving complete texts with a collection of hadith is *Muwatta'* by Malik ibn Anas (d. 179/795), after whom the Maliki school of law was named.[15]

In time, different kinds of hadith compilations emerged, arranged either by subject matter or by transmitter. These are classified into several groups:[16]

- *sahifa*: the earliest type of compilation, being collections of hadith written down by the Prophet's Companions or their Successors
- *rasa'il* or *kutub*: collections dealing with one of eight specific topics (beliefs; laws; piety; etiquette; Qur'an commentary; history; crises; appreciation and denunciation of people and places)
- *musannafs*: large collections arranged into chapters according to subject matter
- *musnads*: technically referring to those collections arranged according to the names of the final Companion in the chain of transmission of a hadith, but also used to refer generally to reliable collations of hadith
- *jami's*: large collections of hadith covering all eight topics (see *rasa'il* above)
- *sunans*: works dealing only with legal hadith.

Naturally, some collections became well respected and more famous than others. Amongst Sunni Muslims, the *Sahih* of Bukhari (d. 256/870) and the *Sahih* of Muslim (d. 261/874) are considered the two most authoritative sources of hadith, although some individual hadith contained therein have been criticized by later scholars. Other important works include collections by Abu Dawud (d. 275/883), Tirmidhi (d. 279/892), Ibn Maja (d. 273/886) and Nasa'i (d. 303/915). The most important *musnad* work is by Ahmad ibn Hanbal (d. 233/847), after whom the Hanbali school of law is named.

Development of hadith criticism

When hadith began to be transmitted formally, a system of checking of isnad (chain of transmitters) developed, which provided the basis for determining whether or not a particular hadith was authentic. Some Muslim scholars argue that the beginnings of the isnad system can be traced back as early as the students of the Prophet's Companions.[17] However, a formal system probably did not emerge until the latter half of the first/seventh century or even the early part of the second/eighth century.

Scholars specializing in the discipline of collecting and scrutinizing hadith (known as Traditionists), as well as jurists dealing with religious law, developed certain principles for the criticism of a hadith's chain of transmitters (isnad) and for its text (matn).[18] In assessing the authority of a hadith based on its isnad, traditionists stipulated that its chain must be traced back to the original reporter through a continuous succession of transmitters whose identity, unquestionable character and high moral qualities were established.[19] Also, if the hadith reported an event that occurred in the presence of a large number of people (particularly if it occurred on a regular basis), it was required to have been originally reported by several transmitters. If such a hadith was reported by one Companion alone, it was considered unacceptable by some early authorities. They reasoned it was impossible for an event witnessed by so many of the Prophet's Companions to be reported only by one transmitter.[20]

As hadith and their chains of transmission began to be systematically scrutinized, a 'science of biography' (of those associated with hadith transmission) developed, known as *asma' ar-rijal*. Details of the lives and characters of various transmitters were recorded, which allowed evaluation of their credibility. The following are some of the criteria utilized for this purpose:

- The name, nickname, title, parentage and occupation of each transmitter in the chain of transmission should be known.
- The original transmitter of the hadith should have stated that he heard the hadith directly from the Prophet.
- If a transmitter received his hadith from another transmitter, the two should have lived in the same period and have had the possibility of meeting each other.
- At the time of hearing and transmitting the hadith, the transmitter should have been physically and mentally capable of understanding and remembering it.
- The transmitter should have been known as a pious and virtuous person.
- The transmitter should not have been accused of having lied, given false evidence or committed a crime.
- The transmitter should not have spoken against other reliable people.
- The transmitter's religious beliefs and practices should have been known to be correct (and not heretical).
- The transmitter should not have carried out or practised peculiar religious beliefs of his own.[21]

However, proving the authenticity of a chain of transmission does not necessarily prove the authenticity of the text of the hadith, as the text may be a faithfully memorized and transmitted forgery.[22] Some general principles utilized in criticism of the hadith text include:

- It must not be contrary to the text of the Qur'an, or the basic principles of Islam.

- It must not be contrary to other hadith on the subject which have already been accepted by authorities as authentic and reliable.
- It must not be against dictates of reason and natural laws, and common experience.
- It must not contain statements about disproportionately high rewards or severe punishments for otherwise ordinary deeds of a person.
- If it exalts a particular people, tribe, place or even a chapter of the Qur'an for a specific reason, generally it should be rejected.
- If it contains detailed prophecies of future events with dates, it should be rejected.
- If it contains observations and remarks attributed to the Prophet, but these are not in keeping with what is generally known about him and his views, it should be rejected.[23]

Grading of hadith[24]

Hadith are graded as accepted (*maqbul*) or rejected (*mardud*). Accepted hadith are then graded into 'authentic' (*sahih*) (either by itself, or because of the presence of other similar authentic hadith) or 'agreeable' (*hasan*) (again either by itself or due to the existence of other similar hadith). Defects which affect the grading of an accepted hadith include factors such as a transmitter narrating a hadith as a statement of the Prophet, when most others have ascribed it to one of his Companions, or a transmitter who has a high moral character but lacks literary skills.

Rejected hadith are also sub-divided, and may be rejected owing to a defect in a transmitter, such as if he or she was known to be a liar. Other grounds for rejection are if there is a discontinuity or missing name in the chain of transmission or for other incidental reasons such as a famous hadith purposely being given a different chain of transmission, so that whoever 'possessed' it would be given credit for being able to teach a novel hadith (i.e. a famous hadith but with a new chain).[25]

Shi'i conception of hadith[26]

The Shi'a[27] also believe that the Sunna of the Prophet is a primary source of law. However, they hold that hadith (known among them as *akhbar*) should be transmitted by a member of the family of the Prophet or by his descendent imams who are considered reliable, truthful and honest. For this reason, many of the transmitters of hadith included in Sunni hadith collections may not be acceptable from a Shi'i point of view. While the texts of hadith can be similar between Sunni and Shi'i collections, this may not be the case for their chains of transmission.

Just as Sunni scholars rely on compilations such as the *Sahih* of Bukhari, so too are there Shi'i collections. Several Shi'i scholars collected hadith that are considered reliable from their point of view. These scholars arranged the contents of those source collections into four accessible books that continue to play a pivotal role among Shi'a today. Scholars who compiled these collections are al-Kulayni (d. circa 329/941); Ibn Babawayh (d. circa 381/991); al-Tusi (d. circa 460/1067).[28]

For the Twelver (Imami) Shi'a, there are four main categories of hadith:

- *sahih* (authentic): a hadith whose chain of transmission is unbroken through narrations from just imams of the Imami Shi'a, or followers of the imams who adhere to the Ja'fari school of jurisprudence
- *hasan* (good): a hadith reported by commendable Imamis whose reliability cannot be confirmed. If the chain contains a single reliable non-Imami then the hadith is classified as dependable and if it contains a single weak reporter then the whole hadith is classified as weak
- *muwaththaq* (dependable – also termed *qawi* 'strong'): a hadith considered reliable by classical scholars, although narrated by scholars of a different school of religious law, or even by transmitters belonging to those who opposed the Imamis
- *da'if* (weak): a hadith where one of the reporters is known to be a fabricator, immoral or unreliable, or is unknown.[29]

Modern critique of hadith

In the modern period, many Western scholars of hadith have argued that much of the hadith literature should be considered the work of early Muslims and should not be attributed to the Prophet. From their point of view, early Muslims incorporated the practice of the Prophet and of his Companions and Successors, as well as of later jurists and their opinions, and then projected these back on to the Prophet.[30]

Ignaz Goldziher (d. 1921) was a Hungarian Orientalist scholar and student of convert Arminius Vambery (d. 1913). Some believe Goldziher also secretly converted to Islam.[31] Goldziher held that hadith were mostly formulated in the early second/eighth century as a result of sectarian and political rivalries and the need for jurists to defend their legal views. The 'worldly' Umayyads, argued Goldziher, were not really interested in the development of religious literature; instead, pious aphorisms and the magnified heroics of the Prophet's military career were what concerned them.[32] He rejected the assertion that Umar II (d. 101/719), the Umayyad caliph, was the first to sponsor a systematic collection of hadith, and argued that hadith literature followed on from the formulation of Islamic jurisprudence.[33] He pointed to the earliest extant work that includes a collection of hadith, Malik's *Muwatta*, and noted that the various versions of the collection display a concept of Sunna as a community practice supported by reference to hadith but not bound by them. In his view, consideration of the consensus of people of Medina (where the

Prophet lived in his final years and where Malik also lived) on a particular issue was such an overriding concern for Malik that he did not hesitate to prefer the 'consensus' over authentic hadith that he included in his collection (*Muwatta*).[34]

According to this view, it was not until the time of Bukhari (d. 256/869) and Muslim (d. 261/875) that strict isnad criticism emerged. However, even for Bukhari – who for his *Sahih* made a skeletal outline of areas of concern, for which he later filled in the necessary traditions – there were not enough traditions of the highest standard to complete his fiqh map.[35] Later compilers found it necessary to relax isnad criticism and rely on lesser-quality hadith in order to find enough to cover every point of Islamic law. Eventually, the status given to the Companions of the Prophet and the Successors meant that it was unbecoming for later Muslims even to question their motives or trustworthiness, thereby allowing the reinstatement of previously rejected material.[36]

Following on from the work of Goldziher, another Orientalist scholar, Joseph Schacht (d. 1969), saw the development of hadith literature (in particular the isnad system) as springing from pressure on jurists to defend their views. He held that the early Islamic period (the first two centuries of Islam) was more complex than Goldziher believed, although the historicity of the early jurists' material was weakened when later jurists formulated hadith chains to justify their conclusions.

To demonstrate this thesis, Schacht developed the 'common link' theory, which was also taken up by another modern Orientalist, Gautier H. A. Juynboll. The common link theory was derived via a process of analysing hadith with similar texts (ostensibly the same prophetic utterance) to draw a map of isnad chains, called an 'isnad bundle'. A common link transmitter is one who passes a particular tradition on to a number of pupils, but who usually only heard it from one immediate authority.[37] Juynboll, like Schacht before him, argued that most hadith have common link transmitters, and thus points of origin[38] in the second/eighth century. Taking a middle position between Muslim and other Western scholars, Juynboll is wary of accepting the authenticity of a hadith (i.e. that it accurately reflects a statement or deed of the Prophet Muhammad), except where a common link transmitter can be found at the Companions level.[39]

There are Muslim scholars today who, while not going as far as Goldziher, Schacht or Juynboll, argue that the traditional Muslim position on hadith is difficult to justify. For example, Fazlur Rahman (d. 1988) held that Western scholars are correct about the development of the Sunna content, but not the Sunna concept itself. For Rahman, the prophetic Sunna was a valid concept from the very beginning of Islam; the problem was that Sunna also came to include the interpretations and agreed practices of the early Muslim communities following the death of the Prophet.[40] The Prophet, from Rahman's point of view, was not primarily a 'pan-legist' (he seldom resorted to acting in a legislative capacity, in his view), but rather was a moral reformer.[41] Rahman argued that the bulk of the hadith corpus is nothing but the Sunna and juristic reasoning of the first generations of Muslims; in other words, the opinions of an individual that over time received the sanction of community consensus (*ijma'*).[42] Such a view of hadith authenticity is generally rejected by mainstream Muslim opinion, for whom hadith refers to the authenticated sayings, deeds and descriptions of the Prophet Muhammad, not of the early generations.

Implications of hadith scholarship today

Although some Muslim scholars have attempted to counter Orientalist claims, the two worlds of scholarship have remained largely isolated and unconnected. Western scholarship does not appear to have had a significant impact on traditional Muslim approaches to the study of hadith. This may be due in part to the condescending tone of early Orientalists (which allowed their claims to be written off as 'anti-Islamic') as well as the failure of Western scholars to grasp adequately the complexities of the traditional methods.

Nevertheless, the implication for hadith scholarship in the 'meeting' of these two worlds is quite significant. A case is the recent experience of the Muslim academic and feminist Amina Wadud, who led a Friday prayer service in 2005, an activity almost always performed by Muslim men only. After publicity about the event held in New York, a number of articles appeared on the internet that drew on interpretation of hadith and points of Islamic jurisprudence to affirm or discredit the legitimacy of female-led prayer.

Nevin Reda, a feminist writer, used a number of arguments to support her thesis that female-led prayer is acceptable in the universe of Islamic interpretation. She pointed to the existence of a hadith in which the Prophet is said to have commanded a woman Umm Waraqa to lead a congregation that included a male assigned to make the call to prayer. It was on this basis that a minority of classical jurists – including the famous Tabari – reportedly allowed women to lead men in prayer, a point that belies the notion that there is consensus on this prohibition (that is, woman leading men in prayer). Reda also referred to Juynboll's method of isnad analysis and rejected the notion that hadith must be accepted as unimpeachable simply because they appear in the classical canons, particularly if they appear to transgress positive Qur'anic teachings on leadership of women.[43]

Zaid Shakir wrote a response to Reda from a traditionalist Sunni perspective, analysing the strengths of the various narrations of the hadith of Umm Waraqa and their legal value for ruling on the permissibility of female-led prayer. He rejected her interpretation of key Arabic terms used in the hadith, as well as Juynboll's thesis about isnad analysis, in order to defend the Maliki, Hanafi, Shafi'i and Hanbali interpretations of prohibition.[44] This case, which received international exposure, shows that modern hadith scholarship is as relevant today as it ever was.

Profile of a hadith scholar

Abu Abd Allah Muhammad ibn Isma'il al-Bukhari, the most famous traditionist in Islamic history, was of Persian origin. He was born in Bukhara in 194/810 and died near Samarqand in 256/869.[45] His father studied under the famous scholars Malik ibn Anas, Hammad ibn Zayd (d. 179/795) and Ibn al-Mubarak (d. 181/797). Bukhari's early education took place at the feet of his mother, with whom he and his brother went in search of knowledge after mastering all the knowledge in his native town of Bukhara.[46] He interrogated more than one thousand scholars of hadith in places such as Balkh, Merv, Nishapur, Hijaz, Egypt and Mesopotamia.[47] The Sahih of Bukhari is considered by Sunnis to be the most important textual source after the Qur'an.

Bukhari's objective was to collect only the most authentic traditions of the Prophet and to compile them into a work divided into several parts, taking a portion of each hadith as a heading.[48] Where relevant, he would repeat hadith in different chapters devoted to different subjects. The number of hadith in his book with full isnads totals well over seven thousand; however, without repetition they total about two and a half thousand.[49] His biographers report that Bukhari reduced this number from six hundred thousand hadith by applying his strict criteria.[50]

For an isnad to be ranked authentic and included in his Sahih, Bukhari applied strict conditions. The transmitters must be of exemplary character and possess a high literary and academic standard. There must be evidence that the transmitters met one another and that each student learned from each teacher.[51] The difference between the Sahih of Bukhari and that of Muslim was on this last point. Muslim accepted that if two transmitters lived in the same locale, it was possible, even if not proved, that they could have learned from each other. Therefore the chain of transmission (for Muslim) was not broken and hadith linked in this manner were acceptable. Bukhari, on the other hand, required positive evidence that the student learned from the teacher and for this reason his Sahih tended to gain wider acceptance by later Muslims as the stronger of the two works.[52]

Chapter 4

Legal thought

This chapter will explore Islamic law and the development of legal knowledge. It will begin by explaining key terms in Islamic law, namely shari'a and fiqh, and providing an outline of the development of law in the first three centuries of Islam. The chapter will then identify the main 'bases' of Islamic law as discussed in Muslim sources, point out some of the early debates in Islamic law and identify its established schools. It will conclude with a brief reference to *ijtihad* and to the current debate on reform of Islamic law.

Shari'a and fiqh

A key term associated with Islamic law is shari'a; in fact many often translate shari'a as 'Islamic law'. However, it is important to give a clear meaning of this term in order to distinguish it from fiqh, another key term associated with Islamic law and also often translated as 'Islamic law' or sometimes as 'Islamic jurisprudence'. The term shari'a is linguistically associated with terms such as 'the path', 'the way' or 'the road'. Inherent, therefore, in its meaning is that it is considered the path set by God for Muslims to follow in order to achieve salvation. Shari'a represents the divine guidance contained in the revelation communicated to the Prophet through the Qur'an and further illuminated by the Prophet in his sayings and deeds (Sunna). In the context of Islamic law, shari'a refers to the totality of this guidance contained in the Qur'an and Sunna and generally expressed in their commands and prohibitions. These instructions take different forms: sometimes they are specific like the dietary and some penal laws; at other times they are principles and values which the Qur'an and Sunna want to instil in believers, such as their consistent reminder to be just and fair in one's dealings, and always to act honestly and truthfully.

The term fiqh is closely associated with shari'a. It originally meant 'understanding' or 'knowledge' of something. It perhaps originated from the use of the term *faqih*, a 'man of understanding', for the camel expert who distinguished the she-camels that were in heat from those that were pregnant. The term fiqh also occurs in the Qur'an in its verb form in this general meaning of understanding. For instance, in recounting the response of the Prophet Shu'ayb's people to his message, the Qur'an states, 'Shu'ayb, we do not understand [la nafqahu] much of what you say'.[1] In reference to those who reject God's commands, the Qur'an states that 'they have hearts, but do not understand [la yafqahun] thereby'.[2] Similarly, the term fiqh and its derivatives are found in the hadith literature. An often cited example is a blessing the Prophet Muhammad bestowed on his Companion Ibn Abbas (d. 68/687) in which the Prophet reportedly said: 'May Allah grant him deep understanding [faqqihhu] of religion'.[3] These usages of fiqh have the broader sense of understanding something, and even when restricted, as in the case of the above hadith, refer to all matters of religion and not just legal matters.

From its broader usage, the term fiqh came to be more narrowly applied. People read the Qur'anic commands and prohibitions and attempted to understand what the Qur'an required of them in terms of what they had to do, mentally or physically, and what they had to avoid. This was carried out in the light of the Prophet's Sunna. With the passage of time, such interpretative activities brought about a positive body of knowledge which included legal, theological and ascetic material. All these shari'a disciplines were referred to as fiqh in the early period of Islam, which roughly covered the first hundred and fifty years (610–750 CE). With the development of theology (kalam) and asceticism (sufism) in the second/eighth and third/ninth centuries, fiqh came to be applied only to the body of legal knowledge. Here three things need to be noted:

- First, the term 'fiqh', from being a mental act, that is, the act of under-standing, came to mean something more concrete – the body of knowledge produced by examining the commands and prohibitions found in the Qur'an and Sunna. This body of knowledge at first included all shari'a disciplines but was later confined to legal matters.
- Second, shari'a and fiqh came to be differentiated. Shari'a was the totality of commands and prohibitions found in the Qur'an and Sunna. Fiqh referred to specific rulings obtained through the understanding and inter-pretation of the shari'a material using other sources, as will be explained later. Thus the source of shari'a, for the Muslim, is God and divine, while the source of fiqh is human.
- Third, in common usage today, shari'a refers generally to the commands and prohibitions not just as they are found in the Qur'an and Sunna but as they have been interpreted and elaborated in fiqh to be acted upon in everyday life. Therefore these terms are often used interchangeably.[4]

For many Muslims, fiqh or Islamic law covers all aspects of a Muslim's life, religious and mundane, individual and social. It gives concrete form to the shari'a principles, norms, values and specific instructions (commandments and prohibitions) related to all these areas. These norms, values and instructions came from the Qur'an and were further elaborated in the Sunna of the Prophet. Muslim scholars needed, especially in the first three centuries of Islam (610–900 CE), to go through these to develop a legal system that would allow for the appropriate manifestation of shari'a. This encompassing conceptualization of shari'a, which resulted in the development of Islamic law, is outlined by Seyyed Hossein Nasr:

> It [shari'a] is a religious notion of law, one in which law is an integral aspect of religion. In fact religion to a Muslim *is* essentially the Divine Law which includes not only universal moral principles but details of how man should conduct his life and deal with his neighbour and with God; how he should eat, procreate and sleep; how he should buy and sell at the market place; how he should pray and perform other acts of worship.[5]

Key terms associated with law

Qur'an: the holy scripture of Islam, which Muslims believe is the revealed book of God

Sunna: example of Prophet Muhammad

Shari'a: Islamic law, meaning 'the path to be followed'

fiqh: Islamic jurisprudence or Islamic law

alim: a scholar of religion

mufti: person who is qualified to issue a fatwa (a legal opinion)

faqih: scholar qualified in Islamic legal theory

qadi: judge in a court

ijtihad: the process of independent reasoning to arrive at a legal opinion

tafsir: explanation of Qur'an, or exegesis

usul al-fiqh: principles and sources of Islamic jurisprudence

ijma': unanimous agreement or consensus of Muslim scholars on a point of law

qiyas: analogy

maslaha: public interest or benefit

urf: custom or habit; customary practices of a community

fatwa: an Islamic legal opinion or solution to a problem

ra'y: private opinion; considered opinion or reason.

Early development of Islamic law

The early development of Islamic law can be divided into four stages. The first is the prophetic stage, the period when the Qur'an was revealed. The Qur'an gave 'laws' related to the individual, such as ritual prayer, fasting and pilgrimage, and to society, such as marriage and divorce, business transactions and punishments. These laws were meant to realize certain ideals: the religious and personal laws were intended to create a God-conscious and morally sensitive person with an acute sense of right and wrong. The laws related to the social sphere aimed at creating a just and compassionate society. These laws were in the form of specific rulings as well as principles and values often without important details. For example, the Qur'an urged believers to be steadfast in prayer (*salat*) and pay the obligatory alms (*zakat*). However, it was silent on the form of prayer or the details related to alms such as the amount, how it should be given and under what circumstances. These details were provided by the Prophet through his actions and instructions (Sunna). Thus, before his death, he left not only a set of ideals, as outlined in the Qur'an, but also a way of achieving them through his Sunna.

After the death of the Prophet, Islamic law developed in the hands of the Companions. As Islam spread outside Arabia and came into contact with other cultures, Muslims were faced with new situations and problems. Utilizing ijtihad (intellectual effort of Muslim jurists to reach independent religio-legal decisions), the Companions found solutions to such problems. For example, Abu Bakr (d. 13/634), the first caliph after the Prophet, was faced early on with a large number of Arab tribes that had once paid zakat but now refused to. The Companions were divided as to the right course of action regarding this as there was no clear guidance in the Qur'an or a precedent from the Prophet. Some, like Umar (d. 24/644), a senior Companion and the second caliph, were ready to accommodate the tribes as Muslims, but others disagreed. Abu Bakr regarded the tribes as rebels or apostates and wanted to fight them until they paid up. After much debate, Abu Bakr finally won.[6] This decision of Abu Bakr greatly contributed to, and influenced, the formulation of the laws of apostasy in Islam.

Important rulers

Rashidun (Rightly guided) caliphs (632–661)

Umayyads (661–750)

Abbasids (750–1258)

Ottomans (1290–1924)

Umayyad caliphs of Spain (756–1031)

Nasrid Kings of Granada in Spain (1238–1492)

Mughals in India (1526–1858)

The next stage of the early development of Islamic law was the time of the Successors, the generation that immediately followed the Companions. The beginning of this period can be identified with the establishment of the Umayyad caliphate in 40/661 and extends to the early part of the second/eighth century. Some important developments that had implications for the development of Islamic law need to be mentioned here.

With the establishment of dynastic rule under the Umayyads, the type of consultation on points of law that existed during the Rashidun period more or less ceased.[7] There was no official consultative body to debate points of law and enact new rulings. The *ijtihad–ijma'* process of the Companions, which helped to keep the development of law within the confines of the state and gave it some unity, had largely gone. Instead the law was now developed by individual jurists at various centres of Islamic learning in Hijaz, Iraq, Syria and Egypt. Although the *ijtihad–ijma'* process gradually ceased, individual ijtihad remained and the creative process of producing knowledge in law continued. Through their study, teaching, debates and discussions of issues related to all aspects of law, scholars continued to augment the existing body of legal knowledge based on the Qur'an, the Sunna and the precedents and opinions of the Companions.

Islam was established outside Arabia not long after the death of the Prophet and came into contact with foreign systems of law. When it was conquered by the Muslims, Syria already had a well-established form of administration – that of the Byzantine empire (Eastern Roman empire). The Umayyads retained this system and this led to Roman law influencing the development of some aspects of Islamic law there. For example, the Umayyads, influenced by the Byzantine market inspector or *agoronomos*, developed the office of the market inspector (*amil al-suq*), who had limited jurisdiction concerning such things as weights and measures used in the market and petty offences committed there. From this evolved the function of *hisba* or the duty of safeguarding the proper standard of religious morality.[8] This stage also saw the emergence of two distinct trends in law: the 'people of reason or opinion' and the 'people of hadith'; the former based their opinions on reason and the texts (Qur'an and hadith) whereas the latter tended to base theirs largely on a literal reading and application of the texts of the Qur'an and hadith.

The final stage of the early development of Islamic law may be described as that of the jurists. This period began around the second half of the second/eighth century hijra and continued well into the third/ninth century, during which the major schools of law were founded.

Sources of Islamic law

Qur'an

The first and most important source for Islamic law is the Qur'an. Although the Qur'an is considered to be the Word of God and has always played a central role in the thinking of Muslims, it is not a *legal* code. It describes itself as 'guidance'. Until the death of the Prophet, the Qur'an continued to be revealed; therefore it was an ongoing source of instruction for the emerging Muslim community. As the community's situation changed, so did the Qur'anic instructions. Given the concern of the Qur'an with rules and regulations for governing the emerging Muslim community, particularly after the migration of the Prophet to Medina in 1/622, Muslims saw from the beginning a close connection between law and the Qur'an.

Sunna

The second source of Islamic law is the Sunna, which is the normative behaviour of the Prophet. Even in pre-Islamic times, the concept of following the 'sunna', the ways of doing things by well-known and respected people, was seen as providing standards for later generations. It is therefore inconceivable that the Prophet's Sunna would have been ignored by the Companions, his immediate followers. In fact, several Qur'anic verses indicate that, even in the area of law (which is more specific than the Sunna), Muslims were asked to abide by the decisions of the Prophet:

> But no, by your Lord, they [Muslims] will not believe until they make you the arbiter in controversies among them, and they find in their souls no objection to what you decide, but accept approvingly.[9]

While the importance given to the Qur'an in the domain of law is easy to understand, there was concern amongst the early Muslims as to how the Prophet's Sunna should be identified from established practices of the Muslim community. When establishing the Prophet's Sunna through hadith became the norm (when hadith collection on a systematic basis began), especially after Shafi'i (d. 204/820), Muslims became more aware of the issue of hadith fabrication. Scholars became cautious in accepting hadith, which led to the debates on whether certain types of hadith could be accepted in legal matters. Abu Hanifa (d. 150/767) was extremely cautious in accepting certain hadith, even if they were 'authentic'. However, Shafi'i argued strongly that whenever an authentic hadith was found on an issue it should be followed and not discarded. For Shafi'i, legal rulings must be based on the Qur'an or the Sunna, a position that came to be widely accepted in Islamic jurisprudence.

Ijma' (consensus)

Ijma' means 'consensus' and is the third source of Islamic law. Shafi'i defines it as the adherence of the congregation of Muslims to the conclusions of a given ruling pertaining to what is permitted and what is forbidden after the passing of the Prophet. In the principles of jurisprudence (*usul al-fiqh*), this concept is generally understood to be unanimous agreement on a specific issue by Muslim scholars (jurists) or the Muslim community as a whole. Usually the issue on which this consensus is arrived at is a legal one; however, consensus can also be arrived at on theological matters. Given the difficulties of arriving at consensus, some have even suggested that consensus can mean agreement of a majority of scholars, not necessarily all scholars, on an issue. For others consensus was possible only in the time of the Companions when the number of Muslims was relatively few. After that such consensus was not possible.

What is considered legitimate and valid consensus is a point of difference amongst the schools of law. Many of the details associated with the notion of consensus are also disputed. Even the textual support that is used by scholars to justify consensus has been challenged. We could say that there is no consensus among Muslims on 'consensus' except on the fundamentals of Islam, such as the unity of God, the prophethood of Muhammad, the five daily prayers, the Qur'an as the word of God, fasting, and pilgrimage to Mecca. Despite this, claims of consensus exist on a range of issues in different schools of law and by a variety of scholars.

Qiyas (analogy)

This is the fourth source of law in Sunni schools of law. Given the limited number of rulings in the Qur'an and Sunna and the unlimited number of situations an individual or society might face, Muslim jurists had to find ways to arrive at rulings that would guide a person's behaviour correctly. This is where *qiyas* (analogy) was useful. In the earliest period of Islamic legal thought, qiyas was used freely. It was a form of reasoning in which jurists based their rulings on a precedent or a similar case. Over time, this form of reasoning was restricted, structured and systematized.

An example of qiyas is as follows. A text in the Qur'an clearly prohibits the consumption of wine. The rationale of this prohibition, according to most jurists, is the effect of alcohol on the mind. On this basis, any product that leads to the same effects, such as narcotics, can be prohibited using the principle of qiyas, thus extending the rule for wine to narcotics even though there is no specific prohibition of narcotics in the Qur'an or Sunna.

Examples of other principles of Islamic law

Respecting and giving recognition to custom (*urf*) is a principle in Islamic law. If people in a particular place follow certain practices and these are not in conflict with clearly spelt out commandments and prohibitions of the Qur'an and Sunna, these customs are to be given due recognition in Islamic law.

A further principle is that if there is no definite text from the Qur'an or Sunna permitting or forbidding something, that thing is generally permitted, an example being the establishment of a coinage in an Islamic state.

The development of the sources and principles of Islamic law was significantly boosted by the legal arguments of Shafi'i. He argued, like the Traditionists (scholars of hadith, the traditions of the Prophet), that a hadith, even a solitary one not backed by any commonly agreed-upon community practice, should be relied on in interpreting law and should not be discarded. For Shafi'i, where a text on a religious matter existed (from the Qur'an or hadith), it had to be followed. He was against the idea of giving any recognition to rulings based simply on opinion or reason (*ra'y*) where a text existed. The emphasis given to reason in places like Iraq (with Abu Hanifa) and to a lesser extent in Medina (with Malik), in Shafi'i's view, should be curtailed in favour of text.

Shafi'i's work became the cornerstone of many later developments in the area of Islamic legal thought. For him, law is inherently religious and cannot be separated from religion. This underpinned his belief that rulings and laws should be based strictly on the Qur'an and Sunna. According to Wael Hallaq, a number of key principles are found in Shafi'i's *Risala*: (1) law must be derived exclusively from revealed scripture; (2) the prophetic Sunna constitutes a binding source of law; (3) there is no contradiction between the Sunna and the Qur'an, nor among verses or hadith within each of these sources; (4) the two sources complement each other hermeneutically; and (5) a legal ruling derived from unambiguous and widely transmitted texts is certain and subject to no disagreement, whereas a ruling that is inferred by means of ijtihad and qiyas may be subject to disagreement.[10]

Schools of law and their consolidation

Hanafi school

This school arose from the teachings of Abu Hanifa (d. 150/767), who lived in Kufa in Iraq. Since the school originated in Iraq, the Abbasid caliphs, who were based in Iraq, gave it their support. However, this support declined over time and the school had to wait until the emergence of the Ottoman Empire to become influential again. This school, particularly in the early stages, was associated with an emphasis on reason (much more than other schools of law). Today, Hanafi law is the dominant form of Islamic law in the Indian subcontinent, Central Asia and Turkey.

Maliki school

Malik ibn Anas of Medina (d. 179/795) was a great Traditionist who became the leading authority within this school. He compiled *Muwatta'*, one of the earliest works that combined hadith and fiqh. To a large extent, Malik favoured the text over reason. He considered the customary practice of the people of Medina, where the Prophet and the early Muslim community established their state, as indicative of a continuous practice going back to the time of the Prophet, and hence authoritative. It is reported that, given Malik's stature as a scholar, the Abbasid caliph al-Mansur (d. 158/775) urged Malik to compile a work of law that could be applied throughout the Abbasid caliphate. However, Malik rejected this suggestion as unworkable given the diversity in Islamic legal thinking. Through his students, Malik's teaching spread across North Africa and Spain. Today the Maliki school is dominant in North and West Africa.

Shafi'i school

This school has its roots in the scholarship of Muhammad ibn Idris al-Shafi'i (d. 204/820) who travelled widely in search of religious knowledge. He studied under several scholars in Mecca and moved to Medina to study with Malik. Later he travelled to Iraq and subsequently moved to Egypt. For Shafi'i, Islamic law should be based on the Qur'an and Sunna. The Shafi'i school remained the most important school until the emergence of the Ottoman Empire, which supported the Hanafi school. Today, the Shafi'i school of law is predominant in Southeast Asia.

Hanbali school

Ahmad ibn Hanbal (d. 240/855), who was a student of Shafi'i, is considered to be the leading figure of this school. He was a great Traditionist who collected approximately fifty thousand hadith[11] in his hadith collection (*Musnad*). In law, the Hanbalis relied more heavily on the text (the Qur'an and Sunna) and relegated analogy (qiyas) and consensus (ijma') to an insignificant role. For them, the views of Companions on religious matters have a much more important position than in other schools of law. The Hanbalis are often characterized as literalistic and somewhat intolerant towards those who hold different opinions to theirs. Nevertheless, some later Hanbalis, such as Ibn al-Qayyim (d. 751/1350), are known to have had a high degree of tolerance towards other streams of Islamic thought. The Hanbali school of law is predominant in Saudi Arabia.

Ja'fari school

This is the major Shi'i school (of Twelver Shi'a) of jurisprudence. They believe that the Qur'an is the primary source of Islamic law and that the Sunna is a secondary source. However, according to the Shi'a, hadith must be narrated and transmitted by those whom the Shi'a consider reliable. This often means the family of the Prophet or someone recognized as sympathetic to the Shi'i tradition. From within this tradition, it is the Shi'i imams who have the ability to interpret the Qur'an and hadith authoritatively.

Over the course of the second/eighth and third/ninth centuries, the schools of Islamic law became firmly established and their principles of jurisprudence strengthened. This period also saw their geographic consolidation. Once the schools were established and veneration of the earlier authorities (particularly the founders of schools) increased, a view emerged that the early authorities had completed all the necessary tasks of legal analysis and defined all intellectual structures necessary to construct law. Therefore, new ways of looking at the text and constructing or interpreting law were discouraged in favour of faithfully following what earlier scholars had done.

Ijtihad and the construction of Islamic law

'Ijtihad' means the exertion of the utmost effort by a trained jurist, taking into account all the relevant texts of the Qur'an and Sunna as well as principles of jurisprudence, to discover, for a particular human situation, a rule or law. Ijtihad is the mechanism by which Islamic law, as revealed in the Qur'an and the Sunna, may be interpreted, developed and kept alive in line with the intellectual, political, economic, legal, technological and moral developments of a society. Explicit rules and instructions in the Qur'an and the Sunna are limited in number, and, since Muslims face new situations and problems at all times and in all places, legal problem-solving is necessary. This ultimately determines the necessity for ijtihad. Ijtihad thus represents an important and dynamic element within the Islamic legal system.

A critical aspect of ijtihad is that if a rule is clearly and unambiguously stated in the primary sources of the shari'a, that is the Qur'an and Sunna, it is considered to be based on an authoritative text. Where such a ruling exists, it cannot, under normal circumstances, be subject to the process of ijtihad. For instance, the prohibition of theft is clearly and unambiguously stated in the Qur'an and therefore there cannot be any ijtihad to determine whether theft should be prohibited or not. Nor is ijtihad applicable to matters such as scientifically ascertainable facts or what is considered common sense. Ijtihad is therefore used when: (1) there is evidence (text) in the primary sources of the shari'a, but neither the meaning of the evidence nor its authenticity is certain; (2) the meaning of the text is certain, but the authenticity is not; (3) the authenticity of the text is certain but the meaning is not; or (4) there is no text at all relevant to the matter.

The historical experience

Ijtihad began as an extremely flexible tool among the Companions (the first generation of Muslims). The most creative period of the development of fiqh through ijtihad occurred during the first four centuries of Islam. This creative process gradually stagnated, however. Law became more rigid with the 'writing down' of Islamic disciplines. Such writing down of formerly orally transmitted matter and the consolidation of legal schools led to a gradual decline in the flexibility available to scholars of all schools.

The early lack of formalism in the first/seventh century gave way to a more systematic and formal approach to 'law' and its construction. By the third/ninth century, the principles of jurisprudence were established in Islamic scholarship thanks to scholars such as Shafi'i. By the end of the fifth/eleventh century, fiqh had reached its zenith in the works of several eminent scholars, such as al-Ghazali (d. 505/1111). From the sixth/twelfth century onwards, many jurists appear to have accepted the doctrine of the closure of the 'gate of ijtihad', meaning that ijtihad as practised early on should no longer be exercised; instead, one had to follow the decisions of earlier scholars where possible. Creativity in law thus became restricted to the explanation of earlier jurists' views. The emphasis on ijtihad as a creative mechanism, so characteristic of the formative period of fiqh, was replaced by imitation (*taqlid*), which hindered the development of law in line with developments in society.[12]

In the following centuries, serious attempts to question major aspects of fiqh were rarely made. Notable exceptions were Izz ibn Abd al-Salam (d. 660/1261) and al-Shatibi's (d. 790/1388) attempts to perform ijtihad primarily from a *maqasid* (the objectives of the shari'a) perspective, but without violating agreed key principles of fiqh.[13] The Hanbali jurist Najm al-Din al-Tufi (d. 716/1316) went beyond all jurists and declared that, first and foremost, the public interest (*maslaha*) should determine what is islamically acceptable and what is not. Contrary to the generally accepted view, he argued that public interest can override even a clear text of the Qur'an or Sunna in cases other than worship (*ibadat*).[14]

Renewal of ijtihad

Over time, the practice of ijtihad stagnated to a large extent. However, from the eighteenth century, the Muslim world experienced what has come to be known as 'Islamic revivalism'. This was, amongst other things, a movement against the perceived corruption of religion and the moral degeneration that was felt to be prevalent within Muslim societies. The early revivalism of this period[15] was characterized by the need to go back to 'original' Islam and by attempts to get rid of the idea of the fixed nature and finality of specific rulings by the traditional schools of law, allowing for the rethinking of the Islamic message through ijtihad.[16]

Encouraged by the push for ijtihad, what came to be known as the modernist movement emerged within Islam in the latter part of the nineteenth century. It called for fresh attempts to revive ijtihad in its original, full vigour. The modernists called for employing ijtihad to derive relevant principles from the Qur'an and Sunna in order to formulate laws suited to modern times. The Qur'an, according to the modernists, was a historic phenomenon that occurred against a socio-historical background. In their opinion, to insist on a literal implementation of the rulings derived from the shari'a sources by earlier jurists, 'shutting one's eyes to the social change that had occurred, was tantamount to deliberately defeating the Qur'an's socio-moral purposes and objectives'.[17]

Modernists called for systematic thinking about Islamic legal issues without claiming finality. This involved making a clear distinction between the shari'a and fiqh, in order to distinguish between the permanence of the shari'a represented by the Qur'an and Sunna and the 'mutability' of fiqh. Additionally, modernists sought to avoid sectarianism and the exclusiveness of legal and theological schools by not necessarily following the specific legal rulings and solutions of any particular school.[18]

The twentieth-century experience

This spirit of ijtihad so characteristic of modernists continued well into the twentieth century, playing a significant role in reviving Islamic legal thought. There were times, however, when the enthusiasm of the modernists for ijtihad was not matched by an equal enthusiasm to master traditional shari'a disciplines. This led to the unfortunate situation where many later modernists used the catchword of ijtihad to sideline the traditional shari'a disciplines in their quest to meet the challenges of modernity. Nevertheless, the modernists, on the whole, played a major role in bringing ijtihad to the forefront of the debate on reform in Islamic thought, and in portraying ijtihad as an essential tool to be utilized in a more flexible and creative manner in solving contemporary problems. Included in the agenda of the modernists was the 'democratization' of ijtihad to make it more accessible by relaxing the view enshrined in classical Islamic jurisprudence that it is only the ulama (scholars of religion), the specialists in shari'a sciences, who can perform ijtihad.

Much confusion remained as to the most appropriate methodology for applying ijtihad. From its very beginning, Islam tolerated, and even encouraged, differences amongst the scholars in areas not clearly and explicitly specified in its basic sources. Consequently, considerable diversity exists as to the question of the most appropriate method of ijtihad. Scholars have been influenced by local circumstances, customs and ideas, which have reinforced this diversity of approach.

Three forms of ijtihad appear to be dominant in the modern period. All of these approaches have been influential at different times in Islamic legal history.

Text-based ijtihad

This is the method of ijtihad generally recognized in classical Islamic scholarship and is still practised among traditionalist scholars. It is based on the foundation texts, as well as ijma' (consensus) and qiyas (analogy), and relies on the rules and principles of jurisprudence. For the scholar, each new problem should be seen in isolation. When a new problem emerges, the scholar identifies relevant texts of the shari'a and then applies the rules and principles of jurisprudence. The text could be a verse of the Qur'an, a hadith or even a view of an early authority. The literal reading of texts and the strict application of principles of fiqh heavily emphasizes conformity and tradition, which are the hallmarks of this method.

Eclectic ijtihad

In eclectic ijtihad, when scholars face a problem or issue, they often attempt to justify a position by selecting texts such as verses, hadith or views of early authorities that support their preconceived positions. Their methodology is ad hoc, often opportunistic, and does not systematically follow clear principles or rules. No major consideration is given to the principles of jurisprudence and scholars often ignore textual or historical evidence contrary to their position. As far as intellectual honesty is concerned, this is the most hazardous and problematic approach of all. It has no clear boundaries, signposts or methods that can be followed.

Context-based ijtihad

This form of ijtihad existed in an embryonic form in early Islam. However, context-based ijtihad as it exists today should be seen as a relatively new phenomenon. It is distinguished by the fact that it attempts to understand a legal problem in its historical and modern contexts. If a problem emerges for which an Islamic view is needed, the scholar first looks carefully at the problem, identifying its features, purpose, and function in the society. If it is found that the problem, or a similar one, existed in the time of the Prophet, the scholar will examine the nature of the historical problem and will be guided by the concept of public interest or common good (*maslaha*). The scholar is concerned with the underlying objectives of the shari'a in relation to the problem, such as fairness, justice and equity. A decision is then made as to the attitude Muslims should adopt vis-à-vis the problem.

Islamic law in the modern period

For many Muslims, the marginalization of Islamic law today in Muslim societies may be traced back to the colonial period, particularly in the nineteenth and the twentieth centuries. During this period a great number of Muslim countries and peoples came under European political and commercial domination. The British ruled Malaya and the Indian subcontinent and also had political mandates over some Middle Eastern countries; the French ruled much of North Africa; the Dutch ruled the East Indies (Indonesia). While the attitudes of European powers towards Islamic law differed, Muslims believe that European political domination of Muslim countries opened the way to the Westernization of law in many of those countries.

The eventual gaining of independence by Muslim countries in the twentieth century saw the birth of new Muslim nation states that largely put aside Islamic law and adopted Western laws. For example, the legal systems of Egypt, Tunisia and Algeria are influenced by the French legal system.[19] In Egypt, Islamic contract and financial law were replaced by French civil law in the late nineteenth century, although these laws were partially amended in the Egyptian Civil Code of 1949 to incorporate shari'a principles. In addition, the abolition of the Ottoman caliphate (in 1924), which upheld Islamic law, and the establishment of the Republic of Turkey led to the marginalization of Islamic law there. The new republic abolished Islamic law and adopted the Swiss and Italian legal codes. The one main area of Islamic law that has been maintained in much of the Muslim world to this day is family law: laws related to areas such as marriage, divorce and inheritance.[20]

Implementation of Islamic law in Iran and Saudi Arabia

While some countries purport to be ruled by shari'a, all Muslim countries have freely chosen to be bound by a minimum set of national and international obligations of membership in a world community of nation states. This includes living under national constitutional regimes (even where there is no written constitution) and legal systems that require respect for certain minimum rights of equality and non-discrimination for all. Nevertheless, some countries fail to provide these.[21]

Legal development in the Muslim world over the last two hundred years illustrates that Islamic law is alive and well in the modern world and is integrating itself into the modern nation state.[22] For example, in Iran, after the 1979 revolution, '[t]he Supreme Judicial Council issued a proclamation

directing courts that all un-Islamic legislation was suspended . . . with
Ayatollah Khomeini's *fatawa* [plural of 'fatwa'] serving as "transitional
laws" '. Its sources of law include Islamic law and constitutional law,
legislation and customs.[23]

In Saudi Arabia, shari'a law plays a prime role in traditional matters, while
matters related to areas such as finance and the petroleum industry are
governed by royal decree.[24] In line with the conservatism that is dominant
in Saudi Arabia, it restricts women's liberties. Women, for example, are
prohibited from driving, working freely and dressing in public as they please,
justified on the basis of 'Islamic' law.[25] Islamic law applies also in matters
of divorce, inheritance and testimony, where women are considered to be at
a judicial disadvantage.[26]

Restriction of Islamic law to family law in most Muslim countries

Family law represents the major area of Islamic law to have survived in
Muslim societies until today without being replaced by Western legal codes.[27]
While other areas of law have been reformed in response to external trends
and the needs of today, family law in many cases has remained much the
same. For many Muslims, this area of law should be protected. For them,
new definitions of family that have been legitimized in much of the Western
world, such as de facto or gay relationships, should not be accepted under
Islamic law. Many Muslim societies consider these definitions to be in
opposition to laws based upon Qur'anic and hadith injunctions.[28]

As family law is derived from Islamic sources in most Arab countries,
there is often a 'contradiction between a woman's constitutional right to
work and a family law that enables her husband to require that she obtain
his permission to work outside the home'.[29] In Turkey, success in achieving
women's equality in the public sphere highlights the asymmetrical gender
roles maintained within the home.[30] State legal systems in Muslim countries
have traditionally left family law issues such as succession and property
law often to informal dispute settlement systems, and have had very little say
in such matters. Modern states such as Pakistan have recently attempted
to regulate these 'extra-legal' spheres of family law, by using statute law.[31]
In countries where the state has incorporated Muslim personal law into the
official legal system (e.g. Pakistan and Bangladesh), clashes have occurred
between the two types of Muslim personal law – the traditional shari'a rules
and the state-sponsored codified Muslim personal law.[32] Restriction of shari'a
to family law has made it 'a highly symbolic location of the struggle between
the forces of traditionalism and modernism in the Muslim world'.[33]

Islamic family law in minority contexts

In countries where Muslims live as minorities, Western traditional juris-prudence leaves no formally recognized space for a personal law system based on different religious and cultural traditions. Muslim law is pushed into the realm of the unofficial, the extra-legal, the sphere of cultural practice or ethnic minority custom, rather than being treated as officially recognized law.[34] The ambivalent approach of Western legal systems in delegitimizing Muslim law but tolerating its social presence has been highly conducive to the hidden growth of unofficial Muslim law in those countries.[35]

In the UK, the notion of legal positivism and its conceptual understanding has been that English law should ignore 'unofficial law' and 'legal postu-lates' or the value systems of other groups of people. While this still permits development of 'conflict of law' rules, it is different from recognizing the presence of foreign laws within the official English legal system.[36] In other multicultural countries, e.g. Australia and Canada, some authors have argued that this fictional uniformity is 'unreal in social terms', and that a 'new conceptualization of equity is required in the world of today to handle ethnic diversity'.[37]

English law has made allowances for Muslims in Britain, but these are neither coherent nor carefully researched.[38] Various forms of Islamic law are recognized as overseas law under the rules of private international law. In Britain, English law treats all ethnic minority laws as customs or cultural practices, and so does not recognize shari'a as an official law.[39] Islamic law is not recognized in Australia; however, some recommendations by the Australian Law Reform Commission have made small concessions towards Muslim needs. There is greater emphasis on conciliation and mediation in resolving disputes, and binding financial agreements between spouses are recognized, but Australian law does not recognize other aspects of family life, such as a Muslim wife's right to divorce, place of domicile, etc.[40]

Reform of family law

Abdullahi An-Na'im argues for the transformation of family law into a normative system that is guided by modern notions of social policy as well as Islamic precepts, but not bound by historical shari'a, or represented as such.[41] For him, 'legitimate and coherent revision and reformulation' of Islamic family law principles in Muslim countries must take into consid-eration 'the broader understanding of shari'a according to the jurist(s) who framed those principles in a totally different historical context'.[42]

Reform of polygamy laws

Modern legislation in a range of Muslim countries on polygamy has departed from the conventional position that made polygamy a prerogative of the husband. Reforms have made polygamy conditional on obtaining a legal order:[43] it is forbidden in the Tunisian Law of Personal Status 1956; allowed with conditions and the permission of the court under the Iraqi Law of Personal Status 1959; under Moroccan and Syrian law it is made dependent on a court order. The Jordanian Law of Personal Status 1976 imposes no obvious restrictions on polygamy, but it allows the wife to stipulate in the marriage contract that the husband shall not take another wife. The Islamic Family Law (Federal Territory) Act 1984 (Malaysia) requires that applicants for polygamy must fulfil certain conditions. The state authorities and shari'a courts are responsible for ensuring that polygamy ensures justice. Egyptian Law No. 100 (1985, Art. 11) added previsions to its previous law No. 25 (1925) entitling a wife whose husband has married again to apply for divorce.[44]

Challenges for Islamic law

Khaled Abou El-Fadl argues that Islamic law is alive in the contemporary period, with many Muslims willingly implementing new rules and regulations. However, 'Islamic law as an epistemology, process and methodology of understanding and searching, as a fiqh, for the most part is dead'. Calls for the rekindling of ijtihad since the beginning of the twentieth century have focused on the need for the production of new rules (*ahkam*), without setting out a specific methodology for further development.[45] One of the challenges for Muslim countries is to accommodate Islamic law to appease the islamized population, and at the same time reconcile Islamic laws with a rapidly changing world. Some contemporary challenges facing Islamic law are Islamic family law, implementation of prescribed Islamic punishments such as amputation for theft and flogging for unlawful sexual intercourse, non-Muslim citizens, women, human rights and the shari'a.

Chapter 5

Theological thought

One of the most commonly used terms for Islamic theology is *kalam*. In Arabic, the word kalam can mean several things. Broadly translated it refers to speech, debate and discussion. The term is used for theology because of this association to debate and argument in theological matters. Kalam is an area of knowledge which deals with basic religious beliefs, proofs and defences against attacks on the foundations of Islamic faith. In this sense it does not deal with an area of law. Rather, it centres on the belief system underpinning Islam. Kalam thus diverges from fiqh (Islamic jurisprudence), which focuses on deeds and actions.

The beginning of this area of knowledge goes back to the earliest period of Islamic history, when Muslims began to debate religious belief. The issues included matters such as the unity of God and His existence and attributes, prophecy and prophethood, scripture and revelation, and resurrection and the afterlife. While many theologians developed arguments for various theological positions and were engaged in theological debates, some Muslims opposed the arguments and debates. They did not believe there was any need for the discipline of theology or for Muslims to engage in such debates at all. For them, the creeds of Islam were manifestly established by the Qur'an and explained by the Prophet. Thus there was no need to prove the beliefs of a Muslim rationally; such a procedure was an innovation in Islam. The well-known statement 'He who is involved in kalam will never receive salvation, for never does a man take to kalam unless his heart was lacking in faith' is attributed to Ahmad ibn Hanbal. Certain Hanbalis simply considered the discipline of kalam as sinful and wrote many epistles discouraging Muslims from expressing an interest in it.

The development of *kalam*

Debates about theological matters and appropriate Islamic belief emerged early within the Muslim community, but were rare during the Prophet's time. In one hadith, there is a report that several Companions were discussing the nature of God's predetermination of events (*qadar*) and the Prophet asked them not to talk about it. The Prophet also reportedly asked Muslims not to debate the nature of God.[1] If these reports are correct and authentic the Prophet was cautioning against too much unnecessary theological debate.

The Qur'an has numerous references to the Creator, God and creation, and asks Muslims to reflect on these topics. The Qur'an argues that God is closely involved in creation by sending messengers and prophets to the people so that they can understand and put into practice the basic teachings that they need in order to function in a godly manner. The Qur'an uses logic and reason so that people can understand its messages in a rational manner. It also provides guidance and information about the meaning of life and life after death. It has a lot to say on questions related to belief and unbelief, good and evil, right and wrong, and salvation. The Qur'an was on the whole comprehensible to the average person in the Arabian peninsula, who was characteristically illiterate, sometimes nomadic, and had little time for sophisticated forms of thought or reasoning. This simplicity permeated an essentially oral culture with hardened attitudes towards life, dominated by tribalism and feuds. For all the Qur'an's clarity, a number of events soon triggered major debates on its interpretation.

Early theological debates: the political context

For Sunnis, at his death, the Prophet Muhammad had not named a successor to rule the community. He was succeeded by two of his close companions, Abu Bakr and Umar, whose caliphates operated without major difficulties. The community was generally happy with their performance and did not dispute their rule much, although there were some who were keen to see someone from the family of the Prophet, preferably Ali, at the helm. It was only after the assassination of the third leader, Uthman (d. 36/656), that Ali was proclaimed caliph. His nomination was not received without resistance, mainly from the people of Iraq and the governor of Syria, Mu'awiya (d. 60/680). Early inter-Muslim fighting at the Battle of the Camel (36/656) between Ali's forces and those of his opponents, and the Battle of Siffin (37/657) between Ali's forces and those of Mu'awiya had lasting effects not only on the unity of the community but also on the future development of the discipline of theology.

During the Battle of Siffin, Ali agreed to arbitration with his challenger Mu'awiya, but a group of Muslims who had sided with Ali in the battle argued that he should not have agreed to arbitration. For them, by agreeing to that Ali effectively relinquished legitimate power to an illegitimate ruler (Mu'awiya). In protest, these Muslims seceded from Ali's camp and opposed both Ali and Mu'awiya, becoming known as Kharijis (seceders or rebels).

The Kharijis held a number of politico-theological positions:

- They rejected the political leadership of both Ali and Mu'awiya (and later of the Umayyads) on the basis that agreeing to arbitration by Ali was against the concept 'judgement belongs to God alone'. They elected their own leader.
- They argued that a Muslim who committed a grave sin (such as unlawful killing of another Muslim, which Umayyad rulers were accused of later) was no longer a Muslim and would go to Hell.
- They adopted an uncompromising attitude towards application of the commandments and prohibitions of the Qur'an.
- They believed that Muslims who did not support their position were unbelievers or religious hypocrites and could be killed with impunity.
- They believed that leadership of the Muslim community was not based on tribal kinship, and that the most God-conscious and pious Muslim among them should be the leader of the community. Furthermore, they held that a leader who is not righteous – one who did not strictly follow the sacred law – could be deposed.

The Kharijis themselves were divided on a range of issues, such as who was a true Muslim and how salvation might be attained. Early on, a multitude of subgroups sympathetic to Khariji positions or associated with Kharijis emerged. Despite the extremist nature of many of their positions, the Kharijis exerted enormous influence on the theological debates of other Muslims. In time, the mainstream Muslims (later to be known as Sunnis) adopted refined versions of several Khariji positions. At a political level, the Kharijis, particularly the most extremist among them, remained hostile to Umayyad rule and suffered violent repression for decades.

A second group, the Shi'a, arose as a result of the early political divisions. They remained loyal to Ali. There is some evidence to suggest that even while Ali was alive, some of those claiming to be his followers exaggerated his status. This tendency to exaggerate the status of key members of the Prophet's family continued after the death of Ali. Two of his sons, al-Hasan and al-Husayn, were also viewed by some as being more than human. Some Shi'a developed strong messianic beliefs, including that an infallible imam would appear at the end of time to restore justice and the rule of God, not only in the Muslim community but also in the world at large. Some of the early extremist Shi'i groups even abolished fundamental practices of Islam and adopted esoteric interpretations of the Qur'an to justify their position. This tendency among the Shi'a to exaggerate the status of the family of the Prophet and to adopt esoteric interpretations of religious texts is referred to as extremism (*ghuluw*) and those who display it are called extremists (*ghulat*) by Sunnis. Out of this chaos emerged the more moderate Shi'a in the form of Twelver (or Imami) Shi'ism, whose name is based on the recognition of twelve descendants of the Prophet as rightful heirs to leadership of the community. Twelver Shi'is came very close to Sunnis on a range of issues, and their legal school, the Ja'fari school, has relatively few areas of major interpretative difference with the main Sunni legal schools. Several Shi'i rebellions were put down by the Umayyads (41–134/661–750) and their governors, thus laying the foundation of a bloody history of persecution between Shi'i and Sunni Muslims.

In addition to the Kharijis and Shi'a, several other groups emerged in the first two centuries of Islam, often in response to the views of the Kharijis or the Shi'a. These early trends were highly fluid, as no systematic theological schools then existed. This period saw the emergence and disappearance of several theological orientations and groups.

The Mu'tazila

Much of the debate on theological matters from the mid first/seventh century to the mid second/eighth century was heavily concentrated in Iraq. This may have been because Iraq witnessed much of the opposition to Umayyad rule, and was a safer place for the Shi'i and Khariji movements.

One of the most influential figures in Iraq at this significant time was Hasan al-Basri (d. 110/728), a well-known teacher and ascetic in Iraqi religious circles. Even though al-Basri appeared on the scene before the Mu'tazili-Traditionist debates began in earnest, he undoubtedly left ideas that influenced their development, and planted the seed of a different religious movement.

Hasan al-Basri had a disdain for politics and all worldly matters. He saw sectarian disputes and acute differences of legal opinion as a threat to the proper practice of the law. His repeated call for the remembrance of the hereafter and his constant denigration of the worldly life made asceticism his cornerstone. Hasan al-Basri was critical of the fatalistic and deterministic visions of the world that were becoming influential amongst Muslims. He said that human beings were responsible for their own actions. Unless human beings have the capacity to act freely, it is hard to argue the point of rewards and punishments. Al-Basri was not debating these issues based on specific philosophical or political positions; rather, his arguments were couched within the text and ethos of the Qur'an.

It was in this context of the early second/eighth century that the first systematic theological school, the Mu'tazila, emerged in Iraq. The person believed to be the first Mu'tazili and the father of the Mu'tazili movement is known as Wasil ibn Ata (d. 131/749). He was a student of Hasan al-Basri. A commonly told story in relation to the emergence of the Mu'tazila is the following. One day, when al-Basri was with his pupils, someone came and asked whether people who committed grave sins should be considered Muslims or, according to the Khariji view, be declared unbelievers. The mainstream view at the time was that such a person was a sinner but still a Muslim. Hasan al-Basri wanted to take the time to reflect on the question and provide a properly considered opinion. But his student, Wasil, apparently became impatient with his slow decision-making and said, 'I do not say that the person who commits a major sin is an absolute believer or an absolute non-believer. For me he is between two states (belief and unbelief). He is neither a believer nor an unbeliever.' Wasil then left al-Basri's study circle, at which the teacher reportedly said, 'He broke away from us'. The word al-Basri used for this was *i'tazala* (broke away, seceded), from which it has been claimed came the name Mu'tazila.

Abbasids and the emergence of kalam

While political dissension and the intermingling with people of other faiths, particularly the Christians, left their mark on earlier theological debates, the coming to power of the Abbasids in 133/750 heralded a significantly different political climate. Unlike the Umayyads, the Abbasids represented the ascent of a non-Arab regime to power. Abbasids claimed to be the defenders of the true spirit of Islam: no distinction was to be made between Muslims on the basis of race (for example, Arabs versus non-Arabs). Scholars of religion from all surrounding areas flocked to Baghdad, the capital of the Abbasids, to play a part in creating a climate of authenticity which the Abbasids were keen to display. The Abbasids' insistence on not disregarding the law and taking legal council attracted the best legal minds to the new caliphate.

Moreover, several other factors also played a significant role in the development of kalam, such as the sophistication in legal reasoning that developed in fiqh, which in turn influenced the construction of theological arguments as well as the translation of Greek philosophical works into Arabic. The interaction and debates between Muslims and followers of other religious traditions such as Christians and Zoroastrians on issues such as prophecy and the prophethood of Muhammad, and the Muslim concept of the unity of God, also facilitated the development of kalam, as such debates often required Muslims to defend their religious beliefs on the basis of rational arguments.

Mu'tazilis versus Traditionists

It was during the Abbasid period that the consolidation of Mu'tazila as a theological school took place. This was strengthened by the support of the Abbasid caliph al-Ma'mun (d. 218/833), and later by al-Mu'tasim (d. 227/842) and al-Wathiq (d. 232/847). The Abbasid caliph al-Ma'mun instituted Mu'tazili theology as the orthodoxy. To ensure its dominance in the theological arena, al-Ma'mun instituted an inquisition (*mihna*) to force some of the state functionaries to adopt the Mu'tazili position on the 'createdness' of the Qur'an. Non-Mu'tazili scholars were persecuted by the inquisition if they did not assent to this doctrine, a situation that continued until the Abbasid caliph al-Mutawakkil (d. 247/861) turned against the Mu'tazila in favour of the Traditionists and reversed the decision of al-Ma'mun.

Key theological positions of the Mu'tazila

Mu'tazili kalam reached its peak during the third/ninth century. Those who were considered the main voices of this school of theology were far from unanimous vis-à-vis the issues that were being debated during that period and later. However it appears that Mu'tazilis were in agreement on at least five theological principles, which set them apart from other theologians and from what came to be regarded as orthodoxy. These were as follows.

Tawhid (unity of God)

Mu'tazilis adopted strict interpretation of 'monotheism'. For them, monotheism required an uncompromising observance of the transcendence and absolute unity of God. For them, God is pure Essence without any attributes, as from their point of view, assigning attributes, as their opponents did, implied multiplicity. While other Muslims argued, for example, that speech was an attribute of God and therefore uncreated, Mu'tazilis believed that it could not be uncreated as this would compromise the unity of God. Given that the Qur'an was the speech of God, the Mu'tazilis argued that the Qur'an was created in time. For them, anyone who believed that the Qur'an was an uncreated attribute of God compromised the absolute unity of God.

It has been said that the Mu'tazili position on the created nature of the Qur'an was partly a reaction to the Christian notion of the incarnation of Jesus, which they saw as infringing the unity of God:

> [T]o say that the Qur'an *is* the divine uncreated Word which manifests itself in time in the form of Arabic speech, is equivalent to saying what Christians say about the Incarnation: that Christ *is* the divine uncreated Word, who manifests himself in time in the form of a human being.[2]

Famously, the Traditionist Ahmad ibn Hanbal (d. 241/855) refused to agree with the doctrine that the Qur'an is 'created', and was imprisoned and flogged for teaching the eternality of the Qur'an. The Traditionists, as exemplified by Ahmad ibn Hanbal, rejected Mu'tazili rationalism and gave precedence to the letter of the scripture. Ibn Hanbal believed that the mode of the attributes of God, according to the teachings of the Qur'an, does not lend itself to human reason, and thus must be accepted without qualification.[3] Asking whether God's attributes, particularly speech, are 'in' Him or 'without' Him was an unacceptable religious innovation in his view. Divine speech is 'essentially' of God, it subsists in Him, and He expresses it. He does not create it inside anything else; it is He Himself who speaks. Therefore the Qur'an, according to Ibn Hanbal, is the uncreated word of God, not just metaphorically, but with words, letters and ideas.[4]

Divine justice

Human beings are capable of creating and performing acts both good and evil, and it is on this basis that they are rewarded or punished in the hereafter. It is not God who creates evil and injustice, for this would mean that God is unjust. God in His wisdom only wills well for people. God does not ask human beings to commit evil. Part of God's well-wishing is to send prophets to guide humanity.

Promise and threat

Believers who depart from this world having obeyed God and repented of all major sins 'deserve' reward in the hereafter. Otherwise, they are damned eternally, although their punishment will be lighter than that inflicted on the infidels of other faiths.

Commanding good and prohibiting evil

Humans ought to be able, through reason, to have knowledge of and perceive good and evil, and acknowledge the gifts that God bestowed before revelation. Divine laws were revealed through the prophets to make the observance of those laws obligatory. Mu'tazilis did not agree on how the laws were to be observed. Some saw that this task was the sole prerogative of an imam (the political-religious leader of the Muslim community). Others believed that it was up to the community to decide, while a third group believed that the task had to be divided between those laws which were the proper domain of the imam, and those which could be decided by the community.

The intermediary state of the sinner

The Mu'tazilis believed that the *fasiq* (sinner who does not repent) from among the Muslim community is in an intermediary state between 'belief' and 'non-belief'. This means the fasiq is neither a believer nor a non-believer.

When the tables were turned against the Mu'tazilis (from 236/850), the intolerance they showed during the inquisition (212–36/827–50) towards those Muslims who did not share their views was visited on the Mu'tazilis by the Traditionists. The downfall of the Mu'tazila meant that the Traditionists, with their literal reading of texts related to theology, were in the ascendancy. Between the two extremes of the Mu'tazila and the

Traditionists, the Ash'ari school of theology emerged to become the most dominant and pervasive theological school within Sunni Islam. On the other hand, the Shi'a came to adopt many Mu'tazili theological views.

Ash'ari and his school of theology

The third/ninth century also witnessed the advent of the important theologian Abu al-Hasan Ali ibn Isma'il al-Ash'ari (d. in Baghdad circa 330/941), after whom the Ash'ari school of theology is named. Born in Basra, he began as a Mu'tazili. However, he later broke away and began teaching doctrines that denied his Mu'tazili past.

In addition to contradicting the Mu'tazila on the question of God's essence and attributes, including that of speech, al-Ash'ari attacked the Mu'tazilis on free will, the nature of the divine law, the definition of evil and the role of reason, all of which had much to do with the concrete attitude of the community.

Although it is not clear why al-Ash'ari broke away from the Mu'tazilis, one of the more famous stories surrounds a dispute he had with a former teacher over the hypothetical case of three brothers (a believer, an unbeliever and a child) and the fates of their souls in the hereafter. His Mu'tazili teacher could not give a satisfactory answer. Al-Ash'ari thought that the answer given highlighted some important weaknesses in the principle of 'the promise and the threat', after which he came to doubt the entirety of Mu'tazili doctrines.[5]

Ash'ari theological beliefs

Knowledge of God

The first duty of the human being is to know God. According to the Ash'aris, it is possible to know through reason, but the obligation to know comes through revelation, which is superior to reason (for example, distinguishing good and evil, or believing in the realm of the 'unseen', cannot be achieved through reason alone). We can know God's attributes through His acts, and examination of the self leads to knowledge of God.[6]

The argument is that, for example, when human beings reflect on the way they were conceived, how they grew from one state to another until they reached perfection, and realized that they could not have instigated or performed this, they will be in no doubt of a creator who is all-powerful, all-knowing, willing, wise and all-merciful. The human being who has a sound intellect, according to al-Ash'ari, would find it inconceivable that these acts were brought about by chance or autonomously, since their manifestly deliberate choice and perfection would deny that claim, pointing instead to their creator.[7]

Attributes of God

God is transcendent and there is nothing like Him in creation. Only those attributes mentioned in the Qur'an may be used in describing God. The distinguishing feature of the Ash'ari conception of God's attributes is that his positive attributes – knowledge, power, will, life, hearing, sight, and speech – subsist in Him eternally and are inherent in His essence (unlike the Mu'tazili view, which held that God's essence and attributes are identical).[8]

The Qur'an

Ash'aris believe that the Qur'an is the eternal, immutable and uncreated word of God. The letters, the ink and the paper however are created.

Vision of God in the next life

The Mu'tazilis rejected the possibility of seeing God in the next life. The Ash'aris believed that while this is not possible in this life, Qur'anic references and many sound hadith refer to the possibility of sighting God in the hereafter. To resolve the problem of the inference that sight would spatially limit God, the Ash'aris said that it is possible in the next life to perceive God, but in a manner unlike our 'seeing' in the physical world through the eye.[9]

Sinners as believers or unbelievers

The notion that a person is neither a believer nor an unbeliever, neither a friend of God nor His enemy, is untenable, according to the Ash'aris. Thus, they reject the Mu'tazili belief in the intermediate state of grave sinners. The Ash'aris believe Muslims can be sinners and may receive God's mercy provided they do not abandon their faith before or after committing sin. Sinful acts therefore do not have any bearing on faith.[10]

Theory of kasb (acquisition)

In contrast to those (such as the Jabris – the determinists) who took a deterministic view of human actions, and the Mu'tazilis, who believed human beings possessed free will and power to act, the Ash'aris adopted a doctrine called *kasb* (acquisition). According to this doctrine, human beings do not possess the power to originate or complete an act; that power belongs to God alone. Rather they are given the ability to choose freely between right and wrong, and thus acquire responsibility for their choices. The Ash'aris held that power is of two types: original and derived. God alone possesses true originating or creative power, whereas human beings have derived power, which cannot create an act in itself. Human beings are, therefore, the loci for God's creative power, which completes the choices they make. Human beings possess 'free choice' and it is God's habit to create the action that completes the choice. From this, the human being is rewarded for choosing good or punished for choosing evil. The result of the doctrine of *kasb* was that Ash'aris believed that God creates good and evil. The theory of *kasb* was controversial within the Ash'ari school itself.[11]

From the Creed of Adud al-Din al-Iji (circa 1281–1355 CE), an Ash'ari theologian

The following is a summary of the key points in Iji's Creed (known as Adudiyya).

- The world is originated, and is capable of becoming non-existent.
- The world has a maker who has been from eternity.
- God is characterized by all the attributes of perfection and is free from all the marks of deficiency.
- God has no similar, no rival, no like, no partner, no helper.
- God does not inhere in anything else; no originated (thing) subsists in His essence.
- God is not a substance, an accident or a body.
- God is not in any place or in any direction.
- God is seen by the believers on the Day of Resurrection.
- What God willed came to be, and what He did not will did not come to be. Unbelief and sins (in human beings) are by (God's) creating and by His willing but not with His approval.
- God is rich (and independent); He has no need of anything.
- There is no judge over God; and nothing is obligatory for Him.
- God is not divided into parts or portions. He has no limit and no end.
- God has angels possessing wings, in twos, threes and fours. The angels include Jibril, Mika'il, Israfil and Izra'il.
- The Qur'an is the speech of God, uncreated.
- The return (to life) is a reality; the bodies will be gathered together, and their spirits will be restored to them.
- Everlastingly abiding in Paradise are the people of Paradise, and in Hell the unbelievers. The Muslim who has committed a great sin does not abide everlastingly in Hell, but finally goes to Paradise.
- The punishment [that is reported to take place] in the grave is a reality.

- The sending of messengers (by God), from Adam to our prophet, with evidentiary miracles (to confirm their claims) is a reality.
- Unbelief is the absence of faith. We do not declare any Muslims unbelievers except where they deny the Creator who is all-powerful, effectively willing and all-knowing, or (where they) associate others with God, or reject the prophethood of Muhammad, or reject the evidence by which the coming of Muhammad is necessarily known, or reject a matter on which there has been definite agreement, such as the five pillars of Islam, or consider forbidden things permitted.[12]

Maturidi school of theology

Closely related to the Ash'ari school of theology is that of the Maturidis. Abu Mansur al-Maturidi (d. circa 333/944) of Maturid, Samarqand, sought to introduce to the eastern provinces of the caliphate what his younger contemporary al-Ash'ari would achieve in Baghdad. A Hanafi in law, al-Maturidi was also keen to use reason within the limits of orthodoxy, and shunned literalism. No writings of Al-Maturidi appear in published form. It is thus easier to speak of Maturidism than to speak of al-Maturidi himself. The creed of Najm al-Din al-Nasafi (d. 537/1142) and its commentary by Taftazani are renowned Maturidi sources to this day. With the Ash'aris, Maturidis held that all of God's attributes are eternal (the alternative would mean that God changes), and criticized the Mu'tazila for divesting His attributes of real meaning.[13] Vision (of God) in the next life does not have to conform to the rules of optics of this world.[14] Faith occurs by assent of the heart.[15] Grave sinners may receive mercy, but judgement lies with God, who may punish them eternally in Hell if He so wills.[16] But Maturidism came close to Mu'tazili thought on a number of issues: al-Maturidi introduced theories on the sources of knowledge, and reserved a particular place for reason in his epistemology, as well as his theology.[17] Reason by itself, not only revelation, could prompt in us the need to know God. Despite its general acceptance of the theory of kasb ('acquisition'), Maturidism also maintains that God endows human beings with both choice and power to act.[18]

Imami Shi'i theology

There are three main groups within Shi'ism – Imamis (Twelver-Imamis), Ismailis and Zaydis – and all have theological positions which often differ significantly from one another. The Imamis and Zaydis are heavily influenced by Mu'tazili theology, so on many theological positions they could be considered an extension of the Mu'tazilis. The Ismailis however, with their emphasis on esoteric interpretation, differ significantly from Imamis and Zaydis. The systematic elaboration of Imami belief was the work of a number of scholars such as Ibn Babawayh al-Qummi (d. 381/991). The earliest full statement of doctrinal belief is the Epistle (*Risala*) on Imami beliefs composed by Ibn-Babawayh.[19] Key Imami theological positions include:

- Insistence on God's unity and acceptance of a distinction between essential and active attributes of God. The active attributes originate in time. For example, God cannot be Provider (*raziq*) until there is a creature for which He makes provision (*rizq*).
- Interpretation of anthropomorphic terms, such as 'face' and 'hand', are applied to God metaphorically.
- Acceptance of common eschatological beliefs, although some are interpreted metaphorically.
- Acceptance of the idea of the createdness of the Qur'an. If the Qur'an is created, it is not necessarily the expression of God's being, and may therefore be modified by an inspired imam.

What is noticeable is that the Imamis come very close to Mu'tazili positions in theology. Much like Sunnis, there have been two contrary tendencies in Imamism: one that uses reason and engages in kalam and another that mostly restricts itself to the Qur'an and Sunna and criticizes the use of reason.[20]

Gradual decline of *kalam*

With its tendency to take the middle ground between the Mu'tazila and the Traditionists, Ash'arism came to dominate the theological scene in much of the Sunni world. The Malikis and Shafi'is, on the whole, became Ash'aris in theology, while a significant section of the Hanafis became Maturidis (who in many respects are similar to Ash'aris). The Imami Shi'a and Zaydi Shi'a came to adopt the Mu'tazili theology. However, within the Sunni world, much of the Traditionist unease with theological debate and rationalism came to dominate, gradually leading to a significant decline and marginalization of kalam among Sunnis. This was perhaps facilitated by figures such as al-Ghazali (d. 505/1111), a Shafi'i, through his attacks on philosophy, and by Ibn Taymiyya (d.728/1328), a Hanbali, through his anti-kalam approach. The sidelining of the Mu'tazilis with their staunchly rationalist outlook after the inquisition of the Abbasid caliph al-Ma'mun, the triumphalism of the Traditionists under Ahmad ibn Hanbal, and the emergence of Ash'arism with its highly traditionalist positions, meant that kalam was unable to sustain itself within a rationalist framework. The Traditionist framework, with its strong bias against rational thought, was no place for a vibrant kalam to flourish.

Kalam in the modern period

In the modern period, reformers such as Muhammad Abduh (d. 1905), one of the key figures of the modernist movement and one-time head of al-Azhar seminary in Cairo, attempted to revive theological thought. The intellectual task that Abduh set for himself was to simplify Islam through a return to its early sources. Two aspects of modern thought played a central part in Abduh's theological thought. One is the theory of evolution, which he employed to demonstrate that the Prophet Muhammad was the culmination of the prophets.[21] The second is the concept of scientific law as a formulation of a relationship between cause and effect.[22]

Fundamental to the idea of prophecy in Islam is the doctrine of its conclusion by the Prophet Muhammad. Theologians taught that God willed that communication with humanity through revelation should end with a specific prophet at a specific time. Rather than supporting this doctrine solely by quoting Qur'anic verses and hadith, Abduh attempted to support it through a sociological rationale. He suggested that revelation varied in accordance with human development. For instance, when human beings were in the stage of 'childhood' (early history),

> [r]eligions in that sort of context could not intelligibly relate them-
> selves to men on subtle aspects of consciousness or 'extend' them with
> rational proofs. . . . The religions took men and gave them straight
> commands and firm restraints, to which they required obedience to
> the utmost degree. Though the meaning and purpose were there to be
> known, obedience was irrespective of actual comprehension and
> intelligent knowledge.[23]

It is then understood that the coming of Muhammad, the 'seal of prophecy', ushered in the age of maturity, or the age of reason to be more precise. Through this evolutionary account, Abduh tacitly urges a rethinking of religion to align it with the changes that were brought about by the spirit of Muhammad's message in the first place.[24]

Steering away from Ash'ari theology, Abduh strove to show that Islam accommodates and urges the upholding of the principle of causality. Abduh charges with committing the sin of association of other beings with God (*shirk*) all those who do not employ the normal procedures of causation, as ordained by God, and holds them responsible for the false reliance on God and a fatalistic view of the world that he believes is behind the stagnation of the Muslim community (umma) at large.[25] Having resurrected the Mu'tazili view of the world, Abduh aimed at the same time to limit the miraculous, of which he was sceptical. Conversely, Abduh wanted to limit the scope of 'reason', lest his thesis develop into a stand for 'rationalism'. He considered the message of the prophets to be complementary to reason: 'How then can reason be denied its right, being, as it is, the scrutineer of evidences so as to reach the truth within them and know that it is Divinely given?'[26] But once it concludes that the utterances of the Prophet are truthful, reason must accept the information or teaching they contain.

The adoption of such theological thought within the seminaries of Muslim religious education has been slow; in fact, the resurgence of neo-revivalism in the twentieth century (in the form of Muslim Brotherhood, for instance), and the significant revival of traditionalism and literalism in the form of Wahhabism and Salafism has further curtailed the revival of theological thought along the lines of Abduh.

Chapter 6

Mystical thought
Sufism

Sufism (or Islamic mysticism) is one way of understanding and approaching God in Islam. It is related to asceticism, rooted in divine revelation and comprehended through shari'a. It is an approach to God that makes use of intuitive and emotional spiritual faculties, considered by Sufis to be dormant unless discovered through guided training. One definition of Sufism, therefore, is that which 'embraces those tendencies in Islam which aim at direct communion between God and man'.[1] Training in Sufism is known as 'travelling the path' and aims at 'dispersing the veils which hide the self from the Real[2] and thereby become transformed or absorbed into undifferentiated Unity'.[3] This mystical training reacts against the rationalization of Islam in law and theology, and focuses instead on spiritual freedom that allows our intrinsic intuitive spiritual senses their full scope.[4]

Early development of Sufism

The basis of asceticism in Islam was fear of God's judgement, resulting in a deep consciousness of sin and human weakness, and consequent desire for complete submission to the Will of God. The first century of Islam was favourable to the spread of asceticism as a result of dissatisfaction with materialism and religious and political dissension. In the second half of the first/seventh century, the ascetic movement was still 'orthodox' and leaders were of the 'pietist type'.[5] The ascetic movement of the first two centuries of Islam – with encouragement to renunciation and otherworldliness – was gradually combined with tendencies towards mysticism, thus developing the earliest form of recognizable Sufism.[6]

Sufi asceticism developed through supererogation (observing rules and rituals beyond that required by religious law), and the renunciation of unlawful and even some lawful things. Examples of Sufi ascetic practices and beliefs include:

- the wearing of a patched robe (*khirqa*)[7]
- eating only 'lawful' food, i.e. that earned by the labours of a Sufi's own hands

- voluntary fasting of varying duration and severity[8]
- holding the view that the true fasting was 'abstention from desire, and that the fasting of the heart was more important than the fasting of the body'[9]
- spending much time in prayer and recitation of the Qur'an as a means of drawing near to God, as well as prayer in the form of remembrance of God (*dhikr*).

Among the most important of Sufism's ideas is renunciation of the world, which means the abandonment of the transient pleasures of this life, and even of desire for eternal bliss. Rabi'a al-Adawiyya (d. 185/801) was the first Sufi to place emphasis on the notion of unselfish love for God. She is said to have prayed:

> O Lord,
> If I worship You
> From fear of Hell, burn me in Hell.
> If I worship You
> From hope of Paradise, bar me from its gates.
> But if I worship You for Yourself alone
> Then grace me forever the splendour of Your Face.[10]

According to al-Qushayri (d. 465/1072), a true Sufi is one who 'should be indifferent to this world and the next'.[11] True Sufi poverty involved the sacrifice of all material goods as well as the exercise of patience and resignation to the will of God,[12] and the glad endurance of affliction in this life for the sake of drawing nearer to God in the hereafter.[13]

Development of Sufi orders

Sufism developed ways of purification through the medium of religious orders: the organized cultivation of religious experience, based on the idea of a master–disciple relationship.[14] A disciple accepted the authority and guidance of a master who had travelled the stages of the Sufi path. Initially, the 'path' (*tariqa*) referred to a gradual and practical method of contemplative and soul-releasing mysticism, which took a disciple through a succession of 'stages' (*maqamat*) in order to experience divine reality.[15] Later it also came to refer to particular Sufi groups with distinct initiation rites and ritual practices that developed over centuries through chains of master–disciple relationships back to a single 'founding' master, in whose honour the tariqa was named.[16]

These developments were not well received by many ulama, the experts in religious law, who viewed them with suspicion. The ulama resented the Sufis' disassociation from what the ulama recognized as legitimate spheres of religious authority, and were incensed by areas such as the Sufi *sama'* (spiritual concert for inducing ecstasy).[17] However, by the fifth/eleventh century, more moderate trends in Sufism came to be recognized as legitimate, mostly owing to the activities of well-respected Muslim scholars who were also Sufis, such as al-Sulami (d. 412/1021), his disciple al-Qushayri and perhaps most notably Abu Hamid al-Ghazali (d. 505/1111).[18]

Al-Ghazali first gained fame as a respected theologian who was appointed head professor at the Nizamiyya College in Baghdad. After suffering a break-down, he turned to Sufism and retreated into the life of an ascetic. He continued to write and teach and harmonized the pursuit of Sufism with what was considered orthodox theology and law, and contributed greatly to the wide acceptance of Sufism in orthodox circles. Official recognition did not mean the suspicions of the ulama disappeared, however, and Sufism continued to develop on separate paths from non-mystical Islam.[19]

Because many would-be Sufis travelled widely seeking masters, the orders established centres (hostels, rest houses, hospices, retreats) throughout the Muslim world.[20] By the fifth/eleventh century, organized Sufi convents had become numerous, contributing to the islamization of borderland and non-Arabic regions in central Asia and northern Africa.[21] Rules of convent etiquette began to develop known as 'companionship' (*suhba*).[22] By the sixth/twelfth century, many Sufi convents had become flourishing establishments,[23] but a new direction developed in the phenomenon of single masters who withdrew from convent life to a small retreat, or took up the wandering life with a group of disciples. By the seventh/thirteenth century, tariqas were associated with a single master, whose teachings, mystical exercises and rules of life were handed down through a chain (*silsila*) of spiritual guides.[24]

The Sufi path

The central aim of all ascetic exercises was a direct spiritual experience: the mystic consciousness of union with God. For Sufis, this goal could be attained only by the faithful following of the sufi path, with its numerous stages, which enabled the soul to be purified, to acquire certain qualities and to rise higher until, with the help of divine grace, it would find its home in God.[25]

Perhaps the first systematic exposition of Sufism as a way of life and thought was *The Book of Flashes (Kitab al-luma')* by Abu Nasr al-Sarraj (d. 378/998), a Sufi scholar from the city of Tus in the Iranian region of Khurasan. Sarraj discusses seven stations (stages of spiritual attainment) along the Sufi path: repentance; watchfulness; renunciation; poverty; patience; trust; and accep-tance. Furthermore, Sarraj lists ten states (spiritual moods given by God): meditation; nearness to God; love; fear; hope; longing; intimacy; tranquillity; contemplation; and certainty.[26] While Sarraj acknowledges that anyone can join Sufism and participate in this mystical tradition, he notes that there is a rigorous set of standards for the seeker in the areas of self-discipline, psychological self-awareness, intuitive or mystical understanding, and emotional and poetic sensitivity.[27]

According to al-Junayd (d. 298/910), the first stage of repentance involves not only the remembrance of sins but also the forgetting of them.[28] The early stages of the path include patience and gratitude, hope and fear. Al-Rudhabari (d. 322/934) compared hope and fear to the wings of a bird in flight: if one fails its flight falters, if both fail it dies.[29] Other stages include poverty, renunciation and dependence on God. Among the higher stages is satisfaction – that the human being is satisfied with all God has ordained for him or her – and, later, remembrance of death. The final stages include love and gnosis leading to the vision of God and the ultimate goal of union with the divine.[30] Other Sufis, such as al-Qushayri and al-Ghazali, gave even more comprehensive lists of the stages of the Sufi path.

Sufi orders[31]

During the first four to five centuries of Islam, Sufi instruction was transmitted via an individual master (known variously as *shaykh*, *pir* or *murshid*) to a group of students. After a while, a more structurally tight-knit organization developed, more often than not named after a founder and based on a spiritual framework encompassing rules of etiquette, behaviour, meditation and other forms of worship.[32] Below are some of the most influential Sufi orders.[33]

The Qadiriyya order

This order was named after Abd al-Qadir al-Jilani (d. 561/1166), who was born in a village in northern Iran. His ideas influenced other founders of mystical orders such as Khwaja Mu'in al-Din Chishti (d. 633/1236) and Abd al Qahir al-Suhrawardi (d. 564/1168). He is said to have remarked: 'My foot is on the head of every saint.'[34] The order was formed several decades after his death, and stories of his miracles were later circulated by biographers such as Ali ibn Yusuf al-Shattanawfi (d. 713/1314).[35] Al-Jilani viewed shari'a as the source of all spiritual advancement and culture, and followed the Hanbali school of law (see Chapter 4).[36] Initially, Qadiri teachings spread in and around Baghdad, then moved into Arabia, Morocco, Egypt, Turkestan, parts of Africa (Khartoum, Sokoto, Tripoli) and India.[37]

It is unlikely that al-Jilani himself instituted a rigid set of prayers and rituals to follow, and different Qadiri groups have different practices, although nominal allegiance is given to the caretaker of al-Jilani's tomb in Baghdad. Pilgrimages are often made to places associated with the Qadiri order and festivities are held in honour of the founder at which gifts are presented to his descendants. Qadiris also perform *dhikr* accompanied by music.[38] Al-Jilani's sermons were collected into a work titled *The Sublime Revelation* (*al-Fath ar-rabbani*). In his fifteenth 'discourse', he said:

> No one knows how to behave correctly with the shaykhs unless he has served them and become aware of some of the spiritual states [*ahwal*] they experience with Allah (Almighty and Glorious is He). The people [of the Lord] have learned to treat praise and blame like summer and winter, like night and day. They regard them both as from Allah (Almighty and Glorious is He), because no one is capable of bringing them about except Allah (Almighty and Glorious is He). When this has become real for them, therefore, they do not place their confidence in those who praise them, nor do they fight with their critics, and they pay no attention to them. Their hearts have been emptied of both love and hate for creatures. They neither love nor hate, but rather feel compassion.[39]

The Shadhiliyya order

In the western Muslim world, i.e. around the Mediterranean, the end of the Almohad empire in the seventh/thirteenth century gave rise to several dynastic regimes. Under one of these – the Hafsids of Tunis – the Shadhili order came into being, named after Abu al-Hasan al-Shadhili (d. 656/1258).[40] His order prospered in Spain, Morocco, Algeria, Tunisia and under the Mamluks in Egypt, attracting notable intellectuals including the prolific author Jalal ad-Din al-Suyuti (d. 911/1505). After its initial start in North Africa, the order gained prominence in the eastern parts of the Islamic world; today it is mainly represented in North Africa with active branches in Egypt and the Sudan.[41]

Early Shadhilis followed the Maliki school of law (see Chapter 4) and emphasized the doctrine of the absolute unity of God (*tawhid*). Their goal was the gnostic realization of God based on strict adherence to religious law and Ash'ari dogma.[42] From early in their history, many sub-branches of the Shadhili order sprang up. They avoided ostentatious dress or spectacular public displays, although visiting the tombs of saints was an important feature of their practice. Later, Shadhilis also played an important role in resisting European colonization of Muslim lands, and generated a number of revivalist movements.[43]

Shadhili mystical practice conforms to the practice of religious law. It includes congregational recitation of poems, prayers and litanies. For example, 'The Cloak' (*al-Burda*), a famous poem honouring the Prophet Muhammad, was written by a Shadhili Sufi, al-Busiri (d. 695/1296). In this he says:[44]

Muhammad, leader of the two worlds
and of Man and the jinn,
Leader also of the Arabs and
non Arabs and their kin.
Our Prophet, Commander of right,
prohibits evil's way,
Yet no one's speech more gentle could be
than his nay or yea.[45]

The Naqshbandiyya order

Named after Khwaja Baha' al-Din Muhammad Naqshband (d. 791/1389), this order has had a far-reaching impact on Muslims all over the world. Its spiritual affiliation is with the first caliph, Abu Bakr, unlike most Sufi lineages, which reach back to the Prophet's cousin and son-in-law Ali.[46]

The order was established in Central Asia, but, despite its early history in the Persian world, the Sunni-focused Naqshbandi order lost influence in Persia with the rise of the Shi'i Safavid dynasty (908–1149/1502–1736). After its founding, the Naqshbandis spread through Turkestan, Syria, Turkey, Afghanistan, Java, Borneo, Africa and China. The Mujaddidi branch, established by Ahmad Sirhindi (d. 1034/1624), gained prominence in India, but also migrated to Turkey. Another significant Indian Naqshbandi influence came in the form of the teachings of Shah Wali Allah (d. 1176/ 1762).[47]

The Naqshbandis did not shy away from involvement in politics. They had a generally favourable relationship with the Ottomans; the Turkish Shaykh Ahmed Ziyauddin Gumush-Khanewi (d. 1311/1894), who developed a large following that exists to the present day, fought in the Ottoman–Russian war of 1877.[48] Other Turkish Sufi shaykhs fought in the First World War and the Turkish War of Independence, while militant Naqshbandis opposed the establishment of the secular Turkish state. In India, Naqshbandis played an important role in developing Mughal ideology; in particular, Ahmad Sirhindi attempted to reform the ruling classes.[49] The Naqshbandis, joined by the Qadiris, were also active in attempting to resist the Russian entrance into Caucasia.[50]

In the present day, a prominent Naqshbandi group has moved into the United States and Europe under the direction of the charismatic Shaykh Muhammad Nazim al-Haqqani and his deputy Shaykh Muhammad Hisham Kabbani.[51] According to the Naqshbandiyya–Haqqaniyya, there are three levels of daily spiritual practice depending on one's stage along the path. Along with the obligatory practices that all Muslims perform (such as the five daily prayers and following the requirements of religious law), an initiate in the Naqshbandiyya–Haqqaniyya order repeats certain phrases, invocations, lists of the divine names and Qur'anic chapters (suras) multiple times, and also prays blessings on the Prophet Muhammad. A disciple at the next level does the same but with increased repetitions. At the third level, the disciple undergoes more rigorous spiritual practice and meditation. Periods of seclusion are required in order to heighten spiritual awakening.[52]

Ibn Arabi and his school

Abu Abd Allah ibn Arabi (d. 638/1240) is probably one of the most influential Sufis in Islamic history. Known as Muhyi al-Din (meaning the reviver of the religion) and al-Shaykh al-Akbar (the greatest master), he was born in Murcia, Spain, in 560/1165.[53] Early in his life, he had a conversion experience following an illness, and, although he did not found a specific Sufi order, his influence on Sufi thought is ubiquitous. Ibn Arabi had the opportunity to meet a number of important scholars and teachers. He travelled through Spain, North Africa and the eastern Islamic world, and made a pilgrimage to Mecca, where he stayed for two years, reportedly experiencing mystical visions and dreams.[54]

He wrote on several esoteric currents existing within the world of Islamic thought, such as Pythagoreanism, alchemy and astrology, and various Sufi trends, which he developed into a vast synthesis shaped by the Qur'an and Sunna.[55] Around eight hundred and fifty works have been attributed to Ibn Arabi, of which seven hundred are extant, and of these about four hundred and fifty are considered authentic. Among them are the famous *The Meccan Opening* (*al-Futuhat al-makkiyya*), *The Ringstones of Wisdom* (*Fusus al-hikam*) and *The Tree of Engendered Existence* (*Shajarat al-kawn*).[56] Two of Ibn Arabi's most important doctrines are the 'Unity of Being' (*wahdat al-wujud*) and the 'Perfect Man' (*al-insan al-kamil*).[57]

Ibn Arabi's theosophy

Crucial to Ibn Arabi's theosophy and metaphysics is the concept of 'Unity of Being' (*wahdat al-wujud*), a term often used by his followers, but not by Ibn Arabi himself. The phrase 'Unity of Being' means that from the perspective of transcendence of God (*tanzih*) there is only one Being; nothing else has true existence besides the indivisible One. The outside, the created world, is not an objective reality. However from another perspective, that of immanence (*tashbih*), all things are the disclosure or self-manifestation of the Existent.

According to Ibn Arabi, an image of the essence of every creature exists in God's knowledge. These images are called 'the subsistent archetypes' (*al-a'yan al-thabita*) because they subsist in God's knowledge and never leave His knowledge or mind. Because these 'ideals' are identical to the attributes of God, which are also identical with His essence, the many-ness perceived on the 'outside' is not real; it just appears to exist objectively. Distinctions appear as Being determines itself; therefore, multiplicity proceeds from unity. The same one Being manifests itself under different forms without undergoing any division or blemish. In the Perfect Man (al-insan al-kamil), the manifestation of all of God's attributes occurs.[58]

While existential determinations are finite and ideal determination is infinite, Ibn Arabi professes the ontological unity of all that exists. Multiplicity perceived by human beings exists only in their imagination and imaginative power. It takes a particular spiritual taste and a sharp eye to be able to witness God's immanence in the world without losing sight of His transcendence.[59]

The distinction between the creator and creation is only relative. In his *Fusus*, Ibn Arabi says:

> If you wish you can say that the world is God, or you can say that it is a creation; if you would rather, you can say that it is God on the one hand and a creation on the other, or you can plead stupefaction because of the lack of differentiation between the two.[60]

According to Ibn Arabi, God's Essence is perceived as a substance that somehow penetrates the world and intermingles with it. On this basis, Ibn Arabi adds that there is nothing essentially evil in creation. This has given rise to the charge of pantheism and contradiction of the values of the shari'a, according to which there is both good and evil.[61]

It is often assumed that Ahmad Sirhindi of India (d. 1034/1624), of the Naqshbandi order, was a vehement opponent of Ibn Arabi, because of Sirhindi's criticism of the notion of 'Unity of Being'.[62] A deeper analysis of his views, however, suggests that those whom Sirhindi takes to task are more the 'pretenders' who think they are on the path of Ibn Arabi, while failing to appreciate his most delicate distinctions. Thus, Sirhindi's criticisms of 'Unity of Being' concern these groups of aspirant Sufis, rather than Ibn Arabi himself.[63] However, Sirhindi was no mere imitator of Ibn Arabi. He had his own mystical visions and spiritual experiences and developed the notion of *wahdat al-shuhud* (unity of witnessing), which he considered different and even superior owing to the fact that his teachings were considered safe for the masses. Ibn Arabi, on the other hand, was 'guided' but might not necessarily guide others. Sirhindi does not personally see himself as superior to Ibn Arabi; in many places he eulogizes the latter and acknowledges his indebtedness, viewing his own insights as a refinement.[64]

In his concept of Being, Sirhindi inclines towards the position of the ulama using the expression 'everything is by Him'. Sirhindi does not maintain that the world has an original existence: it is a 'shadow' of God, a place in which God manifests Himself. God's attributes can be found in creation, and the attributes and essence of the world of creation denote the attributes and Essence of God. Being is the source of all perfection.[65] However, contrary to the views of some followers of Unity of Being, and following the precepts of the Qur'an, Sirhindi sees it as imperative to maintain a distinction between God and His creation. The Essence of God supports the world through the divine names and attributes, which have their own reality.

Critique of Sufis and Sufism[66]

Like other schools of thought and practice at different times, Sufis have been targeted by zealous ulama and political authorities that have objected to their teachings. Often, theological persecutions were related to politics and social instability.[67] For example, during the Abbasid inquisition regarding the status of the Qur'an (whether it was created or not), a well-known Sufi, Dhu al-Nun (d. 246/860), was persecuted along with Ahmad ibn Hanbal for upholding the uncreated nature of the Qur'an. Similarly, the Sufi writer al-Qushayri suffered when the Ash'ari theological school was persecuted in Khurasan between 440/1048 and 455/1063.[68]

It was not only non-Sufis who criticized Sufism. Other Sufis criticized aspects of Sufism, among them key figures such as al-Sarraj (d. 378/988), al-Hujwiri (d. circa 470/1077) and al-Ghazali (d. 505/1111).[69] Among the strongest critics was Ibn al-Jawzi (d. 597/1200), a strict Hanbali jurist and writer. Ibn al-Jawzi held to a literalistic application of the law, jealously aiming to 'purify' the shari'a.[70] He criticized what he saw as Sufi tendencies towards libertinism.[71] Ibn al-Jawzi listed six main areas of libertinism (among certain sections of Sufism) based on a list by al-Ghazali:

- Since all of our acts are predetermined, we need not perform any religious duty.
- God does not need our prayers, and therefore we need not perform them.
- Whatever we do, God is generous and will forgive.
- Since the law does not eliminate human weakness, it is worthless as a means of spiritual advancement.
- Sufis who see heavenly visions and hear celestial voices have reached the goal, and need not perform prayer.
- Sanctity and the state beyond the law are proved by the performance of miracles.[72]

Ibn al-Jawzi also accused Sufism of a tendency towards incarnationism (*hulul*). Incarnationism is the focus on the beautiful human form as the locus of divine manifestation. The divine beauty was often contemplated in the masculine form; thus we find the phenomenon of 'gazing upon youths' as a phenomenon of *hulul*.[73] The fifth/eleventh century Hanbali jurist and heresiographer Abu Ya'la wrote: 'The incarnationists (*al-hululiyya*) have gone to the point of saying that God the Almighty experiences passionate love!'[74] The Indian scholar al-Thanawi (d. 1158/1745) remarked that the incarnationists were:

> [a] sect of vain pretenders to Sufism who say that it is permitted to gaze on young men and women. In that state they dance and listen to music and say, 'This is one of the divine attributes that has descended among us, which is permitted and lawful!' This is pure infidelity.[75]

Another critique of Sufis is related to their ecstatic sayings, which were interpreted as being misrepresentative of God and the Prophet, especially in matters of eschatology or doctrine.[76] Perhaps the most famous example is that of al-Hallaj (d. 309/922), who was executed on the basis of his ecstatic statement 'I am the Truth' (meaning 'I am God').[77]

There are no clear legal principles for dealing with ecstatic sayings in religious law. Their literal interpretation as blasphemous (warranting sanction in religious law) violates the intentions of the Sufis.[78] The demarcation between jurists who hold to the literal interpretation of ecstatic comments and jurists who hold to their spiritual interpretation is the same as that between scholars who reject and those who accept ecstatic sayings.[79]

Sufism today

Sufism is still an important part of the Islamic religious experience in modern times, and has even spread into the West. In the Muslim world, Sufism has been ferociously denounced by puritanical groups such as the Wahhabis and Salafis who view it as an unacceptable innovation. However, Sufism has also spurred revivalist movements in the Indian subcontinent, Central Asia and Africa.[80] In the West, it has been popularized in the poetry of Rumi (d. 672/1273) and has long been the subject of Orientalist interest. One of the world's leading authorities on Sufism was the German scholar Annemarie Schimmel (d. 2003), who devoted a lifelong career to the academic study of Islamic mysticism.[81]

Sufi groups in the West can be divided into three categories.[82] The first comprises those who adhere to Islam and practise Islamic religious law. Examples of this category include branches of the Shadhili, Naqshbandi, Qadiri, Chishti and Nimatullahi orders which have been established in North America, Europe and Australia. A number of prominent Western converts have been involved with groups in this category, including Shaykh Abdalqadir as-Sufi, Shaykh Nuh Hah Mim Keller, and Abdalhaqq and Aisha Bewley. In the second group the shaykh and perhaps some of the disciples may be Muslims and practise Islamic law in some fashion, but this is not required for entrance into the group. Two examples of this category include the Bawa Muhayiaddeen Fellowship and the Threshold Society (a Mevlevi Order). The third group comprises those who have been inspired by historical Sufism or Sufi teachers but whose disciples may not consider themselves as Muslims, nor do they practise Islamic religious law. Examples from this category include the Sufi Order International founded by Hazrat Inayat Khan, and the Golden Sufi Centre headed by Irina Tweedie and Llewellyn Vaughan-Lee.

Chapter 7

Artistic expression

Islamic aesthetics covers a variety of areas, most of which cannot be covered in a single chapter. Consequently, this chapter will be limited to a very brief overview of selected areas under three subheadings: art and artistic representation, decoration and calligraphy; music and singing; and mosque architecture.

Islamic art and artistic representation, decoration and calligraphy

Islamic art can be defined in a number of ways. However for the purposes of this chapter, it is defined as art that is produced as part of the cultural and religious tradition of Muslims.[1] The art of Islam is essentially a contemplative one, which aims to express an encounter with the divine presence.[2] It has been mainly abstract and decorative in nature and style, portraying geometric, floral, arabesque, and calligraphic designs. The general lack of portraiture is due to the fact that the authorities of early Islam reportedly forbade the painting of human beings (including that of Prophet Muhammad) as many Muslims believe pictorial representation of the human form may tempt followers to commit idolatry.

Questions surrounding the legitimacy of different types of art and their relationship to Islam have long been asked. Despite the widespread belief that there is a uniform position amongst Muslims on the issue of the legitimacy of various types of art, it is interesting to note there have been significant differences among Muslim scholars and thinkers, in both classical and modern periods.

Representation, images and idols

One of the issues often discussed in relation to Islamic art is the representation of living beings. There is no clear passage in the Qur'an that states representation of living beings is forbidden, but certain hadith suggest that such representations are unacceptable. For example:

> Ibn Umar reported the Prophet [may peace be upon him] having said:
> Those who paint pictures would be punished on the Day of Resurrection
> and it would be said to them: Breathe soul into what you have created.[3]

and

> Abu Hurayra reported the Prophet [may peace be upon him] as saying:
> Angels do not enter the house in which there are portrayals or pictures.[4]

Later Islamic scholarship, doubtlessly following interpretations of these
hadith, suggested that if artists, sculptors or painters represented living beings
such as people or animals in their work, it would infringe on the creative
agency of God.

To understand the reported prohibition on the representation of living
beings, it is important to position the debate within its historical context.
Islam was introduced into seventh-century CE Mecca, where idolatry and
paganism flourished. The Meccan polytheists worshipped various idols
in the form of living beings constructed of stone, wood and other materials.
The Prophet's twenty-two year struggle (610–32 CE) in Mecca and Medina
was primarily geared to the abolition of paganism and idolatry in Hijaz and
later in other parts of Arabia. The Qur'anic message, asserting the oneness
of God, was fundamentally opposed to idolatry and paganism and it is
reasonable to expect that the Prophet would have taken a critical stance
against the construction of images and idols used for pagan worship. On the
other hand, the Prophet did not seem to have had the same attitude toward
simple or constructed images not meant for idol worship.

Those who argue that there is no absolute prohibition stress the difference
between making idols for religious worship and constructing images for
entertainment, play, or artistic reasons. They say that the anti-representation
position confuses categories and intention, which has led to a polarization
of the debate throughout Islamic history. One argument is that if images were
used in the presence of the Prophet without his objection, there is no reason
why they should be considered universally prohibited.

Aspects of decoration in Islamic art

Despite difficulties in establishing what types of art conform to Islamic norms,
some forms have gained wide acceptance, perhaps owing to their non-
representational nature. The forms are patterns, particularly geometric
patterns and calligraphy.

A central feature of Islamic art is the use of patterns. There are several
common pattern types, the most obvious being geometric in style. Patterns
appear frequently on the surfaces of important buildings and mosques. As
for geometry, some argue that such patterns became part of Islamic art as a

result of the strict proscription of other forms of art. To many, geometric patterns symbolize the infinite and therefore unified nature of the creation of the one God. The main reason for their popularity is that art was governed by the need for abstraction rather than direct anthropomorphic representation. Muslim thinkers recognized in geometry the unified intermediary between the material and the spiritual world. At the more intellectual levels, the desire for abstraction and the search for unity were two of the main passions which caused Islamic culture to turn to geometry.[5]

Calligraphy is perhaps the best-known form of Islamic artistic decoration and is found on a range of surfaces and relates to the total organization of language and writing in the form of image. It took a long time for Arabic calligraphy to develop. Muslim artists gradually developed a variety of calligraphic forms, using for content Qur'anic verses, the names of God, the names and titles of the Prophet and, in the case of Shi'a Islam, the names of the infallible imams.

Before Islam, an Arabic script existed. However, it was not until the Abbasid caliphate (132–656/750–1258) that calligraphy was commonly used in an artistic fashion, after a range of styles and rules governing such styles were developed.[6] There are several Arabic calligraphic styles, which differ from country to country, and generation to generation. Some of the most famous styles used are *kufic*, *naskh*, *thuluth* and *diwan*.

Kufic appears in two major styles, modern or archaic. Kufic was the dominant script at the dawn of Islam and the Qur'an was written for several centuries using its lettering style. The main feature of the kufic script is that it has no vowel system, and can thus be difficult to read. Modern Kufic lends itself to magnificent, geometrical construction based on angular elements, which can be adapted to any space and any material, from simple silk squares to architectural monuments.[7] Naskh is a cursive script that was common in the bureaucracy of the Abbasid caliphate and was often used in books. It influenced many Turkish and Persian scripts. Thuluth was given a liturgical function, being used for the headings of chapters in the Qur'an. It features prominently in architectural arabesques.[8] During the Ottoman dynasty the Turks invented various styles, such as diwan, which appeared from 857/1453 onwards. It has a cursive flow, which blends into a smaller and more compact ornamented variant. Diwan was used widely from the eleventh/seventeenth century onwards.[9]

The material on which calligraphy is inscribed has also contributed to the rendering of certain letters, so that a given style may be found on wood, for example, rather than on ceramic, stone or parchment. The subject matter, whether the Qur'an, poems, official documents or love letters, also affected the style of calligraphy used.

Music and singing

According to varying Islamic religious edicts, music may be forbidden, disapproved or allowed.[10] Despite the various positions adopted, music 'gained sophistication and momentum during the height of the Islamic empire between the eighth and the thirteenth centuries [CE]'.[11] Contact with assimilated cultures during the early centuries of Islam resulted in the cultivation of new Arabic music.[12] The availability of ancient Greek treatises to scholars in the Islamic world helped to develop music (*al-musiqa*) into a speculative discipline, part of the field of mathematical sciences.[13] The political hegemony of the Ottomans from the tenth/sixteenth century over the Muslim world led to the 'gradual assimilation and exchange [of Arabic music with] Turkish music, which had already absorbed musical elements from Central Asia, Anatolia, Persia, and medieval Islamic Syria and Iraq'.[14] Sufi religious music in its instrumental, vocal and dance forms was partly transmitted to the Muslim world through the Mevlevis, a mystical order established in Konya (in today's Turkey) during the seventh/thirteenth century.[15]

The *Grand Treatise on Music (Kitab al-musiqa al-kabir)* was written by Abu Nasr al-Farabi (d. 339/950), one of Islam's most prolific writers on music. His work discusses major topics including the science of sound, musical instruments, compositions and the influence of music. The thirteenth-century theorist Safi al-Din al-Urmawi (d. 690/1291) was another significant contributor to the knowledge and systematization of melodic modes.[16]

Anti-music views

Although there is no clear text in the Qur'an relating to music, Muslims who say that music is forbidden base their interpretation on the verse: 'But there are some people who vend amusing tales to lead astray from the way of God.'[17] In interpreting this verse, the Companion Ibn Abbas (d. 68/687) argued that this verse refers to singing. Mujahid (d. 104/722), one of the early exegetes, on the other hand, said that the verse refers to playing the drum (*tabl*). Alternatively, Hasan al-Basri (d. 110/728) said the verse concerned singing and musical instruments. A contemporary scholar of the Qur'an argues that it covers all forms of prohibited speech, idle talk, falsehood and all nonsensical discussion that encourages disbelief and disobedience towards God, such as backbiting, slander, lies, insults and curses, singing and musical instruments of the devil, which are of no spiritual or worldly benefit.[18]

Another verse quoted in relation to the prohibition of music is: '[God said to Iblis], "Inflame any of them you can with your voice".'[19] The scholar Ibn al-Qayyim said that the phrase 'your voice' refers to any speech that is not in obedience to God. Therefore anyone who plays a flute or other woodwind instrument, or any prohibited type of drum, is the 'voice' of the Devil.[20] The Prophet Muhammad is recorded as saying: 'Among [my nation] there will certainly be people who permit fornication, silk, alcohol and musical instruments.'[21] For Ibn Taymiyya this meant that musical instruments were forbidden.[22] He added that the scholars of the four schools of law were in agreement that all musical instruments were forbidden.[23]

Pro-music views

Those who favour a more permissive position in regard to music argue that the whole universe is a symphonic orchestra of sound, motion, tones, rhythm and beats, synchronized for perfect melodious harmony; perfectly composed, directed and conducted by its creator Almighty God.[24] Qur'anic chanting is the quintessential religious expression of musical form, although non-metric in character, and is based on the established rules of recitation. Various prophetic sayings recommend that the Qur'an should be recited in a harmonious fashion. The call to prayer (*adhan*) was instituted by the Prophet Muhammad himself in the first two years after the migration to Medina. What was originally a simple pronouncement in the streets quickly grew into an ornate and moving chant issued five times a day from the minarets of mosques. The call to prayer was composed of short phrases chanted in melodic tunes that varied from region to region.[25]

Some scholars have suggested that music is allowed based on a hadith of A'isha, one of the Prophet's wives. She says that during one of the Eid days her father, Abu Bakr (the first caliph), entered the residence she shared with the Prophet.[26] There were two young girls with her singing and Abu Bakr angrily exclaimed, 'Musical instruments of Satan near the Prophet?' The Prophet told Abu Bakr to leave them and replied on A'isha's behalf, 'O Abu Bakr! There is an Eid for every nation and this is our Eid.'[27] Another hadith quoted in support of music is one in which the Prophet reportedly recommended that a singer should be sent to the wedding feast of one of the Muslims of Medina.[28]

Singing

The Prophet's alleged prohibition of singing is central to the debate on the permissibility of music. It is argued that such pastimes are a distraction from more important things, and are thus either prohibited or severely condemned, largely based on the Qur'anic verse: 'But there are some people who vend amusing tales to lead astray from the way of God.'[29]

Ibn Hazm (d. 456/1064), the Andalusian scholar who wrote extensively on a range of Islamic subjects, quotes several hadith used by opponents of singing for leisure.[30] This section will outline four of those hadith followed by hadith that go against these four, to a certain extent. The first was reported by A'isha, who quotes the Prophet as saying, 'God has prohibited the female singer and selling of her and the price of her and the teaching of her and listening to her.' In the second hadith that Ibn Hazm quotes, Ali b. Abi Talib, the fourth caliph, reported that the Prophet said, 'When my community engages in fifteen things, misfortune will fall upon it.' Of the fifteen things, some are related to singing and music. The third hadith is from Mu'awiya, who reported that the Prophet prohibited Muslims from doing nine things, including singing and painting. In a fourth hadith, Ibn Mas'ud reportedly said: 'Singing creates hypocrisy in the heart.'[31]

Despite these apparently prohibitive hadith, Ibn Hazm quotes alternative sayings of the Prophet indicating that singing for leisure is permitted. One of the best known is that mentioned above, where the Prophet permitted the young girls to keep singing after Abu Bakr expressed his displeasure.[32]

In another hadith also found in Bukhari's collection, A'isha reports that the Prophet called for some pleasurable activities, using the word *lahw* (idle talk, distractions). He explained this by saying that the Medinan Muslims would enjoy them. There are other hadith which suggest that the Prophet did not mind certain forms of singing. Scholars who reportedly recognized the permissibility of singing and/or playing instruments include students of Malik b. Anas (d. 179/796), who reported that their teacher permitted singing with musical accompaniment; al-Mawardi (d. 450/ 1058), who elaborated on the permission to play the lute in the Shafi'i school; and Shawkani (d. circa 1255/1839), who approved of singing, even when accompanied by a musical instrument such as the lute or flute.[33]

Mosques and architecture

The mosque is the most important structure in which Islamic artistic and architectural features are found. It was one of the earliest areas of activity for Muslims in terms of building. When considering the aesthetics and architecture of mosques, it is important to remember their centrality in Islamic culture. In Muslim communities across the globe, the mosque was and is the central structure around which life revolves; it has a purpose beyond worship. The structure, design and use of decoration in mosques vary greatly throughout the Muslim world. The richness of this variety is evident in the differences among mosques in Asia, Africa, Europe and the Middle East.

The Prophet Muhammad and his followers used the sanctuary in Mecca where the pre-Islamic Ka'ba – considered as a 'house of God' for worship – was situated. Muslims usually attribute the construction of the Ka'ba to the prophetic forefathers Abraham and Ishmael. When the Prophet Muhammad moved to Medina, one of the first things he did was establish a simple place of prayer: a 'mosque'. Although building mosques was an early Muslim activity, mosque architecture developed over time and was significantly influenced by the cultures and civilizations with which Muslims interacted. As the Islamic caliphate grew and newly developed towns or cities were founded – whether Baghdad established in the second/eighth century by the

Abbasid caliph al-Mansur (d. 158/775) or other new cities – the mosque was often placed at the city centre, with the ruler's residence nearby.

Given that one of the five pillars of Islam is prayer, the mosque plays a fundamental part in a Muslim's life. At the most basic level, however, a 'mosque' can be considered any place where a person can pray. According to one hadith, the whole of the earth is considered a place of prayer. This might suggest there is no need to build special places for worship. Prayer can take place in the sitting room of a person's house, in the work place, on the street or in the park.

Despite this general permission to pray anywhere as long as the place is clean, mosques still play a pivotal role. Certain prayers, for example the Friday noon prayer, must be performed in congregation. Even the five daily prayers, according to the Prophet, are better performed in congregation. Five times a day, Muslims in any locality are expected to come together and pray, giving people an opportunity to meet at regular intervals and thus come to know one another. The idea of prayer in congregation has always been an important part of Islamic practice. This does not exclude individual prayer if, and when, the circumstances warrant it. In Muslim towns and cities, therefore, there would often be small places of prayer (*musallas*), or minor mosques, in addition to the large mosques where Friday and Eid prayers are usually held.

Mosque architecture is closely related to prayer requirements. The most prominent and symbolic example of this is the minaret used by the *muezzin* for performing the call to prayer. Inside the mosque, the direction of Mecca is indicated, and there are guidelines for the congregants to line up in rows. Consequently, the mosque has to have a large, usually rectangular interior. Additionally, a special place, called the *mihrab* (niche), is reserved for the imam for leading the prayer.

Over time, mosques developed from the humble beginnings of the Prophet's mosque in Medina to the architectural monuments of Muslim communities in Spain, Iran, Turkey, Central Asia and elsewhere. The mosque is a symbol of the achievements in Islamic aesthetics and architecture.

Key areas of the mosque include the entrance, minaret and courtyard. The presence and style of the courtyard largely depends on the local climate and geography. In larger mosques the courtyard is a place where people can sit and talk about religious or non-religious matters. Important features of the mosque include the area used for ritual ablutions (*wudu'*); the dome, which provides acoustic enhancement; and the pulpit (*minbar*), where the person giving the sermon during Friday prayers can stand and address the congregation. Wudu' facilities are important given the obligatory nature of performing ablutions, which include washing hands, mouth, nose, face, forearms and feet. In the premodern period many larger mosques had some form of running water available. Sometimes toilets and other such facilities were separated from the mosque proper. The idea of mosque purity requires such facilities to be carefully located away from the place where prayer is performed.

The orientation of the mosque's interior towards Mecca is also an important feature of mosque design. The direction of Mecca is shown by the niche at the front of the mosque. In circumstances where there is no actual niche, there may be lines on the floor, or some kind of decoration at the front, representative of the niche, often opposite the mosque's entrance.

Islamic decoration in the art and architecture of mosques

Calligraphy: Calligraphy is considered one of the most important of the Islamic arts. Nearly all Islamic buildings have some type of surface inscription in the stone, stucco, marble, mosaic and/or painting. The inscription might be a verse from the Qur'an, lines of poetry or names and dates. Sometimes single words such as Allah or Muhammad are repeated and arranged into patterns over the entire surface of the walls.

Geometric patterns: Islamic artists developed geometric patterns to a degree of complexity and sophistication previously unknown. These patterns exemplify the Islamic interest in repetition, symmetry and pattern.

Floral patterns: Islamic artists reproduced nature with a great deal of accuracy. Flowers and trees might be used as the motifs for the decoration of textiles, objects and buildings.

Light: For many Muslims, light is the symbol of divine unity. In Islamic architecture, light functions decoratively by modifying other elements or by originating patterns. Light can add a dynamic quality to architecture, extending patterns, forms and designs into the dimensions of time.

Water: In hot Islamic climates, the water from courtyard pools and fountains cools as it decorates. Water not only reflects the architecture and multiplies its decorative themes, but also serves as a means of emphasizing the visual axes.[34]

Chapter 8

Philosophical thought

The word philosophy[1] comes from two Greek terms *philein* and *sophia*, and literally means 'love of wisdom'. From one point of view, philosophy is 'a critical, reflective analysis of what we think we know about ourselves and our universe'.[2] Philosophy is based on the attempt to understand reality rationally, whereas theology is based on an appeal to supernatural revelation.[3] In the West during the Middle Ages, philosophy was considered 'the handmaiden of theology' and philosophical principles were used to justify religious faith.[4]

Greek and Roman philosophy

The lineages and interconnections within the historical development of Greek and Roman philosophy can be clearly seen. It is generally acknowledged that the first Greek philosopher was Thales of Miletus, who lived in the sixth century BCE.[5] Subsequently, Socrates, whose philosophical teachings adhered to an ethically influenced analysis, inspired other philosophers such as Plato, who is best known for his philosophy of ideas and who founded an academy to educate philosophers. Plato's disciple Aristotle was one of the greatest Empiricists and began his own Peripatetic school.[6] Subsequent to Aristotle, a number of philosophical trends arose, including the Stoics (who argued that virtue is the only real good and everything else is an illusion), the Epicureans (who held that pleasure is the highest end) and the Sceptics (who believed that nothing can be known for certain).[7] There were other schools that followed these traditions. Some of these schools had a significant influence on Islamic philosophy. A particular example was Neoplatonism, which began with Ammonius Saccas during the third century CE. He forsook Christianity and developed his own conception of Platonic philosophy with Aristotelian and Stoic influences. The Neoplatonists developed the theory of emanation, in which levels of existence come from the existence of the One (Supreme Being).[8]

Near Eastern philosophy at the dawn of Islam

Greek philosophy and theology were studied by Syrians and Iraqis as early as the fourth century CE and a number of centres of study were still in existence when the Arab Muslims conquered Syria and Iraq. Notable Near Eastern Christian philosophers who wrote commentaries and treatises on important Greek works included Severus Sebokht, Jacob of Edessa and George, Bishop of the Arabs.[9] In the seventh century CE there were important centres of Greek learning at Harran and Jundishapur. Egypt also had educational institutions that were interested in philosophy. There is no doubt that from an early period, probably even from the time of Alexander the Great, Greek philosophy was studied there. In Alexandria, Greek thought came into contact with a range of other Eastern religious traditions. These included Jewish, Egyptian and Christian philosophies. Greek thought did not remain strictly the same as it was in the times of its great masters; rather, it went through a transformation as a result of the interaction with the thought of other cultures in the East.

With the spread of Islam, particularly after the death of the Prophet, Muslims came into contact with a range of civilizations. Their conquest of Iraq and Egypt provided the first major contact between Muslims and the learning that was inspired by the Greeks. Centres of learning already present in those lands played a significant role in transmitting both the Greek philosophical tradition and the medical tradition to Muslims. Scholars from Harran and the Nestorian Christians from Jundishapur (a major centre of Hellenistic learning) were influential in the Abbasid court. They provided a link back to Greek science and knowledge for the Arabs.[10] There were two ways in which Greek philosophy was transmitted to the mainly Arab Muslims of that period: through the translation of Greek philosophical works and as a result of the ongoing interest in medical research.

A range of philosophical works had been translated into Syriac and were being taught in Syria at the time of the Muslim conquest there. The conquest did not stop the study of Greek thought, which was continued largely by Christian scholars. It was after the conquest of Syria that a number of philosophical, scientific and medical works were translated from Greek and Syriac into Arabic from the eighth century CE. The Arab conquerors were fascinated by Greek thought and many of them encouraged the translation of works into Arabic. The earliest era of philosophical works in Arabic should be considered the activities of the translators, such as Hunayn b. Ishaq (d. 260/873).

Indian and Persian philosophy

Unlike Greek philosophy, the Indian and Persian influence on Islamic philosophy is comparatively small; nevertheless some Arabic-speaking scholars engaged with Persian and Indian ideas, particularly in the scientific realms. In the Abbasid era, Indian medical and astronomical works were translated into Arabic. Al-Biruni (d. 440/1048) wrote on Indian philosophical and religious beliefs, and Muslim theories of atomism carry a number of marked similarities to Indian thought. A number of Persian aphoristic works and moral treatises were available to the Arabs through the work of writers such as Ibn al-Muqaffa' (d. 139/756) and Miskawayh (d. 421/1030). Importantly, many great figures in Islamic thought were Persians, including Ibn Sina, al-Razi and al-Ghazali.[11]

Muslim philosophy

The earliest texts translated into Arabic were of a practical nature and concentrated on medicine, alchemy and astrology. This led to a developing interest in more theoretical and speculative works.[12] Arab philosophers emerged during the third/ninth century. The Abbasid caliphs were interested in learning and gave financial and material support to translators and scholars. The first prominent example of an Arab-Muslim philosopher is considered to be al-Kindi (d. circa 260/873).[13] From the time of al-Kindi, Muslim philosophy became a creative phenomenon that moved beyond translation and commentary and developed into a distinct Islamic discipline.[14] Muslim philosophers sought to integrate Greek thought into their Islamic framework and were interested in harmonizing rationality and religious faith. While the scholars of theology (*kalam*) sought to defend the revealed truths of the Qur'an and the Sunna with proofs, those who took the path of philosophy (*falsafa*) resorted to reason exclusively to disentangle the problems that beset the human intellect. They viewed the Neoplatonic conception of the universe as consistent with Islamic beliefs, in particular the apocryphal *Theologia Aristotelis* with its doctrine of emanation.[15] There are two main types of philosophic literature: commentaries on texts and independent creative works. Both followed Greek methods of organizing scholarly work.[16]

Muslim philosophical trends

The development of Muslim philosophy during the Abbasid period must be seen in light of the following: (1) sectarian conflict that developed after the passing of the Prophet and saw schism in the Muslim community which broke up into the Shi'i, Khariji and majority Sunni factions over the question of rightful leadership;[17] (2) the development of the disciplines of jurisprudence, Qur'anic studies and theology;[18] (3) theological arguments between the Traditionists and Qadaris, and the rise of the Mu'tazili school of theology which utilized Greek dialectical tools;[19] and (4) the founding of the institution of the House of Wisdom (*Bayt al-Hikma*), in Baghdad, which provided for scholarly activity including the translation of Greek texts.[20]

Philosophy entered the western part of the Muslim world (in Spain and North Africa) after the third/ninth century. However, it did not flower until the fifth/eleventh and sixth/twelfth centuries after the works of eastern thinkers such as al-Farabi (known in Europe as Alfarabi) (d. 339/950), Ibn Sina (Avicenna) (d. 429/1037) and al-Ghazali (Algazel) (d. 505/1111) became available to Muslims living in Spain and North Africa. Major western figures included Ibn Bajja (Avempace) (d. 533/1138), Ibn Tufayl (Abubacer) (d. 581/1185) and Ibn Rushd (Averroes) (d. 595/1198), who gave a spirited defence of philosophy in his refutation of al-Ghazali's *The Incoherence of the Philosophers* (*Tahafut al-falasifa*).[21]

In the Muslim West, the Almohad dynasty began with Ibn Tumart (d. 524/1130), from a Berber tribe of the Atlas mountains. His successors overthrew the Almoravid rulers of Spain. He encouraged observance of the literalistic Zahiri legal school and belief in a strict transcendent concept of God. The Almohads viewed philosophy as the pursuit of elites; nevertheless leaders such as the caliph Abu Ya'qub Yusuf (d. 580/1184) gave patronage to philosophers like Ibn Rushd and other intellectuals in Spain.[22]

Western Islamic philosophy had a major influence on thinkers in medieval Christian (and Jewish) Europe, as well as the eastern Islamic world, with the export of the writings of philosophers such as Ibn Bajja, Ibn Tufayl and Ibn Rushd. However, a new development in the history of Islamic philosophy occurred with the resurgence of traditionalism as found in the works of figures such as Ibn Taymiyya (d. 728/1328) and the synthesis of mysticism with philosophy.[23] While the impact of traditionalism on philosophy was devastating (within Sunni Islam), from the sixth/twelfth century a new type of philosophy wedded to mysticism can be seen in the rise of hikma (wisdom), particularly within the Shi'i world. Shihab al-Din al-Suhrawardi (d. 587/1191) founded the illuminationist (*ishraq*) school of theosophy. Mir Damad (d. 1041/1631) revived Ibn Sina's philosophy, giving it a Shi'i ishraqi character. Mulla Sadra (d. 1050/1640) harmonized revelation, rational demonstration and gnosis (*irfan*). The new philosophy spread to the Indian subcontinent and influenced figures such as Shah Wali Allah (d. 1176/1762).[24]

Great Muslim philosophers

Al-Kindi

Al-Kindi (Alkindus, d. circa 260/873) was the first significant Muslim philosopher, and became known as 'the Philosopher of the Arabs'. He had encyclopaedic knowledge and exerted a great influence on medieval Europe. Over two hundred scholarly works are attributed to him and cover a range of disciplines: metaphysics, music, logic, medicine, geometry and politics. He was possibly the first Arabic-speaking logician, but many of his works (including those on logic) have been lost.[25] Al-Kindi was an influential thinker within several areas, including Qur'anic exegesis including Mu'tazili methods of Qur'anic exegesis (see Chapter 2) and Greek philosophy (Aristotle and Neoplatonism).[26]

For al-Kindi, philosophy was a 'comprehensive science that embraced all sciences including theology. Its high status was due to its exalted subject matter (divine reality). Al-Kindi attempted to reconcile philosophy (which has finite limits) and religion, because for him both had the same end. Al-Kindi borrowed the Aristotelian concept that religion needs philosophy, which is its rational defence although he was not consistent on the problem of whether philosophical or religious truth is more certain. We can generally say he gave precedence to revelatory truth, with any contradiction between philosophy and revelation being due to human misinterpretation of the Qur'an.[27]

Al-Kindi believed that philosophy is an essential aid in the study and practice of religion. For him, there was no contradiction between the truth that is arrived at on the basis of religion and the truth that is arrived at on the basis of philosophy. One supported the other. He wrote on the proof of God's existence and God's attribute of absolute unity.[28] Al-Kindi saw a dualism between God, who is beyond description and definition and is absolutely eternal, and created-out-of-nothing beings, who are divided into three categories (corporeal beings, beings separable from matter owing to their finer nature, and spiritual beings with no corporeality). Al-Kindi classified 'beings' into individuals and universals.[29] He supported the concept of *creatio ex nihilo* (creation out of nothing) using mathematical and logical reasoning. Al-Kindi argued that the universe is in motion and motion is not eternal; therefore the universe is not eternal.[30] He also advocated a finite creation.[31]

Al-Kindi's structure of the universe was based on Aristotelian and Ptolemaic theories: nature, being orderly, reveals an intelligent design and thus points to God. Human beings are microcosms of that well-organized and orderly macrocosm. Relying on astrology, which was believed to be a legitimate science, he held that heavenly bodies were animate, possessing reason.[32] Al-Kindi also wrote on the nature of the soul, which he regarded as an incorporeal substance that gave an animate substance its essence and definition.[33]

Al-Farabi

Al-Farabi (d. 339/950), called the 'Second Teacher', was a leading figure in a number of philosophical fields including logic, cosmology and metaphysics. He gave the Arabic-speaking world an understanding of Aristotelian logic, developed an Islamic version of the Neoplatonic doctrine of emanation and is well known for his socio-political model of his *The Virtuous City* (*al-Madinat al-Fadila*).[34] Al-Farabi believed that religious and philosophical truths are objectively one, although formally different. Below are some of his key ideas.

Theory of ten intelligences[35]

Among the chief concerns of this theory is the solving of the problem of the One and the many. Al-Farabi holds that the One (that is God) is the Necessary by Himself; hence, He is not in need of another for His existence or His subsistence. Al-Farabi holds that from the Necessary One flows or emanates only one other by virtue of Its self-knowledge and goodness. This emanent is the first intelligence. The first intelligence is possible by itself, necessary by another; and it thinks the One as well as itself. It is one-in-itself, and many by virtue of these considerations. From the first intelligence flows a series of intelligences. The tenth and last intelligence is that which governs the sublunary world. From the tenth intelligence flows prime matter (*hyle*), the origin of the four elements, as well as forms, which when united with prime matter form bodies.[36] It is from this intelligence that the human souls also flow, and the four elements which are fire, air, water and earth. These intelligences are hierarchical.[37] Thus, 'physics is fused with cosmology and the terrestrial world is subjected to the heavenly world'.[38]

Theory of intellect

Al-Farabi classified intellect in various ways and outlined a theory of how intellect gradually rises and acquires perfection. He based this concept of the intellect on Aristotle's *De Anima*, but added his own contribution. This included the acquired intellect, which serves as a link between human knowledge and revelation. Al-Farabi's theory of the intellect has been extremely influential on Muslim and Christian philosophy.[39]

Theory of prophecy

In Islamic thought, the basis of religion is revelation, and al-Farabi (like other Muslim philosophers) was concerned with the compatibility of rationality with religion. Consequently, he stressed the theoretical study of society and its needs and wrote a treatise on politics, including his *The Virtuous City* (*al-Madinat al-fadila*), which visualizes the city as a series of united parts like the organs of the body. He thought that all individuals were allocated a vocation, of which that of 'chief' was the highest station. The chief should have a number of attributes (similar to the philosopher-king in Plato's *Republic*), including the ability to commune with the celestial world through contemplation and inspiration.[40] Through his attempts to argue against the scepticism about prophecy, which was an issue of his time, al-Farabi not only 'explained prophecy on rational grounds and gave it a scientific interpretation'[41] but also made an important contribution towards a deeper understanding of human psychology and epistemology.

Interpretation of the Qur'an

Al-Farabi held that miracles are supernatural but do not contradict natural laws. Prophets have spiritual power which connects them with the agent of intelligence, and through this communication can cause miraculous happenings. He denied literalistic interpretations of Qur'anic concepts such as the Preserved Tablet. Al-Farabi believed that punishment and bliss in the hereafter are felt spiritually rather than materially and physically.[42]

Neoplatonism and al-Farabi

Aristotle views God as perfection and as a pure form that eternally contemplates itself. He also believes that the world itself is eternal and that God is self-sufficient and independent of matter. This view of God is particularly problematic for people of faith, for whom God is central to their beliefs and way of life. Muslims believe in a God who reveals himself through prophets. Neoplatonism rejects this view. Muslims believe in the act of creation *ex nihilo* (out of nothing and in time). On the other hand, Neoplatonists believe that emanation is eternal, and reject the idea of creation as a temporal act.

This problem was not resolved until al-Farabi attempted to reconcile the Islamic concept of prophethood and revelation with the theory of emanation. Al-Farabi's view of how the theory of emanation and creation *ex nihilo* could be brought together relates to the question of knowledge. He argued that human beings have three faculties: reason, sense and representation. These faculties should combine with the active intellect, the tenth intelligence and the source of knowledge. Al-Farabi gives an example of the relationship between the faculty of knowledge and the active intellect being like that between the eye and the sun. In order to see something, it is not sufficient that one have an eye and an object to be seen. The eye cannot see unless there is light from the sun which gives the light to the eye. Al-Farabi saw the relationship between the faculty of knowledge and the active intellect in the same way and just as necessary in order to intuit knowledge.[43] The human faculty of knowledge, also called the potential intellect (*in potentia*), needs to be connected to the source of knowledge, the active intellect. The active intellect is understood by al-Farabi to refer to an immaterial form which was never in matter and can never be.

> It is much like an acquired intellect, but it is the faculty which ultimately changed this substance that was an intellect in *potentia* into an intellect in action, and the intelligibles in potentia into 'actual' intelligibles. The relationship between the active intellect and intellect in potentia,

therefore, is similar to that of the sun and the eye, which can only see things in potentia as long as it remains in obscurity.[44]

Given that the role of the active intellect is not unlike that of the sun for the act of seeing, it can be said that, for al-Farabi, the active intellect makes the intellect *in potentia* actual: 'potential' intelligible things become 'actual' intelligible things.

The intellect *in potentia* also receives knowledge through things such as visions, and these visions can sometimes occur while a person is awake or asleep. This is where al-Farabi is trying to explain prophecy. For him, representation, one of the faculties of the intellect, is a powerful faculty in the human being. And when that is developed to perfection, this faculty can be the medium by which a person can receive awareness of present and future events. Through such a person, prophecy can be received. This explains the revelation that occurred with the Prophet himself.[45]

With rational explications like these, al-Farabi endeavours to provide a basis for an accommodation of religious truth within the philosophical context: the philosophical truth (or the knowledge arrived at by philosophers) is important, as well as the prophetic truth (the knowledge arrived at by prophets). Prophets often simplified their message so that they could be understood by common people, whilst philosophers are often seen as not very good at conveying their knowledge to the masses.

Ibn Sina

Ibn Sina (d. 429/1037), known as Avicenna in the West, is one of the most famous and influential Muslim philosophers. From Ibn Sina's autobiography, it is clear that he received a thorough education and mastered a number of sciences from an early age. It was, however, a commentary by al-Farabi that opened up Aristotle's *Metaphysics* to this great mind. Ibn Sina lived in politically turbulent times and worked as a physician for a number of princes.[46] He wrote, largely in Arabic but also in Persian, on a wide variety of topics and was influenced by Greek philosophy. He developed a mystical 'Oriental Philosophy' and his medical tome the *Qanun* (*Canon*) is generally considered one of the most influential medical texts in both the Muslim world and the West.[47]

The central topic of Ibn Sina's metaphysical scholarship concerns ontology (the study of being). As well as discussing distinctions between essence and existence, substance and accident, he developed a series of categorizations of being:

• Necessary: a being whose absence would be metaphysically impossible or contradictory, such as the Necessary Being upon whom all other existents (the entire universe) depend;

- Possible: a being whose existence may or may not exist without either state being impossible or contradictory. He divided this category into that which is possible in itself, but made necessary by the Necessary Being (i.e. angels); and those beings who are simply possible without any condition of necessity (i.e. evanescent creatures of the material world);
- Impossible: a being whose existence would be impossible or contradictory if it existed, such as a second Necessary Being (God).[48]

Ibn Sina's cosmology was influenced by the Neoplatonic concept of the emanation of an angelic hierarchy based upon intellection, and followed the principle that only from the One can anything come into being. According to Ibn Sina, the Necessary Being (the One) is completely transcendent from multiplicity, and contemplates its being, which then generates the first creation – the First Intellect, or the supreme archangel. As the latter contemplates itself 'as an act', the Soul, which is the form of the extreme sphere, emanates, and as it contemplates itself *in potentia* a body of that same sphere emanates. Then, as the First Intellect contemplates its cause, the Necessary Being, as necessary, this brings the Second Intellect into being through the same process; from this proceeds the soul and the body of the eighth sphere (Saturn) and the third intelligence and so on until the emanation of the active intelligence, which reigns over our souls.[49] The tenth intellect, called the Giver of Forms, is responsible for bringing material forms into existence and illuminating minds.[50]

Ibn Tufayl

Ibn Tufayl (Abubacer, d. 581/1185) was a leading figure of Muslim Spain. He was not only a physician but also a philosopher, mathematician and poet. His allegorical work *The Living Son of the Vigilant (Hayy ibn Yaqzan)* had a profound effect in the West when it was translated into Latin and published in Oxford in 1671, then rendered into English in 1674 and subsequently into other European languages.[51] Ibn Tufayl lived and worked as a secretary to the governor of Granada, Spain, under the Almohads. Later on he became the personal doctor of Abu Ya'qub Yusuf, and his vizier. He was the teacher of Ibn Rushd, and the one who introduced him to the Almohad ruler. Though unsystematic in his writing in comparison to al-Farabi or Ibn Sina, Ibn Tufayl is often regarded as a leading figure in the 'Andalusian Revolt' against Ptolemaic astronomy, and also a bridge between al-Ghazali's creationism and Aristotelian eternalism.[52]

In the allegorical work *The Living Son of the Vigilant* (which is presented as a story), Hayy grows up on an uninhabited island, is nurtured by a deer, and discovers through his own intellectual efforts philosophical truths about reality and the necessity of a Creator. He then meets the mystic Asal, who has arrived from a neighbouring island. Asal teaches Hayy language, and tells him of his scriptural religion, understood to mean Islam, and of the teachings of the Messenger, understood to be Muhammad. Hayy recognizes Asal's religious teachings as true and in conformity with his own intellectual discoveries. Nevertheless, Hayy cannot understand why revelation resorted to parables and figurative language when speaking about the Divine, and why it gave permission for humans to pursue worldly interests. Asal returns with Hayy to the neighbouring island, which is ruled by Salaman. After attempting to teach Salaman and his subjects, who are not inclined to the esoteric philosophy of Hayy, the latter realizes that there is wisdom in obscuring scripture in figurative language and that the masses are content with the outward law. Hayy and Asal return to the uninhabited island to live a life of contemplation.[53]

Ibn Tufayl's story deals with the essential problems of philosophy and with the issue of whether it is right to divulge its secrets or not. According to Badawi, the work revolves around six main arguments:

- There are no contradictions between philosophy and religion (i.e. Islam).
- Metaphysical matters, like those that pertain to the eternity of the world, are open to interpretation and different solutions.
- Truth has two different modes of expression: one symbolic and relying on illustrative images for commoners, and one precise and pure for the elect. One should not use the language of the former to address the latter and vice versa. Using the language of the elect with the common people only serves to confuse them.
- It is possible for a philosopher who has attained the heights of speculation to achieve union with the Active Intellect, which is the ultimate end of wisdom.
- Reason, through no other device but its own and once connected to the Active Intellect, can dwell in the intelligences of the most hidden secrets of nature and can thus arrive at the most sought-after solutions to the most complicated metaphysical problems.
- Human society is corrupt, and there is nothing more suited to it than popular religion. Any attempt to reform it towards a high intellectuality is bound to fail. For those who are endowed with wisdom, there is no refuge other than the heights of pure reason.[54]

Ibn Tufayl criticized both the doctrine of the eternity of the world and creation *ex nihilo*. He took a middle position in which God, the Creator, precedes creation in essence, but not in time. However, he also believed that reason itself has limits and arguing the point can lead to a maze of contradictions.[55] He held a mystical interpretation of the relationship between God and creation, using the metaphor of light.[56]

Al-Ghazali

There is a widely held view that because Abu Hamid al-Ghazali (Algazel, d. 505/1111) strongly attacked Islamic philosophy and philosophers in *The Incoherence of the Philosophers* (*Tahafut al-falasifa*), their role was significantly reduced within the Sunni world. While there is some truth to this view, attacks on philosophy were prevalent well before al-Ghazali, particularly amongst Traditionists.

The rejection of philosophical approaches to Islamic thought needs to be placed within their historical contexts. We must remember the Mu'tazili position in the early Abbasid period in relation to the creation of the Qur'an and the way these views were adopted by the Abbasid state during the caliphates of al-Ma'mun, al-Mu'tasim and al-Wathiq. The decline of Mu'tazili influence and the reversal of Abbasid state policy under al-Mutawakkil provided a strong basis for the Traditionists who were against the Mu'tazili approach to emphasize a literal reading of the key texts (Qur'an and hadith) at the expense of rational theological argument. Therefore, when al-Ghazali appeared on the scene, there had already been a relatively long period of suspicion of and attacks on philosophy and its methods.

Al-Ghazali is among the most influential Muslim thinkers of the post-prophetic period. He was born in Tus, to a scholastic family interested in Sufism. He studied under the distinguished scholar Imam al-Haramayn al-Juwayni (d. 478/1085), and in 484/1091 he became the youngest professor appointed to the Chair of Theology at the Nizamiyya College in Baghdad. He became a celebrated theologian, and initially took a personal interest in the study of philosophy, but later grew disillusioned by it.[57]

He turned to Sufism, gave up his lucrative career and became a travelling ascetic, which gave him spiritual solace. He found his faith and wrote his influential work *The Revival of the Religious Sciences* (*Ihya' ulum al-din*), an autobiographical work *The Deliverer from Error* (*Al-Munqidh min al-dalal*) and the mystical work *The Niche of the Lights* (*Mishkat al-anwar*). He continued to teach and publish until his death in 505/1111.[58]

In his *The Incoherence of the Philosophers*, al-Ghazali took aim at metaphysics as represented by al-Farabi and Ibn Sina. He found twenty areas where he felt that these philosophers' teachings were flawed. He was most concerned with the idea of the eternity of creation, God's knowledge of particulars and bodily resurrection. Some of his arguments against the philosophers were the following:

- If the world is co-eternal with God it violates strict Islamic monotheism.
- Philosophers make God a fashioner rather than an originator.
- It is impossible to prove or disprove the eternality of the world, so there is no reason for rejecting the orthodox tenet of creation *ex nihilo*.

- Philosophers assume an immediate relationship between cause and effect which al-Ghazali said was not logically necessary.
- The complex theory of emanation does not safeguard God's unity and is deterministic.
- The material world does not demonstrate the principle of one proceeding from one, thus at some point one must meet multiplicity.
- The proposal that God does not have temporal knowledge is highly speculative and implies there is no freedom for God to exercise His will, which makes Him impervious to the petitions of His creatures.
- Emanation does not allow for miracles except as they are naturalized through science.[59]

Instead, al-Ghazali asserted that philosophy was in error for attempting to fathom God's will as if it were similar to human will. As finite creatures we can never fully comprehend the relationship between God and His creation;[60] God is transcendent to time and change but also mysteriously immanent to it;[61] a relationship between cause and effect is not logically required, it only appears that way through observation of the succession of events. Because we perceive them as connected, they are necessarily connected only at a psychological level. We cannot limit causes only to those we have observed, and essentially effect follows cause(s) through God's will. However, ordinarily, God chooses not to disrupt the flow of succession of events.[62] Because there is no necessary relationship between cause and effect, it is not illogical to believe in miracles.[63]

Ibn Rushd

Ibn Rushd (d. 595/1198), known in the West as Averroes, was born in Cordoba (Spain) to a prestigious line of scholars and jurists. He succeeded Ibn Tufayl as *qadi* (judge) in the Almohad court of Abu Ya'qub Yusuf (d. 580/1184) and continued under Abu Yusuf Ya'qub al-Mansur (d. 596/1199). Ibn Rushd is famous for his series of commentaries on the works of Aristotle, which greatly influenced a number of medieval Jewish and Christian scholars.[64] He also wrote texts on jurisprudence and medicine. Envious of his close relationship with the ruler, colleagues at the court convinced Abu Yusuf Ya'qub al-Mansur that Ibn Rushd was using impolite language when writing about the ruler, that he doubted certain Qur'anic teachings and most importantly that he held polytheistic views such as that the planet Venus was a divinity.[65] He was persecuted for his philosophical teachings, was exiled, and his books were burnt. He was later pardoned by Abu Yusuf.[66]

Like philosophers before him, Ibn Rushd sought to defend the pursuit of philosophy. He argued that the Qur'an itself recommended philosophical pursuits when it called on human beings to employ rational consideration (*i'tibar*). According to Ibn Rushd, philosophers are the group of the learned to whom the Qur'an refers in the third chapter, where it says that only God and 'those deeply rooted in knowledge'[67] know its hidden meanings, unlike theologians and the masses.[68]

Ibn Rushd held an Aristotelian ontology and his metaphysics were primarily concerned with knowledge related to 'being'. The object of his criticism of the scholars was not just al-Ghazali but also philosophers such as Ibn Sina, who he thought was not always right in his interpretation and understanding of Aristotle. He addressed questions such as the nature of time, the creation of the world, causality, the nature of God's knowledge and the ways to God.[69] As for his beliefs on creation, Ibn Rushd attempted to reconcile the philosophical view of the eternality of the world with the theological view of creation-in-time by seeing the world as both eternal and temporal. The universe has finite bodies, but moves eternally. He rejected the Neoplatonic doctrine of emanation, especially as advocated by al-Farabi and Ibn Sina.[70] According to him, neither Aristotle nor his peripatetic commentators had ever mentioned anything about the order of emanation or about their separated intelligences and their numbers. Keen to stay close to the Qur'anic view of the world, Ibn Rushd's Aristotelian system endeavours to conceive the world as a whole in which only one force moves all. The world according to his vision is like a state ruled by the one monarch. His viziers are subordinate and derive all their authority from the monarch. As such, all make up one system empowered and regulated by one and only one 'primary principle'. There is no room for the hierarchy of the intelligences and the Avicennan principle which stipulates that 'from the one can proceed only the one'.[71]

Ibn Rushd wrote *The Incoherence of the Incoherence* (*Tahafut al-tahafut*), in which he defended the pursuit of philosophy from its detractors, al-Ghazali in particular.[72] He responded to several of al-Ghazali's arguments, for instance that philosophers transgressed the *ijma'* (consensus) of the community, and were guilty of disbelief in relation to the eternality of the world, their denial of God's knowledge of particulars and their denial of corporeal resurrection.[73] Ibn Rushd pointed out that there is no consensus about all doctrinal matters, because of the esoteric nature of some Qur'anic statements. Also, theologians had misunderstood the purpose of the Qur'anic allegories, which are used to encourage the masses to live virtuously. Philosophers, on the other hand, may apprehend their esoteric meanings, but must not make them public.[74] The influence of Ibn Tufayl in relation to this last point is not hard to detect.

Ibn Rushd listed the core requisites of belief to which all Muslims must assent, although the manner of their interpretation is not a matter of consensus: the existence of a Creator God who rules the world; the unity of God; God's attributes of perfection, which are knowledge, life, power, will, hearing, seeing and speech; God's freedom from imperfection; the creation of the world; the validity of prophecy; the justice of God; and the resurrection on the Day of Judgement.[75]

In *The Incoherence of the Incoherence*, Ibn Rushd addressed each point made by al-Ghazali. He accused al-Ghazali of describing God as a kind of eternal 'man' because of his description of God's attributes of knowledge, will, habit and so on.[76] He argued against al-Ghazali's notion of causality, saying that the inability to specify causation would lead to our inability to say and name any 'thing' meaningfully. He said, 'Denial of cause implies denial of knowledge, and denial of knowledge implies that nothing in this world can be really known.'[77] He used the criticism of al-Ghazali's notion of causality to emphasize the natural nature of miracles (for Ibn Rushd, effects must follow causes), which allows the prophets to draw human beings closer to religion.[78]

Mulla Sadra

Akhund Mulla Sadra or Sadr al-Din Shirazi (d. 1050/1640) was one of the most influential Persian thinkers, although he is relatively unknown outside Iran. A student of Mir Damad, Mulla Sadra developed a new philosophical approach which synthesized revelation, rational demonstration and *'irfan* (gnosis). His most important work was the *The Four Journeys* (*Asfar*), which dealt with the four stages of the gnostic journey.[79] Mulla Sadra's thought was influenced by Aristotelian philosophy, Neoplatonic doctrines, Ibn Sina's philosophy, the works of Ibn Arabi and Islamic religious texts, particularly those of Shi'i origin.[80]

Mulla Sadra developed his theosophy (*hikmat*) on the basis of four major themes:

- *Unity and gradation of 'being'*: Mulla Sadra taught that 'being' is a single reality which has various gradations and degrees of intensity. Absolute being manifests itself to bring various orders of being and individual members of those orders into reality. Unlike Aristotle and Ibn Sina, Mulla Sadra held that there is an independent, archetypal reality. Imperfect beings necessitate the existence of higher states of being.[81]
- *Substantial motion*: For Mulla Sadra, change is motion and the world is continually recreated at every instant.[82]
- *Knowledge and the relationship between the knower and the known*: Mulla Sadra held that knowledge and being (the knower and the known) are essentially the same.[83] 'God knows His own essence and His essence is none other than His Being, and since His Being and essence are the same, He is at once the knower, the knowledge, and the known.'[84]
- *The characteristics and eschatology of the soul*: Mulla Sadra held that the soul moves through stages of transformation, acquiring new faculties,

which lead to its perfection. He used an analogy of the womb to describe the afterlife. As a child in the womb is in the material world, but does not yet know of its existence, so are human beings in the next world but most are unaware of it. Although Mulla Sadra accepted the concept of bodily resurrection, he held that it is the imaginative faculty of the soul, in the next world, which creates external forms. Souls in Paradise are able to create beautiful forms, while souls in Hell can only create painful forms, although this latter state is temporary and eventually all will return to God.[85]

Modern philosophical thought

Muslim philosophers of the twentieth century did not lead movements or conceptualize social trends on the scale of nineteenth- and twentieth-century figures such as Muhammad Abduh, Ahmad Khan or Hasan al-Banna. Recent philosophers on the whole are 'intellectuals' whose ideas influence the academy more than the masses, although it is possible to detect an activist streak in some of them. Most recent Muslim philosophers have had formal training in the field of philosophy and obtained doctorates from renowned Western universities. To varying degrees, contemporary Muslim philosophers are critical of the early reformist or revivalist trends because they find their ideas unsystematic and philosophically flawed. The issue for many modern Muslim philosophers has been the challenge of modernity, and the questions this raises. In the next section we will look at three modern Muslim philosophers.

Mohammed Abed al-Jabiri

Mohammed Abed al-Jabiri was born in 1936 in southeastern Morocco. His early education was at a religious school and a private nationalist school. During his youth he developed close ties to the Union Socialiste des Forces Populaires party and its founder Mehdi Ben Barka (d. 1965).

In 1958, he commenced studying philosophy. In 1963, he was among members of the Union Socialiste who were imprisoned for sedition. After his release from prison he completed a doctorate in 1967 on the thought of Ibn Khaldun. Al-Jabiri was deeply dissatisfied with the way the Arab-Islamic society was evolving, particularly in his home country. These concerns led him to education. He occupied several teaching posts prior to and after the completion of his doctorate, and was therefore exposed to the problems within education; this became the main topic of his writings. Among his main works are *Dealing with Our Heritage* (*Nahnu wa al-turath*, 1980), *Contemporary Arab Discourse: a Critical and Analytical Study* (*al-Khitab al-arabi al-mu'asir*, 1982), and *Critique of Arab Reason* (*Naqd al-aql al-arabi*, 1984). Al-Jabiri considered modernity as follows:

> Modernity . . . is not to refute tradition or break with the past, but rather to upgrade the manner in which we assume our relationship to tradition at the level of what we call 'contemporaneity,' which, for us, means catching up with the great strides that are being made worldwide.[86]

This modernity does not call for a fundamentalism whose understanding of tradition is confined to the past:

> Modernity, therefore, means first and foremost to develop a modern method and a modern vision of tradition. We could thus rid our conception of tradition from that ideological and emotional charge that weighs on our conscience and forces us to perceive tradition as an absolute reality that transcends history, instead of perceiving it in its relativity and its historicity.[87]

According to al-Jabiri, Muslim scholars should not make the mistake of understanding modernity simply by mirroring European intellectuals, who come from a different historical context. That view of modernity followed the European Enlightenment, which itself followed the Renaissance.

In opposition to the idea that contemporary advances in knowledge, science in particular, may have rendered the substantive knowledge produced by Islamic philosophical and scientific thought irrelevant, al-Jabiri argued that the study of the 'thinking apparatus' (*al-jihaz al-tafkiri*) was still highly relevant for any society that is serious about understanding classical Islamic thought. Such study would reveal that Muslim philosophers of the past were not merely operating within the Aristotelian or Neoplatonic paradigm. This was particularly true for the philosophers of the western Islamic world (Andalusia and Morocco), who had had 'an epistemological break' with the eastern part. Al-Jabiri maintains that Ibn Sina represents neither Greek philosophy nor Islamic rationalism. He sees Ibn Sina's philosophy (of the Muslim east) as 'irrationalism', and laments that al-Ghazali borrowed the same irrationalism from Ibn Sina, only to promote in the end a Sufism that is totally alien to the spirit of Islam. Both Ibn Sina and al-Ghazali used Aristotelian logic (demonstration based on inferential evidence) only to advance their illuminist vision (*ishraq*), which al-Jabiri considers part of hermetical thought: 'The discourse of the Qur'an is of reason not of "gnosticism" or illuminism.'[88]

In contrast, the 'Averroist spirit', as al-Jabiri calls it, presents Muslims with a stronghold from which to engage with modernity. Ibn Rushd's rationalist approach considers issues from the point of view of mathematics and logic, and thus avoids the polemics raised by theologians and jurists alike through their defective analogical reasoning (*qiyas*).[89] Instead of analogical reasoning, Ibn Rushd uses hermeneutical interpretation (*ta'wil*) which for al-Jabiri is the only sound method: analogical reasoning distorts reality and prevents reason from carrying out its function. It confuses the religious and philosophical realms, thus breaching the meaning of the text, while hermeneutical interpretation ensures that the religious and philosophical are kept apart.[90]

Syed Muhammad Naquib al-Attas

Syed Muhammad Naquib al-Attas was born in 1931 in Bogor, Java. He comes from a scholarly tradition firmly grounded in the traditional Islamic sciences, particularly metaphysics, theology, philosophy, history and Malay literature. His education was extremely varied. In Java he attended a madrasa, where he studied Arabic. After finishing secondary school in 1951, he entered the Malay Regiment as a cadet. He was selected to study at Eton Hall, Wales, and then later at the Royal Military Academy in Sandhurst, England. He later commenced undergraduate studies at the University of Malaya.

His education did not stop at the University of Malaya. In 1962, he received a Master's degree (with distinction) from McGill University, Montreal, in Islamic philosophy, for a thesis entitled 'Raniri and the Wujudiyya of Seventeenth-Century Aceh'. His doctoral thesis was then undertaken at the School of Oriental and African Studies, University of London, on the mysticism of Hamzah Fansuri. After this significant educational journey, al-Attas returned to Malaysia and in 1965 became head of Malay literature at the University of Malaya. Later he was appointed Dean of the Faculty of Arts at the National University of Malaysia. In 1987, al-Attas founded the International Institute of Islamic Thought and Civilization (ISTAC) in Kuala Lumpur and acted as its director until 2000. The institute worked towards creating the principles and methodology of an 'islamization project'.

Al-Attas believed that the duty of the Muslim intellectual was to take a stand against the false claims of European modernity. There was to be no negotiation with the modern Western scientific spirit or a reinterpretation of Islam in light of that spirit. He believed that such apologetics through the intellectual enterprise of picking and choosing was wishful thinking and served only to undermine the traditional understanding of religion.

For al-Attas, Sufism ought to play a central part in islamization, for it is in the Sufi heritage that we are most likely to find the most important contributions on the ultimate nature of reality. Islamic metaphysics, particularly from the perspective of philosophical Sufism, is a unified system revealing the ultimate nature of reality. It shows that there are other levels of existence beside the horizontal, worldly dimension, and Sufism discloses those higher levels of consciousness.[91]

Al-Attas maintains that modern science sees things as mere things and has reduced the study of the phenomenal world to an end in itself. Certainly this has brought material benefits, but this is accompanied by an uncontrollable and insatiable propensity to destroy nature itself. Al-Attas maintains a firm critique that studying and using nature without a higher spiritual end has brought humankind to the state of thinking that people are gods or God's co-partners. He states: 'Devoid of real purpose, the pursuit of knowledge becomes a deviation from the truth, which necessarily puts into question the validity of such knowledge.'[92] Modern sciences ought to be acquired, but their philosophical foundations must be recast in the Islamic metaphysical framework.

> We do affirm that religion is in harmony with science. But this does not mean that religion is in harmony with modern scientific methodology and philosophy of science. Since there is no science that is free of value, we must intelligently investigate and study the values and judgments that are inherent in, or aligned to, the presuppositions and interpretations of modern science. We must not indifferently and uncritically accept each new scientific or philosophical theory without first understanding its implication and testing the validity of values that go along with the theory. Islam possesses within itself the source of its claim to truth, and does not need scientific or philosophical theories to justify such a claim. Moreover, it is not the concern of Islam to fear scientific discoveries that could contradict the validity of its truth.[93]

Contemporary knowledge needs to be understood within the intellectual framework of the secular ideology upon which it is based. Therefore, in educational terms, this required

> a critical examination of the methods of modern science; its concepts, presuppositions, and symbols; its empirical and rational aspects, and those impinging upon values and ethics; its interpretations of origins; its theory of knowledge; its presuppositions on the existence of an external world, of the uniformity of nature and of the rationality of natural processes; its theory of the universe; its classification of the sciences; its limitations and inter-relations with one another of the sciences, and its social relations.[94]

Seyyed Hossein Nasr

Seyyed Hossein Nasr was born in 1931 in Tehran. His early education was in Iran. He then studied physics and mathematics at Massachusetts Institute of Technology (MIT) and undertook his doctorate at Harvard University, specializing in Islamic cosmology and science. He was professor of the history of science and philosophy at Tehran University.

In 1979, Nasr migrated to the United States and taught at several American universities, before finally joining the George Washington University, Washington DC, where he became Professor of Islamic Studies. His landmark work arose out of the Gifford Lectures at the University of Edinburgh, which were published under the title *Knowledge and the Sacred*.

Nasr is one of the most prolific contemporary Muslim thinkers. His interests are diverse, but his central concern is the relation between religion and science. Both fundamentalist and modernist Muslim thinkers, he observes, tend to equate modern forms of knowledge with *ilm*, a traditional understanding of science, which has nothing to do with the one presented by the modern scientific mind:

> [F]or anyone who understood the essence of modernism based on and originating in the secularizing and humanistic tendencies of the European Renaissance, it was easy to detect the confrontation between traditional and modern elements in the Islamic world.[95]

Tradition for Nasr pertains to

> both horizontal continuity with the Origin and the vertical nexus which relates each movement of the life of the tradition in question to the meta-historical Transcendent Reality. Tradition is at once *al-din* [religion] in the vastest sense of the word, which embraces all aspects of religion and its ramifications. . . . Tradition, therefore, is like a tree, the roots of which are sunk through revelation in the Divine nature and from which the trunk and branches have grown through the ages. . . . Tradition implies the sacred, the eternal, the immutable Truth; the perennial wisdom, as well as the continuous application of its immutable principles in various conditions of space and time.[96]

Equally, for Nasr, no amount of legal probing addresses the malaise that Muslim societies are suffering from. The challenge is of a 'metaphysical' nature. Modernism, mainly through its rationalism and empiricism, sees the universe almost as an autonomous machine. This contrasts with the Islamic perspective of science which depicts nature as a 'book', a meaningful book, containing order and the signs of God. Science is, therefore, sacred. Nasr advocates this view in *Knowledge and the Sacred* (1981) and *The Need for a Sacred Science* (1993), and endeavours to make a case for the religious view of the universe and for a sacred science. Nasr's exposition of *tawhid* brings him to discuss not only the spiritual dimension but how that dimension can serve as a metaphysical base for the cultivation of the natural sciences.

Nasr deplores modernism for having reared a human being whom he describes as the 'Promethean Man'. This is someone 'free' of heavenly guidance and master of his own life and destiny whilst completely alienated from his surrounding spiritual universe. Several decades ago, Nasr warned humanity against the environmental crisis that was looming. The damage to the environment is a sign of a human ego gone astray and is symptomatic of the approach of the modern scientific mind, in his view.

Chapter 9

Political thought

Islam requires more than a spiritual commitment; Muslims are required to commit to a structure and framework of law and governance that fits within the teachings of the Qur'an and the Prophet. Underpinning this requirement is the understanding that political leadership needs to be undertaken 'pursuing justice through social cooperation and mutual assistance'.[1] Therefore, it is important to recognize that politics is not subsidiary to Islamic thought and law; rather it is a central component.

The historical context

It is important to understand the context within which Islamic political thought has developed. Divisions among Muslims occurred immediately after the death of the Prophet in 11/632 over the issue of who should become his political successor; in other words, were the various groups of Muslims separate identities with different leaders, or should the community be united under a single leader, and if so, whom?[2]

Immediately after the Prophet's passing, while his close kin were preparing to bury his body, a group of Meccan Muslims (known as the Muhajirun) and Medinan Muslims (known as the Ansar) debated whether a Meccan or a Medinan should be the new head of the community. Although both groups lived in Medina where the Prophet had established his nascent Muslim state, it was the Ansar initially who provided a vital support base for the Prophet to expand Islam. Consequently, it was the Ansar who first gathered to debate which of them might take over the leadership in Medina. Umar and Abu Bakr, two of the Prophet's closest Companions, rushed to the meeting and made an impassioned plea to keep the community united. After some squabbling Abu Bakr, a Meccan from the Quraysh, was elected leader.

No broad consultation had been held to gain universal consensus, and a number of Muslims believed that it was the Prophet's son-in-law Ali who should have been favoured to succeed. Ali had been one of the earliest converts to Islam, and was cousin to the Prophet as well as his son-in-law through marriage to the Prophet's daughter, Fatima. Ali had fought courageously beside the Prophet in all of the battles that helped secure the survival of the then nascent Muslim community, and was the father of al-Hasan and al-Husayn, the beloved grandsons of the Prophet. Close relatives of the Prophet felt embittered that the issue of succession was not discussed with them, and their claim to the leadership of the Muslim community was overlooked.

Other Muslims, who were in the majority, felt either that the Prophet did not give any clear instructions as to how the issue of leadership should be resolved or that the potentially devastating split in the community required the immediate election of Abu Bakr at the meeting organized by the Medinan Muslims, despite the Prophet's possible preference for Ali. The Prophet, according to the Shi'a, had signalled a special position for Ali during a sermon at Ghadir Khumm in 10/632. Opponents of the Shi'a argue that the Prophet seemed to suggest that Abu Bakr might provide leadership when the Prophet appointed his close friend Abu Bakr to lead the community in prayer during the last days of the Prophet's terminal illness. Whatever the case in terms of rightful succession, Ali with some hesitation eventually took the oath of allegiance to Abu Bakr.

Abu Bakr's rule did not go unchallenged. Many Arabs who had accepted Islam, or who had concluded peace treaties with the Prophet during his lifetime, rebelled against the new leadership in Medina. Some rejected Islam and reverted to their former religions, while others simply refused to pay zakat to the caliph, thus avoiding their religiously sanctioned tax obligations to the central authority. For many of them, the Prophet's death meant that the relationship they had with Islam had ended. These tribes believed that their relationship was with the Prophet and that when he died this could not be automatically transferred to the new central authority in Medina, as represented by Abu Bakr. They saw their position as reasonable, taking into consideration the tribal customs that existed at the time, and the way tribal relationships had long been established in pre-Islamic times. Because of the Prophet's stature and importance, the authority he enjoyed when he was alive could not, in the view of the tribes, be automatically transferred to his successor.[3]

Many of the tribal leaders thus did not desire to continue their relationship with the Muslim authorities in Medina; some even claimed status of 'prophet' for themselves. It was in this chaotic context that false prophets emerged, who attempted to claim a power more significant than merely tribal leadership. The situation can be summarized as follows:

> When the Prophet died, many of the tribal leaders felt that there was no need for them to maintain the relationship; some were even ready to fill any vacuum that followed by claiming prophethood for themselves. . . .
> It is in this context that the sudden emergence of false prophets, from Musaylama, to Sajah, and to Tulayha, can be understood. Since the

Prophet's authority and power were based on his prophethood, this also represented to many the shortest way to elevate the status of one tribe above others, as well as to redirect to themselves the material benefits Muslims had achieved under the Prophet.[4]

Some stability did emerge, however, after the issue of political leadership was resolved decisively in favour of Abu Bakr and he concluded successful battles against rebellious tribes. On his deathbed, after a short two-year caliphate, Abu Bakr nominated Umar, who became the second 'rightly guided' caliph. It was during Umar's time that large-scale conquests of much of Syria, Iraq, Persia and Egypt took place.

Upon Umar's assassination in 23/644, following his insistence that a new leader should be chosen by consultation, a committee of six Meccan Muslims (Muhajirun) chose from among their number Uthman ibn Affan, after the leading contender Ali was sidelined. The first half of Uthman's twelve-year rule progressed with little challenge; however the second half was marred by significant discontent, notably amongst some of the community's elite (governors, generals and key decision-makers) who were by this time widely dispersed in the newly conquered and expanding regions. Claims of nepotism were made against Uthman, who had allegedly favoured relatives from his own clan to hold lucrative posts in the administration. It was such discontent that no doubt led to rebellion against Uthman and finally his assassination.

The political chaos that resulted from the assassination of Uthman firmly divided the community. Finally, in 35/656, it was Ali's turn to be chosen as leader; however, his refusal to deal with some of the leaders of the rebellion against Uthman and his inability to unite the community under his leadership led to further fractures. Several leading figures refused to recognize Ali's rule, including A'isha, one of the Prophet's wives. This led to the famous Battle of Camel (36/656) between Ali and his opponents, led largely by A'isha. Her forces, however, were defeated with considerable losses on both sides.

Similarly, the governor of Syria, Uthman's kinsman Mu'awiya, was not prepared to accept the legitimacy of Ali's rule and assembled forces to fight Ali in the Battle of Siffin (37/657). The inconclusive result of the battle led to both leaders agreeing to arbitration, which led to the emergence of a new group (known as Kharijis who were not happy with Ali's acceptance of arbitration and rebelled against him) who challenged both Ali and Mu'awiya.

Debates on imamate and leadership

It was in this contentious environment that the political concept of leadership (imamate) in Islam emerged and was debated. Those who supported the rule of the family of the Prophet developed their conception of imamate over the first three centuries of Islam. The Kharijis, who rejected the arbitration between Ali and Muʿawiya and rebelled against both of them and their supporters, also developed their own particular conception of legitimate rule. In between, there was the majority of Muslims who also developed an understanding of the imamate. In the following sections we will look at these groups and their interpretations of legitimate rule.

Kharijis

For the Kharijis, any righteous Muslim – even a slave – could be leader. The person did not have to come from the family of the Prophet (as the Shiʿa claimed) or the tribe of the Prophet, Quraysh (as the Sunnis claimed). The determining qualifier for the position of imam was quality and piety, and the imam was to be confirmed via oaths of allegiance (bayʿa) from at least two supporters, although the Kharijis did not regard it as an absolute duty upon the community that an imam be elected. The imam was the leader in war as well as a judge and religious head of the community. Among the imam's duties was to 'enjoin the good and forbid evil'.[5] Rule should be based upon the Qur'an and the Sunna of the Prophet.[6] The imam merely applied doctrine established from these sources.

The Kharijis held a fanatical position on upholding moral propriety. Even the imam, upon committing a mortal sin, was an apostate and liable to be killed. The legitimacy of the imam therefore depended on his 'moral and religious probity'. To the Kharijis, both Uthman and Ali were infidels, as both committed grave sins in their eyes. The Kharijis included in their definition of infidelity failing to declare solidarity with a just imam.[7]

While the Kharijis more or less died out as a movement, some of their descendants have survived in North Africa, Oman and East Africa. They are known today as Ibadis, since they consider 'Khariji' to be a pejorative term. In the legal works of Ibadis, imamate is an important issue. They consider the most important qualifications of the imam to be piety and knowledge. Like the early Kharijis, they give no consideration to family or lineage. For Ibadis, it is the senior members (elders) of the community who should choose the leader, who may be deposed for injustice.

The last 'true imam' to unite the entire Omani region under his power was Ahmad ibn Saʿid (d. 1198/1783), founder of the Busaʿidi dynasty that remains in power to this day. His descendants took the title not of 'Imam', with its connotations of religious leadership, but 'Sayyid', an honorific title held by any member of the royal family. Later, they used the title 'Sultan', implying a purely coercive power that relinquished pretensions to spiritual authority.[8]

Shi'a: Twelver (Imami) Shi'ism

While smaller Shi'i groups (the Zaydis and the Ismailis) have different theories about imamate, this section will consider the largest group of Shi'i Muslims: the Twelver (Imami) Shi'is. The name is drawn from their recognition of twelve direct descendants of the Prophet as rightful successors, who are considered divinely appointed and guided imams.

The Twelver Shi'i conception of the imamate is based on several ideas. First, the imam has a divine right to be the leader of the community, on the basis of the interpretation of a number of Qur'anic verses including: 'Your only friends are God, the messenger of God, and the believers, those who pray regularly, give alms, and bow down'.[9] The Arabic word *waliy* (friend) used in this text carries connotations of guardianship, and Shi'i scholars interpret this verse on the basis of traditions narrating that the occasion for the revealing of this verse was when Ali was the only believer to give zakat, which he did while he was in the middle of prostrating during prayer. Hence, they read the verse as 'give alms while bowing down'.[10] Furthermore, Shi'i scholars consider two other important verses to have been revealed at Ghadir Khumm (near Mecca in 10/632), and draw upon a number of traditions that refer to the Prophet investing Ali with a special status:[11]

> The Prophet in Ghadir Khumm invited people toward Ali and took his arm and lifted it so high that the white spot in the armpit of the Prophet of God could be seen. . . . Then he [said] 'For whomever I am the authority and guide Ali is also his guide and authority. Oh God! Be friendly with the friends of Ali and the enemy of his enemies. Whoever helps him, help him, and whoever leaves him, leave him.'[12]

According to Shi'i belief, leading figures of the Muslim community ignored the Prophet Muhammad's clear nomination of Ali as successor. Thus, Ali was the rightful leader from the very beginning, even though he did not achieve temporal power until some years after the Prophet's death.

Second, the imams are protected by God from error and sin, a protection they share with the Prophet, based on the concept that humanity is in perpetual need of a divinely guided leader and interpreter of the faith. The difference between prophets and imams, then, is that the former bring divine books of scripture, whereas the latter interpret the faith and lead the community. Thus, a prophet can be both prophet and imam, while an imam may not necessarily be a prophet.[13]

Third, Twelver Shi'i Muslims believe that the twelfth imam will return to usher in a period of just rule. According to the doctrine of the 'Hidden Imam', the eleventh imam Hasan ibn Ali al-Askari (d. 260/872) had a secret son named Muhammad, who was kept hidden from the hostile Sunni caliph al-Mu'tamid (d. 279/892). Upon his father's death, the five-year-old boy became the imam and communicated to the faithful through a series of representatives. This period of around seventy years is known as the minor occultation. In 329/939, the imam went into major occultation with the death of his final representative. Shi'i Muslims believe that the twelfth imam is alive, albeit hidden, and will emerge in the fullness of time to usher in an age of justice and restore the faith and practice of Islam. In the meantime, Shi'i jurists represent him in interpreting the law.[14]

For Shi'i Muslims, the imam is not merely the political head of the community, he is also its spiritual leader, and the two functions are held within the same person. This differs from the view of the Sunnis who often make a clear distinction between the two roles. Whether or not political leadership was possible to attain at the time, the Shi'a believe it was the direct descendants of the family of the Prophet who were the only legitimate leaders of the Muslim community. Because Shi'i Muslims themselves were divided on the particular list of successors, schisms occurred at various points in history. The Zaydis split over the choice of the fifth imam, while the Ismailis split over the choice of the seventh imam. Other smaller schisms occurred, including the rise of the Druze, Bohras and Nizaris (whose leader is the Aga Khan) from within Ismaili Shi'ism. In 1260/1844 Sayyid Ali Muhammad (d. 1266/1850) made a number of eschatological claims that resulted in the birth of Babism and later Baha'ism, new religious movements that eventually gravitated away from Islam by replacing traditional Shi'i religious laws and beliefs with their own scriptures and versions of shari'a.

The majority of the Shi'a, however, recognize twelve descendants of the Prophet as imams (leaders) of the community:

1   Ali ibn Abi Talib (d. 40/661)
2   al-Hasan ibn Ali (d. 50/670)
3   al-Husayn ibn Ali (d. 61/680)
4   Ali ibn al-Husayn (also known as Zayn al-Abidin) (d. circa 94–5/712–14)
5   Muhammad al-Baqir (d. 114/732)
6   Ja'far al-Sadiq (d. 148/765)
7   Musa al-Kazim (d. 183/799)
8   Ali al-Rida (d. 203/818)
9   Muhammad al-Jawad (d. 220/835)
10   Ali al-Hadi (d. 254/868)
11   Hasan al-Askari (d. 260/874)
12   Muhammad the Mahdi (went into major occultation in 329/970)

With the major occultation of the twelfth imam, the Shi'a had to relate to existing political authorities, and the question arose over whether they should co-operate with the authorities or reject them as interlopers. Differing views were expressed, with some scholars arguing that some form of co-operation was needed, and others denying the importance of such co-operation. The scholar al-Kulayni (d. circa 329/940–1), for example, sought to warn Shi'i Muslims against appearing before the arbitration of 'the judges of tyranny', and followers of this opinion emphasised using arbitrators from amongst their own ranks.[15] Muhammad ibn al-Hasan al-Tusi (d. circa 459/1067), on the other hand, argued that 'the true imams, upon them be peace, have cast the mantle of judgement on the jurists of the Shi'a, during such time as they themselves are not in the position to exercise it in person'.[16] According to Ann Lambton, 'This appears to be one of the earliest occasions when it is stated that the jurists are in fact the successors or deputies of the imams in the giving of judgement'.[17] Al-Tusi further argued that the giving of judgements should be within the mandate of the sultan (the de facto ruler).[18]

The authority of the jurist is derived from the authority of the imam. While interpreting the law on his behalf is important, certain functions cannot be undertaken in his absence. This includes the implementation of the Qur'anic punishments (*hudud*), Friday prayers being made obligatory, the interpretation of legal texts and the commanding of jihad. They can be exercised appropriately only by an infallible imam.[19] However, in reality, Shi'i scholars have, over several centuries, whittled away at these prohibitions and permitted these prerogatives to be used.

Sunnis

Much of Sunni Islam's political theory was developed during the Abbasid period on the basis that Muslims should hold fast to the sacred law, the Sunna of the Prophet and the generally agreed-upon customary practice of the community. It has been a Sunni tendency to reject extremist political positions, such as those emanating from the more anarchist-puritan Kharijis and the theocratic approach adopted by the Shi'a. For Sunnis, the agreed-upon practice of the community inspired by the actions of the Prophet was taken as the most appropriate way of conceptualizing legitimate rule.

The period of the Rashidun ('rightly guided') caliphs, immediately after the death of the Prophet, is considered by Sunnis to be the 'golden period' of Islamic rule. The methods adopted by the community at the time to elect or choose the ruler were considered the best examples of Islamic governance. The acceptable methods of choosing a ruler were based on the election of Abu Bakr; the nomination of Umar by Abu Bakr; and the appointment of a consultative committee by Umar. Given that caliphs in the Rashidun period and recognized rulers from subsequent dynasties who ruled Muslims were from the tribe of Quraysh (and presumably on the basis of a prophetic saying), the Sunni theory held that the legitimate ruler should come from the tribe of Quraysh. This accommodated the view that the Umayyad and Abbasid rulers were legitimate. Given the central place that shari'a has in the Sunni political theory, as long as shari'a is implemented by the ruler, the legitimacy of the ruler should not be questioned.

Among the earliest thinkers to write on political theory was Ibn al-
Muqaffa' (d. 140/757), a Persian convert to Islam who was familiar with
Sassanid statecraft. He translated several works into Arabic, including the
famous *Kalila wa dimna* (a book of classic fables) as well as one of the earliest
systematic and coherent formulations of Islamic political thought called
Risala fi al-sahaba. Among the areas he explored in his work are the interaction of the political and religious leadership, governance structures,
bureaucracy and law.[20] He believed that a leader must have the allegiance of
his people. In order for this to occur he felt that people had to have a proper
conception of the leader's authority. Ibn al-Muqaffa' believed that the
leader must be obeyed on condition that the leader himself follows the law.
He was trying to find a middle ground between the Khariji conception of
the conditional obedience to the imam and the Shi'i belief that the imam they
do not recognize should not be obeyed. In the area of law, it is the imam
(political-religious leader) who can issue laws and decrees, and these are to
be obeyed. No one else has the right to issue orders in regards to war, the
appointment of officials and the collection and distribution of tax.[21] Ibn al-
Muqaffa' also believed that the leader has the right not only to administer
the legal penalties but also to issue judgements upon matters that the revealed
texts do not clearly articulate. The leader should clarify and systematize the
whole framework of the law and should produce an authoritative codification. Ibn al-Muqaffa' was proposing that the development of law for
Muslims should be taken out of the hands of the ulama and their conflicting
schools and entrusted to the caliph:

> If the commander of the faithful should judge it opportune to give orders
> that these divergent decisions and practices should be submitted to him
> in the form of a dossier, accompanied by the [Traditions] and the
> solutions . . . preferred by each school; if the commander of the faithful
> would then examine these documents and formulate on each question
> the opinion which God would inspire in him; if he would hold firmly
> to this opinion and forbid the religious judges to overturn it; if he would
> then make an exhaustive volume of these decisions then we could have
> this hope that God would transform these judgements, in which (at
> present) error and truth are mixed up, into a single just code. We would
> be able to hope that the unification of judicial practices would be a means
> of harmonising justice according to the opinion, and through the mouth,
> of the commander of the faithful.[22]

One of the most important scholars who wrote on Sunni political theory
is al-Mawardi (d. 450/1058). He emphasized the necessity for the imam
to guarantee the existence of the community. Authority is delegated to
the imam by God and he alone has authority to delegate this to others.[23]
Mawardi believed that God ordained to the community, the umma, a

leader who was essentially the vice-regent of the Prophet. The imamate became the principle upon which the community was established and regulated.[24]

From al-Mawardi's point of view, it is obligatory for Muslims to obey those in authority, on the basis of the Qur'anic verses on this issue. Mawardi also seems to think, perhaps similarly to the Kharijis, that this obedience does have certain limits but, following the Sunni tradition, any rebellion against the ruler is considered unacceptable as it leads to chaos (*fitna*). Rebellion can be considered legitimate only in extreme circumstances such as the ruler apostatizing from Islam.

In Sunni theory, the caliph (imam) is the political leader of the community; he may have some religious functions such as implementing the law (shari'a) but is not considered to have any automatic right to be the interpreter of the law. Interpreting the law is the function of the ulama, who are knowledgeable in shari'a. Therefore, there is a distinction between the religious function of interpreting the law and the political function of governance. The political authority and religious authority are thus complementary.

For Sunni Muslims the caliph must be from the Quraysh. For them it is obligatory for Muslims to elect a leader. The caliph should be the best qualified person in the community, and should rule according to the Qur'an and Sunna of the Prophet. In theory, this leader would have both religious and political functions. A sin committed by the leader does not automatically lead to him being removed from office. Even if the caliph is unjust and oppressive, people should not rebel against him.

From the fourth/tenth century onwards, the Abbasid caliph increasingly became a figurehead. His power was gradually diffused into the 'religious' sphere by powerful warlords and sultans who for all practical purposes had usurped the power of the caliph.[25] Therefore, much of the Sunni political theory of the caliphate was fast becoming irrelevant by the late Abbasid period. The Abbasid caliph had no political power; rather, his authority was reduced to that of a mere 'spiritual leader' controlled by those who held effective power. Successive warlords and military figures and, in fact, dynasties, although ruling in the name of the caliph, exploited the caliphate for the purpose of their own legitimacy. The caliph retained an aura of religious authority: his name was mentioned in the Friday sermon and in all religious ceremonies, but the caliphate was changed from an office that united religious and political worlds into one in which his authority was downgraded. Although still religious, it was now subservient to the political realm.[26]

By the early years of the tenth century [CE], the breakdown of caliphal authority was complete. The now powerless Abbasid caliphs recognized the existence of a supreme governing authority besides the caliph, exercising effective political and military power, and leaving the caliph only as formal head of the state and the faith and representative of the religious unity of Islam.[27]

The two forms of authority, religious and political, came to be so clearly differentiated and separated that during the Seljuq domination (fifth/eleventh century) during the Abbasid period, when the caliph attempted to exercise political power, the Seljuq sultan protested against what he regarded as an infringement of the political authority's prerogatives. The caliph, he said

> should busy himself with his duties as imam, as leader in prayer, which is the best and most glorious of tasks, and is the protection of the rulers of the world; he should leave the business of government to the sultans, to whom it was entrusted.[28]

Al-Ghazali (d. 505/1111), a realist, having seen what was happening during this time, attempted to incorporate these circumstances into his theory. Given that the imamate (represented by the caliph) and sultanate (represented by the sultan who in theory was subject to the authority of the caliph) had become completely separate, the former having no effective power and the latter being the effective political power, al-Ghazali put forward a doctrine based on a close association between the imamate and the sultanate.[29] The association empowered both parties. The imam was to be designated by the sultan, who through his exercise of constitutive authority recognized the institutional authority of the imam. And, on the other hand, the validity of the sultan's government was established by his allegiance to the imam, who authorized his rule. In this way, the sultan recognized that the shari'a was the organizing principle of the community.[30] The main feature of al-Ghazali's exposition of the connection between imamate and sultanate was that the manner and relationship of the imam with the sultan must be based on co-operation. Therefore there was the belief that there should, and could, be co-operation between the religious and political leadership.

Al-Ghazali argues that the requirements of shari'a are focused upon the implied existence of an institutional structuring and that this is authorized by the consensus of the community and is the imamate. Further, this requires the setting up of institutions for the fulfilment of the provisions of the shari'a.[31] For him, both the sultanate and imamate are essential as both are needed to fulfil the requirements of the shari'a. He further argues that, without the existence of the imamate, no judgement of a judge, contract or testament would be legally valid.[32] The theoretical framework proposed by al-Ghazali has three aspects:[33] (1) the use of power is necessary to accomplish and maintain order; (2) the governance structures need to be symbolic of the collective unity of the Muslim community (*umma*) and maintain its historical continuity; and (3) the framework derives its functional and institutional authority from the shari'a. For al-Ghazali, religion and power, both temporal and spiritual, were interrelated. The *umma*, the organization of which rested on religion and reason, was ideally a brotherhood in which all are accorded the same status by God and co-operate in physical, religious and moral acts. This would be understood with their acceptance of the same fundamental beliefs. A central problem for al-Ghazali was the theory of sovereignty. People had only one law, the shari'a, which God had given them. Politics was therefore closely aligned with theology, eschatology and law. It was concerned with the art of how to conduct oneself in the community and to administer affairs in conformity with Islamic law.[34]

Two centuries later, Ibn Taymiyya, the Hanbali jurist, was writing on the question of 'politics'. By this time the Abbasid caliphate had been abolished by the Mongols and there was no caliphate which even at a symbolic level was able to unify Muslims. For Ibn Taymiyya the true caliphate came to an end with the end of the Rashidun caliphs. Therefore, the ulama should be the guardians of shari'a, not the caliph. The connection early thinkers made between the protection of shari'a and the caliph did not make sense any more. The caliphate no longer existed, but the ulama did.

Thus Sunni political 'theory' in a sense is a justification of what existed in practice. At the beginning, when the caliph had real power, the role of the caliph was central to the political life of the *umma*. But with the massive changes that occurred from the third/ninth to the seventh/thirteenth centuries, and the gradual loss of power of the caliph to sultans and generals, the Sunni theory came to accept this and revised its earlier views. This transformation continued until Ibn Taymiyya simply ignored the office of caliph altogether in his work, because Umayyad and Abbasid caliphs no longer existed during his time.

Separation of religion and politics[35]

A careful look at the actual practice of the Prophet, and at the laws he implemented in the first Islamic polis, or more accurately 'emirate', in Medina, reveals that he was quite pragmatic in conducting community affairs. In his scheme, there was no distinction between the religious domain and the political domain. Just as the separation of the religious from the political was problematic, it is equally problematic to consider *everything* the Prophet did as leader of the emirate as somehow 'religious'. Law, for instance, was needed to govern the community and he ensured that what was necessary for this to occur was done. When the community needed a particular law, he adopted it, and this was often determined by social and political considerations. When the circumstances required that the laws should be changed, he changed them. Even in the case of the Qur'an, it was the societal need that determined which laws were given and implemented.

In this sense, both the Prophet and the revelation reflected an acute awareness of what was necessary, what constituted the pragmatic reality of the social domain. The Prophet was not just a religious figure; he was also a political figure, judge, administrator and general. There was no separation between his functions as a political leader and his functions as a religious leader. This continued with the Prophet's immediate successors, the Rashidun caliphs, and to some extent during the Umayyad period. During the Abbasid period, such a separation became increasingly evident. The situation was facilitated to a certain extent by the emergence of a class of ulama (specialists in religious law and knowledge). These ulama started to institute through their specialization a demarcation of skills and activities.[36] This was a practical transformation rather than something grounded in a theoretical revolution, as noted by the Indian Muslim thinker Abu al-Hasan al-Nadawi, who said that 'the separation between religion and politics occurred in practice'.[37]

The modern period: state and citizenship

In the modern period, the debate on the imamate and caliphate has been largely ignored; it has become a debate on state and citizenship, which is the result of the acceptance of the idea of the 'nation state' throughout the Muslim world. Associated debates in the contemporary period include those about democracy and human rights.

With the abolition of the Ottoman caliphate in 1924, and the emergence of the secular nation state of Turkey, the caliphate, which was a symbol at that time of a largely fictitious Muslim unity, disappeared, leaving a political vacuum for the discussion of the Islamic state during the following two decades. The model of the Islamic state and of citizenship rights came to be debated from four broad directions: traditionalist, neo-revivalist, modernist and secularist.[38] While this debate was largely a Sunni one, the Shi'a also had their role. In fact, it was a Shi'i state, Iran, under Ayatollah Khomeini (d. 1989), that perhaps has had the greatest influence on the debate about what is meant by the term 'Islamic state' in the modern period.

For the traditionalists, represented by traditionalist ulama, the Islamic state is one in which shari'a is implemented as it was developed by the classical Muslim jurists and theologians. For the traditionalists, non-Muslims, living in an Islamic state, at least in theory, belong to the category of protected minorities (*dhimmi*). The role of the dhimmi in the Islamic state is contentious. Some ulama think, in line with traditional fiqh, that dhimmis should pay the classical *jizya* (poll tax), while others think that, because in the modern nation state non-Muslims are not 'conquered', they should be treated differently, much like people with whom an Islamic state has a peace agreement.[39]

Neo-revivalists believe that the Qur'an and the Sunna are the foundation texts on which a Muslim society and its institutions should be based. This group is largely represented by the Muslim Brotherhood of Egypt and Jamaat-i-Islami of Pakistan. The neo-revivalists also seek a shari'a-based society, but their conception of shari'a differs from that of the traditionalists. They are not as legalistic as the traditionalists but their thinking is dominated by a form of modern 'scripturalism'. They are more flexible on the question of non-Muslims, but would still consider them as having fewer rights than Muslim citizens. For instance, according to Maududi, there are three types of non-Muslims in an Islamic state. The first group is the contractees, those who accept the hegemony of an Islamic state voluntarily, or during a war, and enter into a contract with it. They are to be treated according to the provisions of the treaty. The next group consists of those who are conquered: they are defeated in war by an Islamic state and their territories annexed by it; they have to pay the poll tax. The final group is those who are resident non-Muslims in an Islamic state in any other capacity, and are to be treated according to the general rules of the dhimmi.[40]

For the modernists, the priority in an Islamic state is the implementation of the clearly spelt out rulings and regulations of the Qur'an and Sunna, which apparently are not many. The remainder of Islamic law is subject to change, requiring a new methodology to deal with the new problems and demands of a modern Muslim society. The modernists are even further from the traditionalists on this issue than the neo-revivalists. On the question of citizenship rights, although they are prepared to adopt some of the classical views, they oppose blatant discrimination against non-Muslims. Modernists, like Muhammad Asad (d. 1992), are happy to provide more protection of non-Muslims' rights, although they still would like to see some preferential treatment for Muslims. Asad argues that in an Islamic state 'a certain amount of differentiation between Muslims and non-Muslims' should exist.[41]

The fourth position is that of the secularists, who support a secular state with equal citizenship for all people regardless of religion. Their view of religion is that it is a private matter between a Muslim and God; religion has no place in politics and governance.[42] Since this position is held mostly by Westernized (or 'secular') Muslims whose attachment to Islam is seen as nominal and superficial, their arguments are rejected by the other three groups. The secularist position was expressed by the late Muhammad Ali Jinnah (d. 1948), the founder of Pakistan, in a speech addressing the citizens of the newly created state:[43]

> You are free to go to temples, you are free to go to your mosques, or to any other places of worship in this state of Pakistan. You may belong to any religion or caste or creed – that has got nothing to do with the business of the State. . . . We are starting with this fundamental principle that we are all citizens and equal citizens of one State.[44]

The secularist trend, although it dominates almost the entire Islamic world at government level, has increasingly been challenged by neo-revivalist Islamists during the later part of the twentieth century. From the 1970s onwards, the strong revival of Islam and the persistent call from a large number of Muslims for a major communal role for their faith have gradually undermined the secularist position. The secularization projects of Atatürk of Turkey, the Shah of Iran and Bourguiba of Tunisia, for instance, and attempts to keep Islam at bay, have been challenged, most notably in Iran. Other countries which followed in the footsteps of countries such as Turkey and Tunisia appear to have been having second thoughts about their Islam-resistant policies. This does not mean that Muslims are intending to 'islamize' their societies along the lines of the traditionally developed laws of fiqh. However, in the Islamic world, serious efforts are being made by jurists and intellectuals to rethink traditionally developed laws in areas such as citizenship, albeit within an Islamic framework (incorporating current perspectives of justice, fairness and egalitarianism). For instance, Abdullahi An-Na'im has said:[45]

> Whereas the personal concept of citizenship would confer this status on the basis of some personal attribute or quality such as religion or ethnicity, the territorial conception of citizenship, which has now become the norm, confers the benefits and burdens of citizenship on all those born and permanently resident within the territory of the state, as well as those naturalised under the relevant provisions of the law of the land. It is morally repugnant and politically inexpedient, I submit, to deny a full citizenship to any person who was born and permanently resident within the territory of the state unless such person opts for and requires the citizenship of another state.[46]

Below are the views of two contemporary thinkers on important political issues today.

Khomeini and the Islamic state

Despite the Sunni neo-revivalist Islamist preoccupation with questions of state and citizenship since the 1920s, it was a Shi'i scholar, Ayatollah Khomeini, who managed to realize the idea of an 'Islamic' state. Khomeini, an Iranian dissident scholar active against the Shah of Iran in the 1960s, was forced into exile in France, where he spent fifteen years. In 1979, he returned to Iran as the champion of revolution against the Shah. He expressed the key features of his conception of the Islamic state as follows:

> Islam provides a comprehensive sociopolitical system valid for all time and place. Thus, God is the sole legislator. Government is mandated in order to implement God's plan in this world. Individual believers are not permitted simply to suffer unjust rule in silence. They must actively work to realize God's plan in this world. The only acceptable form of

Islamic government is that directed by the most religiously learned. This is the guardianship of the faqih (*velayat-e faqih*). Thus monarchy or for that matter any other form of government is unacceptable.[47]

According to Khomeini, since Islamic government is a government of law; those acquainted with law, or more precisely with religion, that is, the jurists, must supervise its functioning. It is they who supervise all executive and administrative affairs of the country, together with all planning.[48] Under his rule, in a move away from the classical Islamic legal position on non-Muslims, the Iranian constitution confers equal citizenship on all Iranians.

Rashid Ghannushi: a Sunni Islamist's view of equality

Rashid Ghannushi is distinguished for his leadership of the Renaissance Party.[49] Born in 1941 in Tunisia, Ghannushi studied philosophy at the University of Damascus. Together with a number of other Tunisians he established an Islamic movement which aimed to reform Tunisian society on the basis of Islamic values and principles. Since this movement was against the then President of Tunisia, Bourguiba's secular policies, an increasingly confrontationist tendency developed between the reformists and the government. Ghannushi was sentenced in 1981 to eleven years' imprisonment, but was released in 1984. In 1987 he was again imprisoned, this time with a life sentence, but was released in 1988. Ghannushi began living in Europe as a political exile from the early 1990s.

Ghannushi was one of the leading figures of the Islamist movement of the late twentieth century. He is well versed in both Islamic and Western thought and is a contributor to the debate on the peaceful co-existence of Muslims and non-Muslims. Among his concerns is reconciliation between Islam and modernity. Though an Islamist, he does not share the views of many other Islamists; for instance, he sees no inherent conflict between Islam and the West or between Islam and modernity.[50]

Other unconventional views of Ghannushi, which set him at odds with a number of Islamists, are that women should have equal rights to men in society; that the veil is a matter of choice and should not be imposed upon women by the state; that non-Muslims in an Islamic state should have equal rights with Muslims; and that pluralism is to be accepted. Ghannushi says: 'We at Al-Nahda [party] absolutely believe in and adhere to democracy and what it entails of pluralism and the alternation of power through the ballot box.'[51] Ghannushi sees it as important and necessary to reinterpret relevant texts in order to suit the needs of Muslims of the modern period. He stresses that one of the main objectives of Islam from the beginning was to establish a just order. This implied protecting the weak and oppressed, which is why such people were the first to profess Islam. The focus in all the Qur'anic verses where justice is considered is on all people, not just Muslims.

The authority for Ghannushi's assertions stems from the Prophet Muhammad's treatment of Jews and Muslims as equals in the 'Constitution of Medina', where the city's inhabitants were held to be a 'community' by the Prophet. Ghannushi goes on to say that the Constitution

> embodied in it the Divine justice and Divine law in terms of equality among human beings on the basis of justice, fairness and the relationship of human brotherhood above any ethnic or class or religious consideration.[52]

Continuing to find bases for his ideas in the foundation texts, Ghannushi turns his attention towards those who disagree with equal treatment for non-Muslims and advocate the denial of generally accepted human rights, such as freedom of religious belief. For him, the Qur'an is very clear on the issue of freedom of belief: religion is acceptable only if people believe in it of their free will. This is again referred to in the verse 'There is no compulsion in religion'.[53] In this context, Ghannushi is critical of discussions in classical sources on preventing the people of protected minorities from building or maintaining their churches. He criticizes the jurists whose opinions were used to limit the freedom of non-Muslims:[54]

> Islam rejects the use of methods of compulsion and violence in order to force creeds and ideas upon others, since religious and intellectual convictions are a domain of man's free choice not one of compulsion and force.[55]

Muslims therefore should not force anyone to accept a religion, even Islam. Even in the case of a Muslim who becomes an apostate, Ghannushi is of the view that it is a matter between the apostate and God. Furthermore, he believes that the issue of apostasy and its prescribed punishment in Islamic law is essentially political, not religious, and that apostasy should not be subject to the punishment of death. This is certainly a radical departure from the traditional Islamic juristic position on this.[56]

Ghannushi also addresses a sensitive issue in the debate on the citizenship rights of non-Muslims; that is, whether they should be allowed to take senior positions in government. He examines the practice of previous generations in this area and reviews the judgements of both early and modern scholars. His conclusion is that such appointments should be on the basis of expertise and qualifications, the only exceptions being the most senior imam and the commander-in-chief of the armed forces, traditionally known as Amir al-Mu'minin (leader of the believers) or Caliph. These positions, in Ghannushi's view, are very closely related to 'religious' positions and, hence, should be reserved to Muslims. They should, however, be the only reserved appointments.

Chapter 10

Renewal, reform and Muslim modernism

Renewal in religion (*tajdid*) has always been part of the Islamic tradition. A renewer (*mujaddid*) came to be one who renovated belief in and the practice of the Sunna (as opposed to *bid‘a*, which means innovation in religious matters). Although orthodoxy does not recognize the rise of further prophetic figures after the Prophet Muhammad, Muslims accept that, at different times and in different parts of the Islamic world, renewers of religion emerged who challenged the status quo and argued for change. Among such renewers we may include Ahmad ibn Hanbal, al-Ghazali and Ibn Taymiyya.

Premodern reform movements

Continuing with the tradition of 'renewal', several reform movements emerged in the Muslim world from the seventeenth to the nineteenth centuries CE in places such as Arabia, India and North Africa. They were primarily related to internal pressures and circumstances and had little to do with the impact of the West. These reformers argued against blind imitation as well as against fanatical following of the earlier schools of law[1] because blind imitation led to divisions within the Muslim community. They also argued for the revival of ijtihad. Significant reformers include Shah Wali Allah of India, the Wahabbis of Arabia, and the Sanusis of North Africa.

India: Shah Wali Allah

Shah Wali Allah (d. 1176/1762) was born in Uttar Pradesh in India. He traced his ancestry to the tribe of the Prophet Muhammad, the Quraysh. He was trained in Islamic disciplines by his father but after his father's death studied in Arabia (particularly in Medina) for a little over a year between 1143/1730 and 1145/1732. His contribution to Islamic scholarship is enormous, due to his mastery of disciplines as diverse as hadith, Qur'anic exegesis, Sufism, law and theology. Over a thirty-year period, he is reported to have written more than fifty works, in Arabic and in Persian (the two languages most connected with Islamic writings in India at the time). He was the first to translate the Qur'an into a popular language, Persian, which at the time was condemned by some ulama as an unacceptable innovation.[2]

One of his key concerns was the decline of Muslim political power in India and ways to improve the condition of Muslims there. He argued for the political unity of Muslims in India, and for following the Islam of the earliest Muslims (*salaf*). For him it was important for Muslims to move beyond their differences and unite to restore the fading Muslim power in India. Shah Wali Allah's ideas include the rational nature of Islamic law; the close connection between the teachings of the Prophet and his social and political environment; the need to bridge the gap between Muslims who followed different schools of law, theology and spirituality; the need to revive the spirit of ijtihad; recognition of acceptable and unacceptable practices within Sufism and support for positive aspects of Sufism; critique of foreign accretions into Islamic thought and cultural practices that were not in line with his understanding of true Islam, such as excessive spending and rituals in marriage ceremonies, probably under the influence of Hindu culture; the need for social justice, helping the needy and disadvantaged and supporting all sections of the community.

There are certain similarities between his thought and that of Muhammad ibn Abd al-Wahhab, particularly in his focus on ijtihad and return to the pure Islam of the *salaf*. Shah Wali Allah's ideas were influential in the setting up in 1866 CE of the Islamic religious education institution in Deoband (known as Dar al-Ulum in India), which brought together ideas of Shah Wali Allah and of those who were influenced by Muhammad ibn Abd al-Wahhab (d. 1207/1792).[3] One could also argue that Sayyid Ahmad Khan (d. 1316/ 1898) and other major thinkers of the Indian subcontinent were also influenced by the ideas of Shah Wali Allah. Even some twentieth-century thinkers such as Sayyid Abu'l-Ala Maududi (d. 1978) seemed to find a precursor to their own beliefs and calls for reform in Shah Wali Allah's elucidation of the shari'a.[4]

Arabia: Wahhabi reform

Muhammad ibn Abd al-Wahhab (d. 1207/1792) was born in Nejd, in central Arabia. Although his religious education was largely in Medina, he travelled widely in Arabia and modern-day Iraq and Iran. He saw that Islam in much of Arabia had descended into a superstitious folk religion that was very similar to pre-Islamic practice in Hijaz. He felt that this compromised the unity of God that Prophet Muhammad had taught. He sought to purify Islam by focusing on polytheism (*shirk*) and unity of God (*tawhid*) and rejecting all forms of innovation (*bid'a*). In the area of law, Muhammad ibn Abd al-Wahhab followed the Hanbali school and was influenced by its figures such as Ibn Taymiyya (d. 728/1328) and Ibn al-Qayyim (d. 751/1350), even though initially his teachings were rejected by local Hanbali scholars.[5] His followers came to be referred to by the somewhat pejorative term 'Wahhabi'. Followers of Ibn Abd al-Wahhab themselves use terms such as 'unitarians' (*muwahhidun*) or followers of the way of the 'righteous earliest Muslims' (*al-salaf al-salih*).[6]

Muhammad ibn Abd al-Wahhab's writings are generally on issues about which a number of key reformers of the twelfth/eighteenth century were concerned: the return to the pure Islam of the Qur'an and the Sunna; the rejection of popular religious practices such as the veneration of saints and treating their tombs as shrines; the rejection of the blind following of earlier scholars; and an emphasis on ijtihad. Ibn Abd al-Wahhab argued for a return to the methodology of the *salaf* and the literal reading of the Qur'an as far as the names and attributes of God were concerned. He rejected Sufi practices almost entirely as heretical and against Islam.

In order to promote his teachings, Ibn Abd al-Wahhab sought assistance from a local tribal chief of Nejd, Muhammad ibn Sa'ud (d. 1179/1765). They formed a political, military and religious alliance that provided the basis for Ibn Abd al-Wahhab to spread his teachings throughout much of Arabia. After establishing their base in Nejd, the Wahhabi army set their sights on the Hijaz. Led by Abd al-Aziz (d. 1218/1803), the son of Muhammad ibn Sa'ud, the Wahhabi army attacked the Shi'i holy site of Karbala in 1217/1802. A few years later they successfully took Medina and Mecca and began destroying sites and prohibiting practices that conflicted with Ibn Abd al-Wahhab's teachings.[7]

The movement, with its hardline approach to popular practice, fighting innovation and labelling other Muslims as not sufficiently Muslim (i.e. as innovators or polytheists), frightened the Ottomans. The Ottoman Sultan asked Muhammad Ali of Egypt to crush the movement and its political base. Medina and Mecca were retaken for the Ottomans in 1227/1812 and 1228/1813 respectively.[8] Within two years, the Wahhabi conquests came to a crushing halt.

In 1902, Abd al-Aziz b. Sa'ud (known as Ibn Sa'ud, d. 1953) who was a direct descendant of Muhammad b. Sa'ud, supported by a paramilitary movement called the Ikhwan, defeated the rival Rashidi clan in Riyadh. He gained control of Nejd and continued raids on other parts of Arabia. By 1924, Ibn Sa'ud's control over much of Arabia was complete, and in the following year control of the two holy cities of Mecca and Medina was taken over by the Wahhabis, ending Hashimi rule there. In 1932, Ibn Sa'ud renamed the areas of Nejd and Hijaz, and the Kingdom of Saudi Arabia was officially established.

Muhammad ibn Abd al-Wahhab's main work is a booklet, *Book of the Unity of God* (*Kitab al-tawhid*), which focuses on notions of unity of God (*tawhid*) and polytheism (*shirk*). On the basis of a literal reading of the Qur'an and hadith texts, he associates polytheism with seeking help and intercession from anyone other than God. In his view, polytheism could also be associated with areas such as visiting tombs of 'saints' and seeking their help and even the celebration of the birthday of the Prophet Muhammad. Wahhabis also believe that music is prohibited.

Echoing Ibn Taymiyya's views, the Wahhabi movement highlighted a 'return to pristine Islam', calling for a strict observance of and adherence to the teachings associated with the idea of unity of God. Ibn Abd al-Wahhab also called for the strict observance of the shari'a and did not hesitate to by-pass the formulations of the four schools of law (*madhhab*). Ijtihad, therefore, was on the agenda of this movement and its founder, and with the same vigour once displayed by Ibn Taymiyya. However, unlike Shah Wali Allah, Ibn Abd al-Wahhab was less keen to consider the impact of time and space and cultural specifics on formulating laws or assessing past ones. Ibn Abd al-Wahhab was sceptical of philosophy and rational intellectualism and was more comfortable in standing by the 'letter' of the texts rather than by their 'spirit'. Furthermore, his insistence on the early generations' formulation of Islam as the sole criterion of authenticity, with no room for further inter-pretation, suggests that for him Islamic reform meant a movement back in time, returning from a desolate present situation to a better old one, in order to re-experience Islam anew.

North Africa: The Sanusiyya

The Sanusiyya movement[9] also emerged in the context of a regeneration of the moral and social fibre of Muslim society, particularly in North Africa. The Sanusiyya movement was founded by Muhammad ibn Ali al-Sanusi (d. 1276/1859). He was born in modern-day Algeria and studied Islamic disciplines there with a number of local religious leaders. He then moved to al-Qarawiyyin in Fez, which was well known for its teaching and to which students from various parts of the Muslim world – in particular North Africa – came to study. Later, he studied with scholars in Egypt and Hijaz. He not only sought knowledge of the religious disciplines but also came under the influence of Sufis from the Tijaniyya, Shadhliyya and Qadiriyya orders. He did not belong to one particular order, just as he did not belong to one particular school of law.

The more al-Sanusi looked into the Muslim societies around him, the more he recognized their bad state, from religio-moral and socio-political points of view. He saw Muslims as politically fragmented. The more he contem-plated and reflected upon this state of affairs, the more he realized how important it was for Muslims to return to the purity of the Islam of the Prophet and earliest Muslims (*salaf*).

Al-Sanusi was aware of the Ottoman administration and its unjust rule in North Africa. This led to difficulties with the Ottoman administration. He had to move frequently not just in search of knowledge but also because of his political views. Thus, he moved from Fez to Algeria, Tunisia, Libya,

Egypt and Hijaz, staying in each region and often teaching. This meant that he developed contacts in a range of regions, and students formed the core of his disciples.

His difficulties with the authorities (both religious and political) continued. In Egypt, his teachings aroused the ire of the ulama of Azhar seminary. The political authorities were also suspicious of him given that his teachings were critical of their atrocities and injustices. His interest in reform, ijithad and a pristine Islam, coupled with his political concerns, kept him firmly focused on the religious and moral conditions in the societies in which he found himself. His difficulties with the religious and political authorities did not prevent him from establishing a series of *zawiyas* (hostels for accommodating members of Sufi orders and their travelling visitors) and attracting numerous disciples. For example, in Hijaz he established his Sufi order in 1253/1837, and his first zawiya in Libya in 1259/1843. His zawiyas increased in number and spread widely, particularly in North Africa. By the time he died in 1276/1859, Muhammad ibn Ali al-Sanusi had become so influential that the Ottoman authorities had to give his institutions some form of recognition. His work was continued by his son Muhammad, who became the leader of the Sufi order established by al-Sanusi.

Among the important teachings of the Sanusiyya include a return to the Islam of the early Muslims, the purification of Islam from various heresies and innovations, and the return to a simpler, purer form of religion and practice with a strong emphasis on the spiritual dimension (hence Sufism). However, the Sanusiyya also rejected certain Sufi practices such as music, dance and singing, which some Sufis use to facilitate their spiritual journey towards God. The Sanusiyya were keen to combine Sufism and following of the law without blind imitation and legalism. Thus, they emphasized a more moderate, less fanatical version of Islam and a more liberating understanding of the faith. Their flexibility is demonstrated by the fact that they did not adhere to one particular school of law, just as they did not follow one particular Sufi order. They were more eclectic and tried to use the best of a range of approaches and schools.

Colonialism and jihad movements

A key aspect of renewal and reform was the emergence of several jihad movements in the nineteenth century as a direct result of the European colonial penetration into Muslim lands. Thus, in response to British colonization of the Indian subcontinent, a number of ulama declared that India no longer was an 'abode of Islam' (*dar al-islam*) but an 'abode of war' (*dar al-harb*). In the early 1800s, Hajji Shariat Allah argued that India was an abode of war and declared jihad against the British in Bengal.

In West Africa, Shaykh Uthman ibn Fudi (d. 1232/1817), also known as Shehu Usman dan Fodio, initiated a successful jihad which resulted in the rise of the Sokoto caliphate, the largest independent state in nineteenth-century Africa.[9] Disillusioned with what he saw as ignorance of the masses, and an unwillingness on the part of the ulama to challenge corrupt rulers, Shehu began a reform movement that sought to empower the disenfranchized. In Shehu's case, his jihad was directed primarily at intransigent Muslims, rather than pagans or colonialist occupiers. Several members of his family played important roles in the jihad and resulting caliphate, including his daughter, the famous poet and educator Nana Asma'u (d. 1280/1864).[10]

Also in Africa, the Sanusis in the North waged a jihad against the French and Italians. In Sudan, Muhammad Ahmad, otherwise known as the Mahdi of Sudan, declared a jihad against the British and killed General Gordon in 1885. These military aspects of reform were important, as the views often shaped a significant part of the anti-colonial agenda of Muslims in the twentieth century. The idea of jihad and jihad movements was to play a significant role, after the end of the Cold War, from the 1990s onwards.

Muslim modernism

With the modern era (nineteenth century CE onwards), the tradition of religious renewal continued more intensively than ever before. The era ushered in the military and political confrontation of the Western powers with the Muslim states in which the Muslims were defeated.[11]

Muslim modernism is in part a continuation of the reformist movement of the eighteenth and nineteenth centuries and in part a way to address the challenges posed by modernity while remaining faithful to the basics of the religion. The impact of the West (and Western modernity) required responses commensurate with the extent of the challenge. Among the first 'modernists' may be included Jamal al-Din al-Afghani (d. 1315/1897) and Muhammad Abduh (d. 1905) in the Arab world, and Sayyid Ahmad Khan (d. 1315/1898), Muhammad Iqbal (d. 1938), and a range of modernists in the Indian subcontinent. Thinkers along these lines also came from parts of Ottoman Turkey, for example Namik Kamal (d. 1306/1888).

Reform was a key theme for modernists. Figures such as Jamal al-Din al-Afghani argued that Muslims should have a reform movement like the ones that had taken place in Christian Europe. The modern context demanded a reappraisal of the intellectual heritage of Muslims and this meant giving up the blind imitation of early scholars. Among other key ideas of the modernists were a return to the pristine Islam of the earliest Muslims (salaf); revitalization of the Islamic intellectual tradition; interpretation or reinterpretation of the tradition and sources in order to meet the challenges posed by modernity; that there is no conflict between reason and revelation; that Muslims should make all efforts to learn from the West, in particular scientific knowledge and technological know-how; an emphasis on catching up with the West; and reform of important institutions such as educational institutions and their curricula.

India: Sayyid Ahmad Khan[12]

Sayyid Ahmad Khan (d. 1315/1898) was born in India. He was influenced by his maternal grandfather, Khawajah Farid, who was the prime minister of Emperor Akbar Shah at a time when the Mughal Empire was in serious decline. Khawajah Farid, an important connection between the declining Mughal Empire and the British in India, was not only a senior figure in the administration of the Emperor but also served the British. He was sent to Iran as an attaché of the British embassy. His connection to the British through his grandfather was an important factor in Ahmad Khan's own relationship with the British.

Ahmad Khan was also influenced by his mother, who was well known for her piety and generosity. Like Shah Wali Allah before him, Ahmad Khan was very concerned about the situation of Muslims in the subcontinent. He saw Muslims as preoccupied with issues that put them at a disadvantage vis-à-vis others in the subcontinent, such as Hindus. Commenting on the aggressiveness with which the new forces took over in India and the predicament in which the Muslims found themselves as a consequence of their capitulation, Khan observed: 'The speed with which decline has set in is so rapid that it seems imminent that within a few years the Muslims will not be found anywhere except serving in stables and kitchens or mowing the grass'.[13]

He tried to put forward the view that Muslims were loyal citizens of the British Raj, especially after the mutiny of 1857. Following the mutiny, the British authorities viewed Muslims in India with deep suspicion. Ahmad Khan argued that, because of the similarities between the religions of Muslims and British (Christians), Muslims were more inclined to be loyal citizens of the British Raj than were others in India. He even wrote a commentary of the Bible and sought to counter the number of fatwas of his time, in many of which the ulama stated that India had become an 'abode of war' (dar al-harb). Khan presented the view that, as long as the basics of Islam could be practised, India should be considered not 'abode of war' but 'abode of Islam'. He strove to show that Muslims in India were faithful to the British. In this context, he even argued that Indian Muslims had no loyalty to the Ottoman sultan and that the authority of the sultan was confined to the lands under his control, not India. He questioned the legitimacy of the claim of the title of 'caliph' by the Ottoman sultan, as historically Sunni Muslims believed that the legitimate caliph should be from the tribe of the Prophet, Quraysh. Ottomans who did not descend from Quraysh therefore were not really in line with the Sunni requirements for a legitimate caliph.

Ahmad Khan interacted with the British in a range of ways. He travelled to England in 1869 to experience British life and understand more about British thinking. He borrowed a substantial amount of money to pay for his trip and stayed for about one and a half years. During that time, he was well received by many senior figures and was made Companion of the Star of India by Queen Victoria. While in England, Ahmad Khan visited key figures of the British establishment as well as universities and important schools, learning from their experience in education. When he returned to India, one of his key projects was the establishment of an educational institution, named the Muhammadan Anglo-Oriental College, in Aligarh in 1877.

In order to modernize Islam, Khan wanted to go back to early Islamic traditions and disciplines and reinterpret key aspects of Islam. He wanted Indian Muslims to adopt modern ways of learning and knowledge and move away from the antiquated ways of teaching and learning of the madrasas. The education system of madrasas was, in his view, outmoded and in dire need of change. Modern science was crucial to his educational vision, and much of what he termed his 'new *kalam*' (new theology) sought to harmonize the tenets of contemporary natural sciences and philosophy with the doctrines of Islam. In addition to madrasa reform, he argued for the adoption of modern science and methods of research based on experience and observation, and a move from deductive to inductive methods.

Khan thought that the resistance of ulama to such ideas was counterproductive and not in the interest of the Muslim community. He saw no contradiction between modern science and the teachings of the Qur'an. For him, the Qur'an was the word of God and nature was the work of God: modern science was thus in harmony with Islam, the Qur'an and its teachings. Any attempt to discredit modern science by relying on the Qur'an only served to defeat the purpose of the Qur'an, which exhorts humans to reason about and meditate on the universe. In his attempt to modernize the religion, he relied heavily on the Qur'an itself and interpretation of the Qur'an by the Qur'an, dismissing a large number of hadith whose authenticity he generally doubted. He rejected the possibility of miracles as they were not compatible with the laws of nature, and in his view nothing in the Qur'an contradicted those laws.

In the social sphere, particularly law, Khan believed in ijtihad as a necessary instrument for realizing the real objectives of religion, infusing it with a dynamic spirit and making it responsive to new situations and requirements. In line with his motto of 'unmixed Islam', he thought that ijtihad might require the going beyond (or the critical reading of) the schools of thought that formed the established orthodoxy.

Khan thought that much of the confusion in Muslim religious thinking was because no direct recourse was made to the Qur'an. Instead, a superstructure of all sorts of commentaries – juristic, mystical, for example – had been allowed to grow up around the Qur'an, choking it. He even regarded hadith as part of that superstructure.

Khan was criticized by many ulama for embarking on reform without adequate knowledge of Islam's sources and for not being a qualified scholar of religion (*alim*). Nevertheless, he made his mark as an important modernist, and founded the Muhammadan Anglo-Oriental College, modelled on Oxford and Cambridge, which later became Aligarh Muslim University.[14] His name should be included among the great contributors to the modern renewal of Islamic thought today, particularly in the context of the Indian subcontinent, one of the key regions that contributed to the development of modern Islamic thought.

Egypt: Muhammad Abduh[15]

Egypt encountered Europe earlier than many other Muslim lands. The Napoleonic invasion of Egypt, though brief (1798–1801), provided an important impetus to engage with Europe intellectually and technologically. The modernization programme of Muhammad Ali of Egypt (ruled 1805–48) with its heavy focus on military and technological know-how led to the awareness in Egypt of major developments that were taking place in Europe and also the degree to which Muslims were behind.

Muhammad Ali wanted to modernize his armed forces, and for this he borrowed heavily from the West in the areas of education, technological expertise and military-related matters. He sent a large number of Egyptians to study in the West, supported the translation of a range of texts into Arabic, and continued with modernization. All of this gave Egyptians a glimpse of the differences between the Western world and the Muslim world and strengthened the position of those who were arguing for imitation of the West in the march towards development and catching up. At the same time, this pro-Western approach attracted significant criticism from the more traditionalist ulama of Egypt, who saw in this imitation a danger to the very identity of Muslims. In Egypt these trends developed gradually, competing with each other and creating a split within the society between those who were Westernized, particularly many young people who wanted rapid change, and others who were traditionalist and resistant to change.

Muhammad Abduh (d. 1905) is one of the most studied Muslim modernists. He began his career in Egypt, the most important intellectual hub for Muslims at the time. Abduh was heavily influenced by Jamal al-Din al-Afghani, the founder of the modern pan-Islamic movement which sought to unite the Muslim world under the banner of the faith. In 1289/1872, Abduh and Afghani met in the Azhar in Cairo and formed a relationship that continued for a considerable time, part of which was spent in Paris in exile. Later, Abduh moved away from Afghani's views, abandoning the radical views he held in the 1870s and 1880s, and began to propound a range of views that provided the basis for much of Muslim modernism in Egypt in the late nineteenth and early twentieth centuries. He was appointed the Mufti (the highest religious authority) of Egypt in 1899 and used his position to advocate reform of Islamic education as well as law. His views however were resisted by a large number of ulama in Egypt.

Muhammad Abduh emerged at a time when the two trends sparked by Muhammad Ali's policies in Egypt were seen as irreconcilable: one adopting modernization and Westernization and the other rejecting them. One of Abduh's tasks, he believed, was to bridge the gap between the two. Though he himself was a scholar of religion (*alim*) from the Azhar seminary, he argued for change, a return to the purity of early Islam, for adopting the sciences and learning from modern ideas and institutions without sacrificing one's religion. He stood for a middle way, by insisting on the need for change while arguing that the change should be guided by 'Islam'. Total Westernization at the expense of Islam was not an option.

In line with other modernist figures, Abduh argued for a return to the Islam of the earliest Muslims (salaf), the simple, uncomplicated and pure Islam of the Prophet and the Companions, and for exercising ijtihad to solve today's problems. He wanted to avoid blind imitation of the early scholars, to go back to the earliest sources of Islam, the Qur'an and Sunna, in order to understand what Islam really is and to minimize unnecessary restrictions imposed by opinions of the scholars of the premodern period. More importantly, given the relative simplicity of Islam in the earliest period, any move to return to the original sources would also reduce the sectarian differences that plagued Muslim communities in his time, not just in Egypt but also elsewhere. Such sectarian differences were in his view largely the result of blind imitation of one's own legal school. He also argued for minimizing the intolerance that existed among Muslims and for emphasizing the unity of Muslims.

On the question of good and evil, Abduh believed that reason could be relied upon to differentiate between the two, as the Mu'tazilis before him argued. For him, good is beautiful and evil is ugly; both can be discerned by reason. In this context, Abduh believed that actions are to be judged on the basis of their consequences. An action that leads to pain and suffering or harm is ugly, and one that leads to benefits and pleasure is beautiful. Here also, reason has the ability to discern what is ugly and what is beautiful. From Abduh's point of view, if the ulama had in the past given the weight to reason that it deserved in the law, the problems Muslims faced in the modern period with regard to premodern Islamic law could have been avoided.

Among the issues he emphasized was the idea that there was no conflict between reason and the revelation of Islam. He believed that scientific discoveries of today were in line with the Qur'an. Even the theory of evolution was not too far from the Qur'an's teaching. In line with this emphasis on reason, he even interpreted the 'miracles' of the Qur'an in ways that made them compatible with natural occurrences; his interpretation of *jinn* (sprites) as 'microbes' is an example of this thinking.

Abduh strongly advocated the teaching of modern sciences, arguing that early figures such as al-Ghazali also held that disciplines like logic and other useful areas of knowledge were important and should be studied. As early as the 1870s, Abduh suggested, without much success, that the teaching of sciences should be introduced into the Azhar seminary curriculum.

Through the simplification of Islam, Abduh hoped to reduce sectarian differences, particularly during the colonial period, to purify religion by removing what he deemed were the obstacles that marred the medieval history of Islam, and to allow a place for reason and modern knowledge alongside the early, authentic sources.

He also argued that Islam itself was the religion of nature (*fitra*), which meant that it could not and would not go against nature, natural laws and the sciences that were emerging based on the study of nature. If there was opposition, it was not because of Islam but because of erroneous inter-pretations of Islamic primary sources. Part of this acceptance of reason was the view that, as the Mu'tazilis had argued earlier, it is possible to arrive at what is morally acceptable or unacceptable using reason.

From modernism to neo-modernism: Fazlur Rahman

The modernist movement, championed by figures such as Sayyid Ahmad Khan and Muhammad Abduh, influenced greatly the development of Islamic thought in the twentieth century. While many might consider thinkers such as Fazlur Rahman[16] as 'modernists', it would be more appropriate to consider him as a 'neo-modernist'. Neo-modernists are more concerned with the essence than the form of Islamic teachings. For instance, they are more inter-ested in whether Muslim women lead ethical, productive lives than in whether or not they wear the headscarf (*hijab*). They also believe that social change currently taking place must be reflected in the interpretation of Islamic foundation texts. Furthermore, they subscribe to the need for fresh ijtihad with a new methodology to deal with contemporary problems. Neo-modernists believe that social and economic matters, rather than political power, should remain the priority for Muslims. They are less hostile to Western and other outside influences and more willing to acknowledge the legitimate interests of secular groups and co-operate with those groups on a sustained basis. Rahman's writings deal with all these areas, taking positions that would be unpalatable to modernists like Abduh and even Khan. Rahman's ideas were to play a significant role in the development of Islamic thought in the late twentieth century, largely as a result of his published works and the students who studied with him at Chicago. He was one of the most daring and original contributors to the discussion on the reform of Islamic thought in the twentieth century.

Fazlur Rahman was born in 1919 in the Hazara district, in what is now Pakistan,[17] in an area with strong connections to Islamic religious education. His father, Mawlana Shihab al-Din, was a scholar of religion, a graduate of Deoband seminary in India. Under his tutorship, rather than in a seminary, Rahman received his religious education in Qur'anic exegesis, hadith and law, theology and philosophy. He attended Punjab University in Pakistan, and obtained Bachelor's and Master's degrees in Arabic. He then went to Oxford, where he wrote his dissertation on Ibn Sina's philosophy.[18] Though his primary interest early in his academic career was Islamic philosophy, he was widely read in Islamic law and history, ethics, Qur'anic exegesis and hadith. Having completed his studies at Oxford, Rahman moved to Durham University in northern England, where he taught Islamic philosophy from 1950 to 1958. He then left to take up the position of associate professor at the Institute of Islamic Studies at McGill University in Canada, where he remained for three years. He was invited to Pakistan by General Ayyub Khan, then President of Pakistan, who was searching for a liberal reform-minded Muslim intellectual to head the Islamic Research Institute in order to advise the government on religious matters and policies. Rahman's stay in Pakistan was short-lived (1961–8). He had to leave Pakistan for the United States as a result of opposition to his views, which were not palatable to the conservative religious establishments in Pakistan. He was appointed Professor of Islamic Thought at the University of Chicago in 1968, and he remained there until his death in 1988.[19]

At Chicago he played a significant role in training a number of post-graduate students from countries such as Indonesia and Turkey. While Rahman's thought is not generally known in the Arab world or in traditionalist religious circles elsewhere, it is in Turkey and Indonesia that Rahman has been most influential. Many of his students occupy senior academic positions in Islamic studies in those countries. In the United States, where he spent the last twenty years of his life, several students of Islam took up his ideas and attempted to reinterpret specific parts of the ethico-legal content of the Qur'an. A good example is Amina Wadud, whose work *Qur'an and Woman* is an example of the application of Rahman's ideas to the interpretation of the Qur'an.

His writings are extensive and much broader than his primary field of Islamic philosophy. They include reform of Islamic education, Qur'anic hermeneutics, hadith criticism, early development of Islamic intellectual traditions, reform of Islamic law and Islamic ethics. An extensive array of books and articles attest to the depth and breadth of his scholarship.[20] A prominent theme in all of his work is reform and renewal, and the importance of method in this reform. Among the most important projects for him was the reform of Islamic education. Unlike many reformers of the modern period, Rahman was not involved in a mass movement, and did not seek out political conflict. He eschewed a propagandist approach, avoided activism and was more comfortable in confining himself to the teaching and research environment of a university.[21]

Trends in Islamic thought today

The modern period has witnessed the emergence of several trends in Islamic thought. Given the diversity of Islamic thought today, it is difficult to adopt a typology that would cover such a wide range of trends and thinkers. However, I have tried to encapsulate, at least at a fairly broad level, the key trends that exist today. In previous chapters, specific aspects of Islamic thought in the modern period, from theology, philosophy, to politics, to Qur'an have been covered and therefore, in this chapter, I will not address those issues in detail. Instead, I will simply outline broad trends of Islamic thought today.

Legalist traditionalists

Legalist traditionalists follow strictly the premodern schools of Islamic law and associated theological teachings. They uphold solutions arrived at by premodern jurists and theologians of the relevant school, and view calls for reform of Islamic law and criticism of traditionalism with a degree of horror. This trend is dominant in the traditionalist seminary (madrasa) system across the Islamic world, for instance in the Middle East, Africa, the Indian subcontinent and the Malay world.

Blind following of one's school (theological or legal) remained a prominent feature of Islam from the fifth/eleventh century right up to the modern period. Historically each locality decided which school of law it would adopt. Thus, for instance, the Ottoman Empire adopted the Hanafi school of law. In the twentieth century, Saudi Arabia adopted the Hanbali school, while Malaysia adopted the Shafi'i school. Until recently, a Muslim was expected to follow his or her school of law in matters related to rituals and other areas of Islamic law such as family law. In some communities, even mosques were at times classified as Hanafi, Maliki, Shafi'i, Hanbali or Shi'i (Ja'fari). Efforts were made during the twentieth century to bring these schools of law together. Concerned scholars therefore sought to emphasize the commonalities and similarities among them and that they all represented 'orthodox' Islam. Despite this, past interpretations of law are still dominant among certain sectors of Muslims today.

Yusuf al-Qaradawi as a legalist traditionalist thinker[1]

Yusuf al-Qaradawi was born in Egypt in 1926. By the age of ten he had memorized the Qur'an. His education was at Azhar seminary from the elementary to the university level, and he obtained his Ph.D. there in 1973. At the time of writing, he was serving as the Dean of the College of Shari'a and Islamic Studies at the University of Qatar.

He has published over forty books dealing with various aspects of Islamic life, literature and poetry. Al-Qaradawi is considered as one of the most temperate Islamic thinkers, and as one of those who combine traditional knowledge of the shari'a with an understanding of contemporary problems. His writings have found general acceptance among all sectors of the Muslim world, and many of his works have been translated into several languages.

The following example (a fatwa) shows al-Qaradawi's thinking on a controversial issue, the leadership of women in prayer. He follows a legalist traditionalist line. In his response to a question relating to whether it is permissible for a woman to lead the prayer (*salat*), al-Qaradawi states:

> Throughout Muslim history it has never been heard for a woman to lead the Friday Prayer or deliver the Friday sermon, even during the era when a woman, Shajarat al-Durr (d. 659/1259), ruled the Muslims in Egypt during the Mamluk period.
>
> It is established that leadership in prayer in Islam is to be for men. People praying behind an imam are to follow him in the movements of prayer – bowing, prostrating, etc. – and listen attentively to him reciting the Qur'an in prayer.
>
> Prayer in Islam is an act that involves different movements of the body; it does not consist merely of saying supplications as is the case with prayer in Christianity. Moreover, it requires concentration of the mind, humility, and complete submission of the heart to Almighty Allah. Hence, it does not befit a woman, whose structure of physique naturally arouses instincts in men, to lead men in prayer and stand in front of them, for this may divert the men's attention from concentrating in the prayer and the spiritual atmosphere required.
>
> Islam is a religion that takes into account the different aspects, material or spiritual, of man's character. It does not treat people as super angels; it admits that they are humans with instincts and desires. So it is wise of Islam to lay down for them the rulings that avert them from succumbing to their desires, especially during acts of worship where spiritual uplifting is required.
>
> Hence, it is to avoid stirring the instincts of men that the shari'a dictates that only men can call for prayer and lead people in prayer, and that women's rows in prayer be behind the men.[2]

Political Islamists

Political Islamists are concerned with developing an Islamic socio-political order in the Muslim communities. They reject, at least in theory, the modern ideologies of nationalism, secularism and communism. They also reject 'Westernization'. Islamists argue for reform and change in Muslim communities, emphasizing 'Islamic' values and institutions over what they see as Western values and norms. They are interested in establishing an Islamic state. A few argue for a revolutionary approach to what they consider to be 'non-Islamic' governance of Muslim states even if this means using violence. Others argue for a gradual approach through education, beginning at the grassroots level.

Political Islamists are particularly keen to project an alternative programme to expand the scope of what Islam means and its role in society. Those who belong to this category of Muslims are reacting to a situation in which the role of Islam in society as they see it is constantly being eroded. In their view, the causes of this erosion lie largely in the colonial period. In the post-independence period, the modern state gave way to areas such as marginalization of Islamic law, and the dominance of non-Islamic priorities.

Notable movements associated with political Islam include the Muslim Brotherhood of Egypt and the Jamaat-i-Islami of Pakistan. They have similar approaches to social change and adopt an ideology that emphasizes a more activist Islam that challenges the existing authorities, whether state or religious. They are determined to change Muslim societies from within. Any obstacle to the change they argue for may become a target of their challenge.

Most significantly, several militant groups of activists have emerged from these movements although the movements themselves are considered 'mainstream'. The militant activists declare that the nation-state as it exists in the Muslim world is illegitimate. Their argument is that, for a state to be legitimate, it has to derive its authority or legitimacy from God, that is, from revealed religion, rather than from the people. God's sovereignty should be supreme in the state, in which case the state should enforce and implement Islamic law, not, as they say, 'man-made law'. Since most Muslim states do not implement 'Islamic law' these states are not seen as legitimate and are under challenge by the militant activists.

A mainstream political Islamist: Sayyid Abul A'la Mawdudi[3]

Mawdudi (d. 1979) was born in Hyderabad in India. He received his early education at home and then studied at a high school that attempted to combine a modern Western education with a traditional Islamic education. Although his higher education was interrupted, by the early 1920s he knew enough Arabic, Persian and English, besides his mother tongue Urdu, to study subjects of interest independently. Thus, most of what he learned was self-acquired and his intellectual growth was largely a result of his own efforts.

He proved to be a highly prolific writer. Initially, he concentrated on the exposition of ideas, values and basic principles of Islam. He paid special attention to the questions arising out of the conflict between the Islamic and the contemporary Western worlds. He also attempted to discuss some of the major problems of the modern age and sought to present 'Islamic' solutions to those problems. All this brought a freshness to the Muslim approach to these problems and lent a wider appeal to his message. He relentlessly criticized modern ideologies that he believed had begun to cast a spell over the minds and hearts of Muslims.

Around the year 1941, Mawdudi developed ideas regarding the founding of a more comprehensive and ambitious movement; this led him to launch a new organization under the name of Jamaat-i-Islami (Islamic Society). After emigrating to Pakistan in August 1947, Mawdudi concentrated his efforts on establishing a truly Islamic state and society in the country. Consistent with this objective, he wrote profusely to explain the different aspects of the Islamic way of life, especially its socio-political aspects. Mawdudi was often arrested and had to face long spells in prison. In 1953, he was sentenced to death by the martial law authorities in Pakistan on the charge of writing a seditious pamphlet against the Qadiyani (Ahmadi) community in Pakistan.

Mawdudi covered a range of disciplines such as Qur'anic exegesis, hadith, law, philosophy and history. He discussed a wide variety of problems – political, economic, cultural, social and theological – and attempted to state how the teachings of Islam were related to those problems. His main contribution, however, was in the fields of Qur'anic exegesis (*tafsir*), ethics, social studies and the problems facing the movement of Islamic revival. His greatest work is his monumental tafsir in Urdu of the Qur'an, *Tafhim al-Qur'an*, a work he took thirty years to complete. Its chief characteristic lies in presenting the meaning and message of the Qur'an in a language and style that appeals to people of today and shows the relevance of the Qur'an to their everyday problems, on both the individual and the societal planes.

Here is Mawdudi on the nature of 'Islamic state':

> Another distinguishing feature of the Islamic state is that the basic conception underlying all its outward manifestations is the idea of Divine sovereignty. Its fundamental theory is that the earth and all that it contains belongs to God Who alone is its Sovereign. No individual, family, class or nation, not even the whole of humanity can lay claim to sovereignty, either partially or wholly. God alone has the right to legislate and give commands. The state, according to Islam, is nothing more than a combination of men working together as servants of God to carry

out His Will and purposes. This can happen in two ways: either some person should receive the law of the state and its basic constitution directly from God or he should follow the lead of another person who is the recipient of such law and constitution. In the working of the state all those will participate who believe in this law and are prepared to follow it. They will all work with a sense of individual and collective responsibility to God, not to the electorate, neither to the king nor the dictator. They will proceed on the belief that God knows everything overt and covert; from His knowledge nothing is hidden; and from His grip man can never hope to escape, not even after death. The responsibility for running the state has been vested in men not for the purpose of enforcing their own orders or imposing their own will on others, enslaving people of other nationalities, calling upon them to bow down their heads in submission, enabling them to construct spacious palaces by fleecing the weak and downtrodden; in short, for the pursuit of their pleasure and self-glorification. On the other hand, men who are at the helm of the state should have a feeling that this is a burden laid on them that they may enforce the Divine law and administer social justice to the creatures of God. They should feel that if they make even a small mistake in following and enforcing the law or become guilty of even a grain of selfishness, prejudice, partiality and dishonesty, they shall be hauled up before the throne of God on the Day of Judgment, even if they escape punishment in this world.[4]

Secular Muslims

Secular Muslims see Islam as largely confined to the domain of personal belief and a relationship between God and the individual. Many value personal piety. They see no need for an Islamic state or for the implementation of what is referred to as Islamic law. Their typical opponents include anyone calling for establishing an Islamic state or an Islamic socio-political order, or those seeking the implementation of premodern Islamic law in society. The following is from a document called 'A Secular Muslim Manifesto' by a French Muslim, which shows the kinds of issues many secular Muslims are interested in:

• We are women and men of Muslim culture. Some of us are believers, others are agnostics or atheists. We all condemn firmly the declarations and acts of misogyny, homophobia, and anti-Semitism that we have heard and witnessed for a while now here in France, and that are carried out in the name of Islam. These three characteristics typify the political Islamism that has been forceful for so long in several of our countries of origin. We fought against them there, and we are committed to fighting against them again – here.

- We are firmly committed to equal rights for both sexes. We fight the oppression of women who are subjected to Personal Status Laws, like those in Algeria (recent progress in Morocco highlights how far Algeria lags behind), and sometimes even in France via bilateral agreements. We believe that democracy cannot exist without these equal rights. . . . It is also for this reason that we oppose wearing the Islamic headscarf, even if among us there are differing opinions about the law banning it from schools in France.
- We believe that recognition of the existence of homosexuality and the freedom for homosexuals to live their own lives as they wish represents undeniable progress. As long as an individual – heterosexual or homosexual – does not break the laws protecting minors, each person's sexual choices are his or her own business, and do not concern the state in any way.
- Finally, we condemn firmly the anti-Semitic statements made recently in speeches in the name of Islam. . . . We see the use of the Israel–Palestine conflict by fundamentalist movements as a means of promoting the most disturbing forms of anti-Semitism.
- Despite our opposition to the current policies of the Israeli government, we refuse to feed primitive images of the 'Jew'. A real, historical conflict between two peoples should not be exploited. We recognize Israel's right to exist, a right recognized by the PLO congress in Algiers in 1988 and the Arab League summit meeting in Beirut in 2002. At the same time we are committed to the Palestinian people and support of their right to found a state and to be liberated from occupation.[5]

Theological puritans

Theological puritans are concerned primarily with theological matters such as 'correct belief'. They seek to purify society of what they consider practices antithetical to Islam, such as reverence for saints and saint-worship, magic, certain Sufi practices and what they call innovation in religious matters (bid'a). They are also concerned with the literal affirmation of God's attributes without any interpretation. They rely heavily on the teachings of figures such as Ibn Taymiyya (d. 728/1328) and Muhammad b. Abd al-Wahhab (d. 1207/1792) and the modern proponents of their teachings. Their hallmark is a degree of puritanism and literalism, coupled with accusations against other Muslims for being engaged in 'innovation in religious matters' (bid'a).

Muhammad b. Salih al-Uthaymin[6] is a scholar from Saudi Arabia and is considered one of the leading figures associated with this trend of Islam today. One of the areas in which a literal reading to the texts of the Qur'an and hadith is applied is in the area of the relationship between Muslims and non-Muslims. Here al-Uthaymin issues a fatwa on the residence of a Muslim in a non-Muslim country:

Question: What is the ruling about residence (*iqama*) in the land of the unbelievers [non-Muslim country]?

Answer: Residence in the land of the unbelievers (*dar al-kufr*) is a dangerous matter for the religion (*din*) of a Muslim as well as his manners and morals. We as well as others have witnessed a lot of deviation in those who lived there and came back. They have returned back sinners and some have even apostatized . . .

Residence in the land of the unbelievers has two necessary conditions to it: (a) the resident is secure about his religion (*din*) in the sense that he has knowledge [of the requirements of the religion] . . . (b) that he is able to express his religion in the sense that he is able to establish the outward manifest symbols (*sha'a'ir*) of Islam without any hindrance so there is no obstacle in establishing the prayer, including the Friday prayer and the prayer in congregation; there is no obstacle in administering *zakat*, fasting, pilgrimage and other symbols of Islam. If he is unable to do so, he is not allowed to reside and must migrate.

After fulfilling these basic conditions, residence in the land of unbelievers can be divided into the following types: (a) that he resides [to preach Islam]; (b) that he resides to study the state of the unbelievers and to know what they are about in corruption of creed (*aqida*), false worship, immorality, and confused behavior so he may warn people [Muslims] of the reality of their affairs . . . (c) that he resides for some need of a Muslim country [such as] establishing (diplomatic) ties e.g. embassy staff . . . (d) that he resides for a specific permissible need, for instance trade or medical treatment . . . (e) that he resides for education . . . [In this case there are certain conditions]: the student must have knowledge of the shari'a that would enable him to distinguish between truth and falsehood and fight falsehood with truth; . . . [and] there is some need of the knowledge for which he is residing over there, for instance, there is some benefit for the Muslims in his acquiring of it . . . (f) that he resides to live and settle. This [last] case presents more dangers than the ones before and leads to greater harm because it involves complete mixing with the unbelievers who demand nationalistic allegiance, which increases the numbers of the unbelievers. Raising his family with people of disbelief leads to adopting their morals and habits, and maybe even blind imitation in [matters of] belief and worship. This is why a hadith mentions that the Prophet said, 'Whoever joins a polytheist (*mushrik*) and lives with him is like him'. Even though [the hadith] has a weak chain of transmission (*isnad*) it sets a perspective since settlement leads to resemblance.[7]

Militant extremists

The late twentieth and early twenty-first century militancy among Muslims is associated with a range of activities including localized national liberation struggles, international struggles such as the First Afghan War (as a result of the Soviet occupation of Afghanistan), and anti-Western activities by extremist militants such as Usama bin Laden. In the early twenty-first century, it is anti-Western activities that dominate much of the debate on militancy and extremism among Muslims, particularly as a result of the events of September 11 and the bombings in both Muslim and Western countries by a global network of militant extremists. These are driven by a view of the world that is characterized by a deep sense of injustice against Muslims. This is supported by a narrative that reinforces this sense of injustice beginning with the Crusades and moving on to colonialism and post-colonial domination of Muslims by the West. The grievances also include 'stealing' of Muslims' resources, controlling and keeping Muslims weak, preventing them from acquiring any means to challenge this domination (economic, military, political) and occupying Muslim lands to achieve these objectives. Other grievances are what they consider to be double standards in dealing with Muslims, preventing the spread or growth of Islam through supporting anti-Muslim missionary activities, betrayal by fellow Muslims who 'collaborate' with the West, and a deep sense of powerlessness in a world that they believe is aimed at 'obliterating' Islam and Muslims. The militant extremists also emphasize the universal brotherhood of all Muslims; they do not seem to support the concept of the nation state and are motivated by a particular understanding of jihad whose theatre is global. They believe that less resourceful people can defeat a powerful enemy, as was the case in the First Afghan War in which the Soviet Empire was defeated. Finally, they believe in using terror to achieve their objectives. The following is from a fatwa issued by Bin Laden and several supporters of him urging Muslims to kill Americans and their allies:

> In compliance with God's order, we issue the following fatwa to all Muslims:
> The ruling to kill the Americans and their allies – civilians and military – is an individual duty for every Muslim who can do it in any country in which it is possible to do it, in order to liberate the al-Aqsa mosque [one of Islam's holiest places, in Jerusalem] and the holy mosque [in Mecca] from their grip, and in order for their armies to move out of all the lands of Islam, defeated and unable to threaten any Muslim. This is in accordance with the words of Almighty God: '[A]nd fight the pagans all together as they fight you all together,' and 'fight them until there is no more tumult or oppression, and there prevail justice and faith in God.'

This is in addition to the words of Almighty God: 'And why should you not fight in the cause of God and of those who, being weak, are ill-treated and oppressed – women and children, whose cry is "Our Lord, rescue us from this town, whose people are oppressors; and raise for us from thee one who will help!"'

We – with God's help – call on every Muslim who believes in God and wishes to be rewarded to comply with God's order to kill the Americans and plunder their money wherever and whenever they find it. We also call on Muslim ulama, leaders, youth, and soldiers to launch the raids on Satan's US troops and the devil's supporters allying with them, and to displace those who are behind them so that they may learn a lesson.[8]

This fatwa has been criticized by a large number of Muslims from around the world and many counter fatwas have been issued.

Progressive ijtihadis

Progressive ijtihadis come from a range of backgrounds and intellectual orientations. They can be considered intellectual descendents of modernists along the following lines: modernists → neo-modernists → progressives. A range of names is used today for progressives, which may include 'liberal' Muslims, 'progressive' Muslims, 'ijtihadis', 'transformationists' or even 'neo-modernists'. It is not a movement but a broad trend with a variety of voices in it. It includes Muslim modernists, liberals, feminists, and even reform-minded traditionalists. Many leading figures of progressive ijtihadis are based in the West and in Muslim countries where there is a reasonable degree of intellectual freedom. The most important characteristics of those associated with this trend are as follows:

- They adopt the view that many areas of traditional Islamic law require substantial change and reform in order to meet the needs of Muslims today. For them, some areas of traditional Islamic law are not even relevant today, or are in need of replacement by legislation more in keeping with the concerns of contemporary Muslims.
- They seem to subscribe to the need for fresh ijtihad and a new methodology of ijtihad to deal with modern problems.
- Many combine traditional Islamic scholarship with modern Western thought and education.
- They hold firmly to the view that social change, whether at the intellectual, moral, legal, economic or technological level, must be reflected in Islamic law.
- They display neither dogmatism nor a strict attachment to a particular school of law or theology in their approach.

- They place a great emphasis on social justice, gender justice, human rights and harmonious relations between Muslims and non-Muslims.

Progressive ijtihadis want to bring change in their communities and beyond through reinterpretation of the Islamic texts and tradition. They have moved well beyond the Muslim modernist apologetics and even some of the neo-modernist limitations of how Muslims should engage with the modern world. Some progressive ijtihadis argue their aim is to enact or perhaps re-enact the values of justice (*adl*), goodness and beauty (*ihsan*) in their societies and the world at large. This overarching vision, which they perceive to be at the heart of the Qur'anic ethos, requires an engagement with both the Islamic tradition and modernity on the issue of human rights, particularly around the theme of social justice, gender justice and pluralism. Towards the aims of pluralism and living in peace in a pluralist world, the progressive ijtihadis believe that Muslims deserve an interpretation of Islam that enables them to restore and in some areas maintain their compassionate, humane, selfless and generous selves in interpersonal relations and exchanges with others.

Progressive ijtihadis are both thinkers and activists. The progressive stance implies a striving towards a universal notion of justice in which no single community's prosperity, righteousness and dignity should come at the expense of another.[9] As activists for change, they see themselves neither as ideologues nor as revolutionaries but as social critics. Concerned about the rise of exclusivism and the violent actions done in the name of Islam, they aim to retrieve the Islamic discourse from what they consider to be 'fanatics', and hope to engender a reinterpretation of Islam that will steer Muslims away from such a mindset. They like to see an open and safe space to undertake a rigorous, honest and potentially difficult engagement with tradition, and yet remain hopeful that conversation will lead to further action.[10]

Examples of progressive ijtihadi writings

On the fallibility of Islamic jurisprudence

In the following, a progressive Muslim points out the fallibility of Islamic jurisprudence:

> Acknowledging the deeply patriarchal and discriminatory elements in Islamic jurisprudence is not cause for despair. It does not mean accepting that God intends Muslim women and men to live in hierarchical, authoritarian marital relationships. On the contrary . . . a thorough exploration and analysis of traditional jurisprudence will reveal the extent to which its rules are seriously flawed; they cannot be divine. The role of human agency in the creation of these laws is evidenced by the diversity of legal views as well as the creation of a system of male marital privilege and

sharply differentiated spousal rights that does not simply emerge wholly formed from the Qur'an. This system is the result of an interpretation, indeed of numerous acts of interpretation, by particular men living and thinking at a specific time. Their jurisprudence is shaped not by any malicious misogyny, or so I choose to believe, but rather by assumptions and constraints of the time in which it was formulated.[11]

On the need for a fresh interpretation of the Qur'an

Amina Wadud, from the United States, is a professor of Islamic Studies and specializes in gender and Qur'anic studies. She argues for an interpretation of the Qur'an that is appropriate to contemporary realities, a concern of many Muslim women who feel that Qur'anic exegesis in the past did not sufficiently take into account the concerns and needs of women. In her *Qur'an and Woman*, she argues:

No interpretation is definitive. I have attempted here to render a reasonably plausible interpretation to some difficult matters. The basis for this plausibility is the significance I draw from the text with regard to the modern woman: the significance of her life-style to her concerns and interactions in her context. I am also influenced by prior text. I have demonstrated the relevance of the Qur'an to the concerns of the modern woman. In doing so, I provide a reading that transcends some of the limitations in previous interpretations. On one hand, some limitations exist in the text – such as when it specifically addresses the social situation in Arabia at the time of revelation – on the other hand, most limitations are reflections of the interpreters who restrict the universality of the divine message to their individual perceptions. It is failure to understand this disparity between particular usages in the Qur'an and its general usages that have led to some of the variations in opinions concerning the overall Qur'anic world-view. I believe the Qur'an adapts to the context of the modern woman as smoothly as it adapted to the original Muslim community fourteen centuries ago. This adaptation can be demonstrated if the text is interpreted with her in mind, thus indicating the universality of the text. Any interpretations which narrowly apply the Qur'anic guidelines only to literal mimics of the original community do an injustice to the text. No community will ever be exactly like another. Therefore, no community can be a duplicate of that original community. The Qur'an never states this as the goal. Rather, the goal has been to emulate certain key principles of human development: justice, equity, harmony, moral responsibility, spiritual awareness, and development. Where these general characteristics exist, whether in the first Muslim community or in present and future communities, the goal of the Qur'an for society has been reached.[12]

Participant Muslims arguing for rethinking of citizenship

Among the multitude of trends within the broad category of 'progressive ijtihadis' there are those we may call 'participant Muslims' in the West who are at the forefront of the emerging Western tradition of Islam. This tradition should be seen as potentially one of the most important developments in modern Islamic thought. Much intellectual and creative energy is needed to construct a vision of Islam that is comfortable with the changes that are taking place in all areas of life today in the West: political, social, economic, technological and philosophical. This strand of Islam is coming to terms with a range of new issues, from democracy, human rights, gender equality, secular law, freedom of expression and religion, and equality before law for all. It has no historical precedent or clear-cut methodology as yet. It exists in practice but it is only recently that Muslims in the West have started to develop methodological tools and principles to provide an intellectual foundation for the strand. It is a product of a fusion of Islam with the Western environment, and Western secular liberal democratic values. It has been most visible since the 1990s through the writings of a number of Muslim scholars based in the West such as Tariq Ramadan of Switzerland, Bassam Tibi of Germany and Muqtader Khan of the United States.

This Western tradition of Islam has the potential to dominate the Muslim religious scene in the West and is driven mostly by the indigenization of Islam in the West. It is espoused largely by second- or third-generation Muslims and converts to Islam. Many professional and middle-class Muslims belong to this strand. It relies on the vernacular such as English, French, German or Dutch rather than on Arabic. Its frame of reference is the local environment of the West and its inspiration comes from that context. For these Muslims in the West, France (for example) is not a foreign country. It is their home, psychologically and physically.

This Western tradition of Islam is challenging traditional understandings of a range of important issues in order to suit the social, cultural, political and intellectual context of Muslims in the West. These Muslims are using ijtihad to put forward bold solutions to contemporary concerns, while not turning their backs on their traditions. As yet restricted to the West, but little known to Westerners in general, this type of thinking is likely to have a significant impact on the wider Muslim world in time.

Tariq Ramadan argues that this strand of Islam is an affirmation of the self-confidence of young Muslims[13] and of their Islamic identity in the West. It is a profound revival of Islamic spirituality and practice.[14] For participant Muslims, Islam is a dynamic, changing way of life capable of adapting to a vast array of socio-historical and political settings. Emphasizing this, the American scholar Muqtader Khan says of American Muslims:

> These young people are not Americans who are Muslims or Muslims who are born in America. They are American Muslims. They believe in

Islam, they are democratic, they respect human rights and animal rights, and they share a concern for environment. They are economic and political liberals and social conservatives. They believe in the freedom of religion and the right of all peoples, ethnic as well as religious, to be treated equally.[15]

Tariq Ramadan speaks about the need for Muslims to adapt to their Western socio-cultural environment (which requires engaging in ijtihad):

> This also means developing a new and confident attitude based on a plain awareness of the essential dimensions of the Islamic identity. This feeling should lead Muslims to objectively and equitably assess their environment. Mindful of the prescriptions of their religion, they should not neglect the important scale of adaptation which is the distinctive feature of Islam. It is this that has permitted Muslims to settle in the Middle East, in Africa as well as in Asia and in the name of the same and unique Islam, to give to its implementation a specific shape and dimension. Once again, as for the form of its implementation, it should be a European-Islam just as there is an African-Islam or an Asian-Islam.[16]

Concluding remarks

The above discussion does not provide a comprehensive list of trends of Islamic thought as it is almost impossible to do so in a short introductory text like this. It shows, however, the range of trends and issues that today's Muslims are trying to come to terms with. Challenges that might not have existed in the past have emerged over the course of the late twentieth and early twenty-first centuries, and Muslims, whether in Muslim majority or minority contexts, are attempting to meet such challenges. Examples include reform of Islamic law to gender rights, human rights, globalization, being Muslim in Western societies and inter-faith issues. The discourses are also global. Scholars and thinkers are geographically spread from West Africa to Southeast Asia and to Muslim communities in the West. In this, Muslim thinkers in the West are essential contributors. Given the high degree of intellectual freedom that exists in Western societies, many such scholars have no difficulty in publishing and debating their ideas away from many Muslim majority contexts where intellectual freedom is still a significant problem. Perhaps for this reason, Muslims in the West and those in other intellectually free societies will be in a position to contribute to Islamic thought more so than those who are based in repressive environments where censorship and restriction on freedom still dominate thinking. The future development of Islamic thought may depend to a certain extent on the degree of intellectual freedom in Muslim societies.

Glossary

Abbasid caliphate   second major dynastic caliphate, which began in 132/750.

abrogation   the theory that some earlier verses of the Qur'an and practices of the Prophet were superseded by later verses and practices.

adhan   the call to prayer, performed five times a day.

ahkam   see *hukm*.

ahl al-kitab   'people of the Book'. Usually referring to Jews and Christians.

ahl al-sunna   'people of the Sunna'. The largest group of Muslims, who among other things acknowledge the 'rightly guided' caliphs as legitimate political successors to the Prophet.

akhbar   traditions of the Prophet as narrated through Shi'i authorities.

alim   (pl. *ulama*) a Muslim learned in religious knowledge.

Allah   God.

Almohad dynasty   see Muwahhid dynasty.

Ansar   converts to Islam from Medina, whose early members helped settle the Prophet and the Meccan Muslims after their migration to Medina.

aqida   (pl. *aqa'id*) a theological creed or set of beliefs.

aql   human intellect, intelligence, rationality.

arabesque   a geometrical pattern used in Islamic art.

Ash'ari school   one of the main schools of Sunni theology.

athar   traditions concerning the Companions.

aya   a sign from God, also used to denote a unit of division of the Qur'anic text equivalent to a verse.

Babism   a nineteenth-century religious movement based on the self-declaration of Iranian merchant Sayyid Ali Muhammad (the Bab) to be the Mahdi.

Baha'ism   a religion that evolved out of Babism, via the teachings of Baha' Allah, who claimed to be the Bab's successor.

bay'a   a pledge of allegiance.

Bayt al-Hikma   the 'House of Wisdom'. A third/ninth century scholarly institution established during the Abbasid period.

bid'a   an unwarranted innovation in religious practice.

Byzantine empire   Greek-speaking Eastern Roman empire.

caliph   a political successor to the Prophet Muhammad, leader of the Muslim community.

caliphate   the office or jurisdiction of the caliph, which after the Rashidun caliphs became hereditary and often much-disputed.

Companion   a Muslim believed to have met, heard or lived with the Prophet.

dar al-harb   'abode of war'; enemy territory; a nation with whom the Muslim state does not have a treaty of peace or non-aggression.

dar al-islam   'abode of Islam'; a nation ruled by Islamic law.

dhikr   devotional prayer for the remembrance of God.

dhimmi   a member of one of the protected religious minorities in a Muslim land.

din   religion; way of life; religious obligations that humans owe to God and for which they will be judged.

diwan   in its artistic sense, a cursive form of calligraphy.

Druze   a sect that emerged from an Ismaili background in the fifth/tenth century, recognizing the imamate of the Fatimid caliph al-Hakim bi Amr Allah, but which developed a number of distinctive doctrines including belief in reincarnation.

Eid   a festival, feast day. The two main Islamic celebrations are the Eid that comes immediately after the month of Ramadan (first day of the tenth month of the Islamic calendar) and the Eid that comes during the time of pilgrimage to Mecca (tenth day of the twelfth month of the Islamic calendar).

falsafa   philosophy.

faqih   (pl. *fuqaha'*) a Muslim trained in jurisprudence.

fasiq   a grave sinner.

fatawa   see fatwa.

Fatimid dynasty   Ismaili dynasty that ruled parts of North Africa and parts of Egypt from 297/909 until 567/1171.

fatwa   (pl. *fatawa*) an opinion on a point of religious law given by a mufti in response to a question by a petitioner.

fiqh   Islamic jurisprudence, human interpretation of religious law.

fuqaha'   see *faqih*.

hadd   (pl. *hudud*) the maximum punishment as defined in the Qur'an or Sunna for certain grave crimes.

hadith   a report containing information about the sayings, practices and descriptions of the Prophet Muhammad. A hadith *qudsi* is a tradition containing revelation from God phrased in the Prophet's own words.

hajj   the pilgrimage to Mecca, one of five essential practices, which all physically and financially able Muslims must undertake at least once.

Hanafi school   a major Sunni school of religious law developed from the teachings of Abu Hanifa and his followers.

Hanbali school   a school promoting the law and theology of Ahmad ibn Hanbal and his followers.

hasan   a grading category of hadith in which a tradition is considered good, but not perfect.

hijab   a curtain, veil; used to refer to modest dressing and behaviour, and in particular a Muslim woman's headscarf.

Hijaz   geographical area along the northwestern coast of the Arabian peninsula, containing the holy cities of Mecca and Medina.

hijra   the emigration of the Prophet and his followers from Mecca to Medina in 622 CE, marking the beginning of the Islamic *hijri* calendar.

hudud   see *hadd*.

hukm   (pl. *ahkam*) a ruling or judgement, a command of God.

hululiyya   a derogatory term used for those accused of believing God to be incarnated or infused in creation, a doctrine known as *hulul*.

ibadat   rituals to do with the worship of God.

Ibadi   belonging to a Muslim group descended from the Kharijis, found mostly in North Africa, Oman and East Africa.

Iblis   the Devil, Satan.

ihsan   beauty, goodness. Used by Sufis to refer to an ideal state of worshipping God.

ijaza   a licence from a scholar giving permission to pass on a particular text or body of knowledge learned by his or her student.

ijma'   the consensus on a point of belief or law by the Companions, religious scholars or the whole community.

ijtihad   exercise of independent reasoning by a jurist to arrive at a solution to a legal problem; effort made by a scholar to derive a ruling on a question of law.

ilm   knowledge, in particular religious knowledge such as *ilm al-kalam*, which is theology.

imam   a leader or model, such as a leader of prayer; an important scholar; caliph; and, in Shi'i belief, one of a number of descendants of the Prophet believed to be his legitimate successors.

imamate   the theory of leadership.

iman   faith; in particular, belief in God, angels, books of revelation, prophets, the judgement of deeds and the all-encompassing knowledge of God.

al-insan al-kamil   'the perfect man'; Sufi theory that certain human beings, such as the prophets, are the locus for the manifestation of divine attributes.

ishraq   the illuminationist school of theosophy founded by Suhrawardi.

islah   reform, the idea of returning to Islam's original message that has been obscured owing to misinterpretation or distortion.

Islamism ideological reform movement that calls for the implementation of Islam in all walks of life, particularly the social and political.

Ismaili belonging to the *isma'iliyya*, a Shi'i group that recognized Isma'il b. Ja'far al-Sadiq to be the rightful seventh imam, rather than his brother Musa al-Kazim.

isnad a chain of transmitters given at the beginning of a hadith, relating the names of authorities who transmitted the text of the hadith, one from the other.

isra'iliyyat Jewish and Christian religious material used for early Qur'anic exegesis.

Ithna Ashari Twelver Shi'a; the main body of Shi'i Muslims who acknowledge a line of twelve descendants of the Prophet Muhammad as his legitimate successors.

Jabri belonging to the *jabriyya*, a group that arose in the Umayyad period, asserting that human beings do not possess free will, and that all acts are predetermined by God.

Ja'fari school the main Shi'i school of law.

jahiliyya a state of ignorance, particularly referring to the pre-Islamic era.

jami' a type of hadith collection containing traditions divided into eight major topics: beliefs; laws; piety; etiquette; Qur'an commentary; history; crises; and appreciation and denunciation of people and places.

janna 'garden'; a state of felicity in the afterlife.

jihad an effort or struggle, including personal striving against sin; a religious war to prevent or overcome oppression.

jilbab a type of female dress.

jinn a sprite, an imperceptible being who, like humans, is capable of good and evil.

jizya the tax paid by protected minorities living within a Muslim state who are exempted from military service and paying the *zakat*.

Ka'ba the cube-shaped building in Mecca considered by Muslims to be the holiest place on earth, and which serves as the direction to which Muslims turn for prayer.

kalam word, speech, theology.

kasb the doctrine in which human beings are considered to acquire the ability to act, so it can be said that God alone has creative power.

khanqah Sufi meeting house.

Khariji belonging to the Kharijis, a group of Muslims who condemned Ali for accepting arbitration with Mu'awiya.

khirqa a patched cloak worn by ascetics.

khutba a sermon delivered by an imam as part of the Friday and Eid congregational services.

kitab a book.

kufic a style of Arabic script. Also used for a type of rectangular, calligraphic pattern used in art.

kufr   that which covers truth; ungrateful disbelief; unbelief.

legalist traditionalist   one who attempts to follow premodern teachings and interpretations of religious law.

madhahib   see *madhhab*

madhhab   a school of thought, such as a school of law or theology.

madrasa   a school or college for the study of the religious sciences.

Mahdi   an eschatological figure expected to appear before the end of time who will fill the world with justice.

Maliki school   a major Sunni school of religious law named after Malik ibn Anas.

Mamluk dynasty   a medieval sultanate ruled by former slaves, which arose in the seventh/thirteenth century in Egypt.

maqam   (pl. *maqamat*) stations or stages along the mystical path to God.

maqasid al-shari'a   the underlying aims or purposes of religious law.

masjid   a place of prostration, mosque.

maslaha   a principle of deriving law based on public interest or welfare.

ma'sum   infallible, sinless.

matn   the text containing the content of a tradition (hadith).

Maturidi school   a school of Sunni theology.

messenger   a prophetic figure bearing a divine scripture.

mihna   inquisition, particularly referring to the forced assent of scholars to Mu'tazili theology during the Abbasid period.

mihrab   a prayer niche in a mosque, marking the direction of Mecca, and before which the imam stands to lead the congregation in prayer.

minbar   a pulpit in a mosque from where a sermon is given.

muezzin   one who gives the call to prayer.

mufti   a scholar authorized to give a fatwa on a question of religious law.

Mughal dynasty   Indian empire founded by Babur, who was descended from Tamerlane and Genghis Khan, in the tenth/sixteenth century.

Muhajirun   the Prophet's early followers in Mecca who made the emigration to Medina.

mujaddid   one who renews the faith.

Mujaddidi   belonging to the *mujaddidiyya*, a Sufi order founded by Ahmad Sirhindi of India.

mujtahid   one capable of performing *ijtihad* and deriving interpretations of religious law.

Murji'i   belonging to the *murji'a*, those who took the theological position of suspending decision on whether a Muslim could become an unbeliever, leaving it to God on the day of judgement.

murshid   a Sufi guide or leader.

murtadd   an apostate.

musalla   a small or private place of prayer.

musannaf   a large collection of traditions (hadith) arranged according to subject matter.

mushaf the physical text of the Qur'an in written form.

mushrik an idolator, polytheist.

musiqa music.

Muslim a follower of the religion of Islam, someone submitted to the will of God.

musnad a collection of traditions arranged by order of the names of the final Companion in the chain of transmission. Also used generally for a reliable collection of traditions.

mutakallim (pl. *mutakallimun*) a theologian, one learned in theology (*kalam*).

Mu'tazili belonging to the *mu'tazila*, an early theological school that emphasized the absolute transcendence and oneness of God. Particularly known for their belief in the created nature of the Qur'an.

Muwahhid dynasty medieval dynasty ruling in North Africa and Spain, founded by reformist Ibn Tumart. Also known in English as the Almohad dynasty.

muwahiddun unitarians. Also used for followers of Muhammad ibn Abd al-Wahhab.

Naqshbandi belonging to the *naqshbandiyya*, a major Sufi group who trace their connection to the prophetic teachings, through the line of Abu Bakr.

naskh in its artistic sense, a cursive form of calligraphy; abrogation of one ruling by another.

Nizari belonging to the *nizariyya*, a major Ismaili group, whose leader is the Aga Khan.

Ottoman caliphate major Turkish dynasty that ruled until 1924 when the caliphate was dismantled.

people of the Book those who possess a pre-Qur'anic scripture. Generally refers to Jews and Christians, although the term has at times been extended to other groups such as Zoroastrians and Hindus.

pluralism an approach that recognizes different religions as legitimate paths to God, in contrast to exclusivism, which holds that only one religion or ideology is true.

polygamy the practice of having two or more spouses at the same time.

prophet one who has received inspiration and a divine commission to call others to God.

qadar the divine decree, the measure or determination of everything in existence.

Qadari belonging to the *qadariyya*, those early theologians who asserted human free will and rejected any concept of predestination.

qadi a judge.

Qadiri belonging to the *qadiriyya*, a Sufi group named after Shaykh Abd al-Qadir al-Jilani.

qiyas a Sunni instrument for deriving law through analogical reasoning.

Qur'an   Muslim holy scripture, the word of God as received and transmitted by the Prophet Muhammad.

Quraysh   a prominent tribe that controlled Mecca in the time of the Prophet Muhammad, who belonged to one of its clans.

Rashidun caliphs   'Rightly guided caliphs'. For Sunni Muslims, the first four successors to the Prophet – Abu Bakr, Umar, Uthman and Ali – are considered to have ruled in accordance with the Prophet's guidance, unlike later successors who turned the caliphate into a worldly, hereditary dynasty.

Safavid dynasty   Persian Shi'i dynasty established in 907/1501 by Shah Isma'il I.

sahaba   see *sahabi*.

sahabi   (pl. *sahaba*) a Companion of the Prophet.

sahih   a grading category of hadith in which a tradition is considered sound or authentic.

salaf   'pious ancestors'; generally considered to be the first three generations of Muslims after the time of the Prophet.

Salafi   one who claims to follow the salaf (pious ancestors).

salat   ritual prayer, one of five essential practices that all Muslims are commanded to observe, and which involves recitations and movements repeated in cycles, five times a day.

sama'   a concert or poetry recitation used by Sufis to induce ecstatic worship.

Sanusi   belonging to the *sanusiyya*, an African Sufi revivalist movement founded by Muhammad ibn Ali al-Sanusi, which fought against the French and the Italians.

sariqa   theft.

sawm   fasting, one of the five essential practices that Muslims must observe.

sayyid   title given to descendants of the Prophet. Also used by royals in the Busa'idi dynasty, instead of the title of imam.

Seljuq dynasty   a medieval, eastern Turkic dynasty.

Shadhili   belonging to the *shadhiliyya*, a major Sufi group, named after Abu al-Hasan al-Shadhili.

Shafi'i school   a major Sunni school of religious law that developed from the teachings of Muhammad ibn Idris al-Shafi'i.

shahada   the first essential duty of the Muslim, which is to witness that there is no god but God, and that Muhammad is the messenger of God.

shari'a   religious law, which Muslims derive from the Qur'an and the practice of the Prophet Muhammad; Islamic law.

shaykh   a respected elder, religious leader, Sufi guide.

shaytan   Satan, devil; Iblis is referred to as a *shaytan*.

Shi'i   belonging to the Shi'a. The term Shi'a is associated with the phrase *Shi'at Ali* (meaning 'partisans of Ali'). The Shi'a are those who believe that Ali and his direct descendants are the Prophet Muhammad's rightful successors. The term Shi'a is used for the people who belong to this group while Shi'i is used as an adjective – for instance, Shi'i belief or Shi'i Muslim.

shirk   polytheism, associating partners with God.

silsila   a chain of spiritual authorities. Used by Sufis as recognition of authority within a Sufi order.

sira   biographical history, particularly of the Prophet and the early Muslims.

Successor   a Muslim who lived during the time of the Companions and met at least one of them; second generation of Muslims.

Sufi   one who practises *tasawwuf* or 'Sufism', the mystical branch of Islam.

Sunna   the normative practice, primarily of the Prophet Muhammad; his sayings, deeds and tacit approvals.

Sunni   belonging to the *ahl al-sunna* (those who follow Sunna), those who acknowledge among other things the Rashidun caliphs as successors to the Prophet.

sura   a division of the Qur'an, roughly equivalent to a chapter.

tafsir   exegesis, or interpretation of the Qur'an.

tajdid   the renewal of religion.

tanzih   the doctrine of the absolute transcendence of God.

taqlid   blind following of the opinions of specialists in theology and law.

tariqa   the mystical path to God; Sufi order.

tawhid   central Islamic doctrine teaching the absolute oneness of God.

ta'wil   a form of allegorical interpretation of the Qur'an.

Tijani   belonging to the *tijaniyya*, an African Sufi group founded by Ahmad al-Tijani in the late eighteenth century CE.

traditionalist   one who is 'traditional' in one's outlook or approach to Islamic law.

Traditionist   belonging to the *ahl al-hadith* 'people of the traditions', an influential second/seventh century movement that asserted the primacy of relying on traditions, rather than personal opinion or human reasoning, in understanding religious faith and obligation; scholar of tradition (hadith).

Twelver Shi'a   see Ithna Ashari.

ulama   scholars of religion; scholars.

Umayyad caliphate   first major hereditary dynasty, founded by the governor of Syria, Mu'awiya, which ruled from 41/661 until 132/750.

umma   community, in particular the Muslim community.

urf   local custom or customary law.

usul   origins, roots, fundamental principles as they relate to the religious sciences such as *usul al-din* (the principles of religion) or *usul al-fiqh* (the bases of law).

wahdat al-shuhud   'oneness of witnessing'. Ahmad Sirhindi's answer to *wahdat al-wujud* (oneness of being), which asserts that the unity of being experienced by the created order was one of perception, not reality.

wahdat al-wujud 'oneness of being'. A doctrine often attributed to Ibn Arabi, that God is the true existent, and creation is the manifestation of His attributes in the perspective of diversity.

Wahhabi belonging to the *wahhabiyya*, those who follow the teachings of the twelfth/eighteenth-century puritan reformer Muhammad ibn Abd al-Wahhab, considered by them to be a pejorative term.

wahy divine inspiration, such as that received by prophets.

Zahiri belonging to the *zahiriyya*, a Sunni legal school that emphasized literalist interpretation of the texts.

zakat the purification of wealth through the payment of alms, one of five essential practices that Muslims observe.

zawiya a small, private place of worship that became known as a Sufi convent for worship, learning and sanctuary.

Zaydi belonging to the *zaydiyya*, a Shi'i group that acknowledged Zayd ibn Ali as the fifth imam.

zuhhad ascetics, who reject material comfort in order to seek God.

Notes

I Transmission of religious knowledge and Islamic thought

1 This chapter is largely based on the author's earlier works, particularly A. Saeed, *Interpreting the Qur'an: Towards a Contemporary Approach*, London and New York: Routledge, 2006; A. Saeed, 'Approaching the Qur'an', in A. Rippin (ed.), *The Blackwell Companion to the Qur'an*, Oxford: Blackwell, 2006, pp.36–50; A. Saeed, 'Qur'an: Tradition of Scholarship and Interpretation', *Encyclopedia of Religion*, Farmington, MI: Thomson Gale USA; A. Saeed and H. Saeed, *Freedom of Religion, Apostasy and Islam*, Aldershot: Ashgate, 2004.
2 Masc. sing. *sahabi*.
3 This term 'people of the Book' refers to people who received divine revelations such as Jews and Christians.
4 Masc. sing. *tabi'i*.
5 W. Montgomery Watt, *The Majesty that Was Islam: The Islamic World 661–1100*, 1974; London: Sidgwick; New York: St Martin's, 1990, p. 65.
6 Ahmad Amin, *Fajr al-Islam* Cairo: Maktabat al-Nahda al-Misriyya, 1975 pp. 258–9.
7 Watt, *Majesty*, p. 69.
8 Watt, *Majesty*, pp. 70–1.
9 Amin, *Fajr al-Islam*, p. 280.
10 *Aqa'id*, sing. *aqida*.
11 *Madhahib*, sing. *madhhab*.
12 R. K. Khuri, *Freedom, Modernity, and Islam: Toward a Creative Synthesis*, Syracuse: Syracuse University Press, 1998, p. 224.
13 O. Bakar, *Classification of Knowledge in Islam*, Cambridge: Islamic Texts Society, 1998, pp. 121–4.
14 Bakar, *Classification of Knowledge*, pp. 207–9.
15 F. Robinson (ed.), *The Cambridge Illustrated History of the Islamic World*, New York: Cambridge University Press, 1996, p. 219.
16 Robinson, *The Cambridge Illustrated History*, p. 221.
17 F. Rahman, *Islam*, 2nd ed., Chicago: University of Chicago Press, 1979, p. 184.
18 M. Chamberlain, *Knowledge and Social Practice in Medieval Damascus, 1190–1350*, Cambridge: Cambridge University Press, 1994, pp. 83–5.
19 Rahman, *Islam*, p. 184.
20 Robinson, *The Cambridge Illustrated History*, p. 230.
21 Chamberlain, *Knowledge*, p. 88.
22 Chamberlain, *Knowledge*, p. 89.
23 R. S. Humphreys et al., 'Tarika', in P. J. Bearman et al. (eds), *Encyclopaedia of*

Islam Online, 12 vols, Leiden: Brill, 2004, 17 June 2005 <http://www.encislam.brill.nl>.

24 A. Saeed, *The Official Ulema and Religious Legitimacy*, 2003, pp. 14–28

2 The Qur'an: the primary foundation text

1 A significant part of this chapter is based on the author's earlier works, particularly A. Saeed, *Interpreting the Qur'an: Towards a Contemporary Approach*, London and New York: Routledge, 2006; A. Saeed, 'Qur'an: Tradition of Scholarship and Interpretation', *Encyclopedia of Religion*, Farmington, MI: Thomson Gale, 2005; A. Saeed, 'Contextualizing', in A. Rippin (ed.), *The Blackwell Companion to the Qu'ran*, Malden, MA: Blackwell Publishing, 2006, pp. 36–50.
2 Q.26: 192–5.
3 Q.96: 1–5.
4 Q.99: 4–5; and Q.41: 12.
5 Q.16: 68–9.
6 Q.28: 7.
7 Q.5: 111; and Q.4: 163.
8 Q.8: 12.
9 Q.42: 51.
10 Q.20: 9–12.
11 Q.26: 195.
12 Q.10: 15.
13 M. H. Tabataba'i, *The Qur'an in Islam: Its Impact and Influence on the Life of Muslims*, London: Zahra, 1987, p. 65.
14 Q.4: 82.
15 Q.26: 192–5.
16 *Al-Muwatta of Imam Malik ibn Anas: The First Formulation of Islamic Law*, rev. and trans. Aisha Abdurrahman Bewley, Islamic Classical Library Edition, 1991, Inverness: Madinah, 2001, p. 77.
17 F. Rahman, *Islam*, 2nd ed., Chicago: University of Chicago Press, 1979, pp. 31–2.
18 M. Sells, trans., *Approaching the Qur'an: The Early Revelations*, Ashland: White Cloud, 1999, p. 3.
19 Q.98: 1–3.
20 Q.18: 27.
21 Q.21: 10.
22 Rahman, *Islam*, p. 31.
23 F. Rahman, *Islam and Modernity: Transformation of an Intellectual Tradition*, Publications of the Center for Middle Eastern Studies, 15, Chicago: University of Chicago Press, 1982, p. 5.
24 Q.16: 64; Q.6: 154–7; Q.2: 176; Q.3: 7; Q.4: 105; and Q.29: 47.
25 Q.1: 1–7.
26 Q.58: 12.
27 Q.93: 1–11.
28 Q.51: 56, my emphasis.
29 Q.2: 155, my emphasis.
30 Q.1: 5, my emphasis.
31 Q.112: 1, my emphasis.
32 Q.2: 285.
33 Q.17: 88.
34 Q.18: 50.

35 Q.7: 11–18; and Q.2: 30–8.
36 Q.4: 1.
37 Q.18: 37; and Q.22: 5.
38 Q.7: 11–25; and Q.2: 30–9.
39 Q.2: 120–21.
40 Q.5: 69.
41 Q.2: 111.
42 Q.5: 48.
43 Q.16: 44.
44 J. D. McAuliffe (ed), *Encyclopaedia of the Qur' an*, Leiden: Brill, 2002, p. 104.
45 F. E. Peters, *Judaism, Christianity, and Islam: The Classical Texts and Their Interpretation*, vol. 2, Princeton: Princeton University Press, 1990, p. 142.
46 A. Rippin (ed.), *Approaches to the History of the Interpretation of the Qur'an*, Oxford and New York: Oxford University Press, 1988.
47 N. Calder, *Studies in Early Muslim Jurisprudence*, Oxford: Oxford Uiversity Press, 1993, pp. 131–4.
48 Abu al-Abbas Ahmad ibn Umar al-Qurtubi, *Talkhis Sahih al-Imam Muslim ibn Hajjaj al-Qushayri al-Naysaburi*, vol. 1, Cairo: Dar al-Salam, 1414 [1993], p. 25.
49 Meir M. Bar-Asher, *Scripture and Exegesis in Early Imami Shiism*, Islamic Philosophy, Theology and Science: Texts and Studies, 37, Leiden: Brill, 1999, p. 16.
50 Bar-Asher, *Scripture and Exegesis*, p. 12.
51 F. E. Peters, *Judaism, Christianity, and Islam: Volume 2: The Word and the Law and the People of God*, Princeton and London: Princeton University Press, 1990, p. 155
52 Saeed, 'Qur'an: Tradition of Scholarship'.
53 Saeed, 'Qur'an: Tradition of Scholarship'.
54 Saeed, 'Qur'an: Tradition of Scholarship'.
55 Saeed, 'Qur'an: Tradition of Scholarship'.
56 Saeed, 'Qur'an: Tradition of Scholarship'.
57 Saeed, 'Qur'an: Tradition of Scholarship'; Amina Wadud-Muhsin, *Qur'an and Woman*, Kuala Lumpur: Fajar Bakti, 1988; Asma Barlas, '*Believing Women' in Islam: Unreading Patriarchal Interpretations of the Qur'an*, Austin, TX: University of Texas Press, 2002.
58 Saeed, 'Qur'an: Tradition of Scholarship'; Wadud-Muhsin, *Qur'an and Woman*; Barlas, '*Believing Women*'.
59 Saeed, 'Qur'an: Tradition of Scholarship'; Wadud-Muhsin, *Qur'an and Woman*; Barlas, '*Believing Women*'.
60 Rahman, *Islam and Modernity*, p. 6; Saeed, 'Qur'an: Tradition of Scholarship'.
61 *The Message of the Qur'an*, trans. Muhammad Asad, Gibraltar: Dar-al-Andalus, 1980.
62 *The Meaning of the Holy Qur'an*, trans. Abdullah Yusuf Ali, new rev. 9th ed., Beltsville, MD: Amana, 1999, reprint of *The Holy Qur'an*, 1989.
63 Abul A'la Mawdudi, *Towards Understanding the Qur'an*, trans. and ed. Zafar Ishaq Ansari, 7 vols, trans. of *Tafhim al-Qur'an*, London: Islamic Foundation, 1988–2001.

3 The Sunna of the Prophet

 1 M. Z. Siddiqi, 'Hadith – A Subject of Keen Interest', in P. K. Koya (ed.), *Hadith and Sunnah: Ideals and Realities*, Kuala Lumpur: Islamic Book Trust, 1996, p. 3.

2 F. Rahman, 'The Living Sunnah and *Al-Sunnah wa'l Jama'ah*', in Koya, *Hadith and Sunnah*, p. 177.
3 Muhammad Mustafa Azami, *Studies in Hadith Methodology and Literature*, American Trust, 1977, Kuala Lumpur: Islamic Book Trust, n.d., p. 32.
4 *Al-Muwatta of Imam Malik ibn Anas*, rev. and trans. Aisha Abdurrahman Bewley, Islamic Classical Library edition, Inverness: Madinah, 1991, p. 77.
5 E. Ibrahim and D. Johnson-Davies, 'Introduction', *Forty Hadith Qudsi*, selected and trans. E. Ibrahim and D. Johnson-Davies, Millat Book Center, n.d., p. 9.
6 *Forty Hadith Qudsi*, p. 126 (with slight alteration in the translation).
7 M. Ali, 'Collection and Preservation of Hadith', in Koya, *Hadith and Sunnah*, p. 24.
8 M. Z. Siddiqi, *Hadith Literature: Its Origin, Development & Special Features*, ed. and rev. Abdal Hakim Murad, rev. ed., Cambridge: Islamic Texts Society, 1993, pp. 19, 21; Khaled Abou El Fadl, *Speaking in God's Name: Islamic Law, Authority and Women*, Oxford: Oneworld, 2001, pp. 215–16.
9 Q.4: 59.
10 Q.33: 21.
11 Umm Asim, the mother of Umar II (as he is called), was a granddaughter of Umar ibn al-Khattab (d. 24/644). See P. M. Cobb, "Umar (II) b. 'Abd al-'Aziz', in P. J. Bearman et al. (eds), *Encyclopaedia of Islam Online*, 12 vols, Leiden: Brill, 2004 <http://www.encislam.Brill.nl>.
12 Ali, 'Collection', p. 33.
13 Koya, 'Introduction', in Koya, *Hadith and Sunnah*, p. xvi.
14 Siddiqi, *Hadith Literature*, p. 7; Ali, 'Collection', p. 34.
15 Ali, 'Collection', pp. 35–6.
16 Siddiqi, 'Hadith', pp. 14–18.
17 M. M. Azami, *Studies in Early Hadith Literature*, Indianapolis, IN: American Trust Publications, 1978, p. 61.
18 M. Z. Siddiqi, 'The Sciences and Critique of Hadith (*'Ulum al-Hadith*)', in Koya, p. 94.
19 Siddiqi, 'Sciences and Critique', p. 94.
20 Siddiqi, 'Sciences and Critique', p. 95.
21 M. U. Kazi, *A Treasury of Ahadith*, Jeddah: Abul-Qasim, 1992, pp. 12–14.
22 Siddiqi, 'Sciences and Critique', p. 95.
23 Siddiqi, 'Sciences and Critique', p. 96.
24 Azami, *Studies in Hadith*.
25 Azami, *Studies in Hadith*, pp. 61–6.
26 A. H. al-Fadli, *Introduction to Hadith*, trans. Nazmina Virjee, London: ICAS, 2002.
27 There are several Shi'i groups, however here 'Shi'a' refers to the largest Imami (Twelver) group of Shi'i Muslims.
28 Al-Fadli, *Introduction to Hadith*, p. 22.
29 Al-Fadli, *Introduction to Hadith*, pp. 25–7.
30 F. Rahman, 'The Living Sunnah', in Koya, p. 132.
31 Siddiqi, *Hadith Literature*, p. 125.
32 I. Goldziher, *Muslim Studies*, ed. S. M. Stern, trans. C. R. Barber and S. M. Stern, trans. of *Muhammedanische Studien*, London: Allen & Unwin 1971, pp. 189–93.
33 Goldziher, *Muslim Studies*, pp. 193–6.
34 Goldziher, *Muslim Studies*, pp. 199.
35 Goldziher, *Muslim Studies*, pp. 216–18, 230.
36 Goldziher, *Muslim Studies*, pp. 249–50.
37 G. H. A. Juynboll, *Muslim Tradition: Studies in Chronology, Provenance, and Authorship of Early Hadith*, Cambridge: Cambridge University Press, 1983,

p. 1; G. H. A. Juynboll, 'Some *Isnad* – Analytical Methods Illustrated on the Basis of Several Women-Demeaning Sayings from *Hadith* Literature', *Al-Qantara: Revista de Estudos Árabes*, 10, fasc. 2, Madrid, 1989, pp. 343–84, reprinted in *Studies on the Origins and Uses of Islamic Hadith*, Aldershot: Ashgate, 1996, pp. 351–2.

38 Given that it is incredible that on important aspects of religious belief and law the Prophet would choose only a single Companion to convey such information, who themselves would choose only a single Successor to receive it, who then themselves would choose only a single successor in the next generation to receive it before it became widespread, it is most likely that the point where the hadith became widely transmitted was its real point of origin.

39 Juynboll, *Muslim Tradition*, p.1; Juynboll 'Some *Isnad* – Analytical Methods', p. 382.

40 Rahman, 'Living Sunnah', p. 133.

41 Rahman, 'Living Sunnah', p. 136.

42 Rahman, 'Living Sunnah', p. 160.

43 N. Reda, 'What Would the Prophet Do? The Islamic Basis for Female-Led Prayer', *Muslim Wakeup!* 10 March 2005, 24 June 2005 <http://www.muslimwakeup.com/main/archives/2005/03/women_imamat.php>.

44 Z. Shakir, 'An Examination of the Issue of Female Prayer Leadership', *Progressive Muslim Union of North America*, 23 March 2005, 24 June 2005 <http://www.pmuna.org/archives/female_imam-3.pdf>.

45 M. Z. Siddiqi, *The Hadith for Beginners: An Introduction to Major Hadith Works and Their Compilers*, New Delhi: Goodword, 2001, pp. 110–12.

46 Siddiqi, *Hadith Literature*, p. 54; Azami, *Studies in Hadith*, p. 87.

47 Siddiqi, *Hadith for Beginners*, p. 110.

48 J. Robson, 'Bukhari, Muhammad b. Isma'il', in Bearman; Siddiqi, *Hadith for Beginners*, pp. 115–16.

49 Azami, *Studies in Hadith*, p. 89.

50 S. S. Faridi, 'The Fallacies of Anti-Hadith Arguments', in Koya, p. 205.

51 Azami, *Studies in Hadith*, pp. 89–90.

52 Azami, *Studies in Hadith*, p. 90.

4 Legal thought

1 Q.11: 91.

2 Q.7: 179.

3 'The Book Pertaining to the Merits of the Companions (Allah Be Pleased With Them) of the Holy Prophet (May Peace Be Upon Him) (*Kitab al-Fada'il al-Sahaba*)', *Sahih Muslim Book Thirty One*, trans. Abdul Hamid Siddiqui, MSA-USC, 26 September 2005 <http://web.archive.org/web/ 20041011231951/ http://www.usc.edu/dept/MSA/fundamentals/hadithsunnah/muslim/031.smt.html>.

4 A. Hasan, *The Early Development of Islamic Jurisprudence*, Islamabad: Islamic Research Institute, 1970, pp. 1–10; F. Rahman, *Islam*, 2nd ed., Chicago: University of Chicago Press, pp. 100–9.

5 S. H. Nasr, *Ideals and Realities of Islam*, London: Allen & Unwin, 1966, pp. 95–6.

6 S. R. Mahmasani, *Turath al-Khulafa' al-Rashidin fi al-Fiqh wa-al-Qada'*, Beirut: Dar al-Ilm li al-Malayin, 1984, p. 244.

7 A. A. B. Philips, *The Evolution of Fiqh: Islamic Law & the Madh-habs*, Riyadh: Tawheed, 1988, p. 46.

8 N. J. Coulson, *A History of Islamic Law*, Islamic Surveys 2, Edinburgh:

Edinburgh University Press, 1964, pp. 28–9; J. Schacht, *An Introduction to Islamic Law*, Oxford: Clarendon, 1964, pp. 25.

9 Q.4: 65.

10 W. B. Hallaq, *A History of Islamic Legal Theories: An Introduction to Sunni Usul al-Fiqh*, Cambridge: Cambridge University Press, 1997, pp. 30–1.

11 Some sources put the number of hadith compiled in Ahmad's Musnad as thirty thousand. M. Z. Siddiqi, *The Hadith for Beginners: An Introduction to Major Hadith Works and Their Compilers*, New Delhi: Goodword, 2001, p. 105.

12 S. Waqar Ahmed Husaini, *Islamic Environmental Systems Engineering*, London: Macmillan; Indianapolis: AmericanTrust, 1980, pp. 18–19.

13 The most important work by al-Shatibi in this area is his famous *al-Muwafaqat fi Usul al-Shari'ah*.

14 Najm-Din al-Tufi, *Risalat al-Imam al-Tufi fi Taqdim al-Maslaha fi al-Mu'amalat ala al-Nass*, annotated by Jamal Din al-Qasimi al-Dimashqi, ed. Mahmud Abu Rayya, Cairo: n.p., 1966.

15 Muhammad ibn Abd al-Wahhab (d. 1792) started his so-called Wahhabi movement in Arabia. In Yemen, Muhammad ibn Ali al-Shawkani (d. 1834) represented an expression of intellectual revival. Shah Wali Allah (d. 1762) and Sayyid Ahmad of Rae Bareli in India, Hajji Shariat Allah in Bengal (born circa 1764), Muhammad ibn Ali al-Sanusi (d. 1859) were also among the leading 'revivers' of this period.

16 Rahman, 'Islam: Challenges and Opportunities', Edinburgh: Edinburgh University Press, p. 317.

17 F. Rahman, *Islam and Modernity: Transformation of an Intellectual Tradition*, Chicago: University of Chicago Press, 1982, pp. 2–19.

18 S. Ramadan, *Islamic Law: Its Scope and Equity*, London: Macmillan, 1961, pp. 71–3; Subhi Rajab Mahmassani, *Falsafat al-Tashri fi al-Islam: The Philosophy of Jurisprudence in Islam*, trans. F. J. Ziadeh, Leiden: Brill, 1961, pp. 51ff, 92–8; M. Iqbal, *The Reconstruction of Religious Thought in Islam*, Lahore: Bazar, [1958], pp. 129, 151ff, 171–3; S. Husaini, *Islamic Environmental Systems*, pp. 23.

19 A brief summary of the legal systems of many Muslim countries is given in Abdullahi A. An-Na'im (ed.), *Islamic Family Law in a Changing World: A Global Resource Book*, London: Zed; New York: Palgrave–St Martin's, 2002.

20 Details and examples in An-Na'im, *Islamic Family Law*.

21 An-Na'im, *Islamic Family Law*, p. 16.

22 O. Arabi, *Studies in Modern Islamic Law and Jurisprudence*, The Hague: Kluwer Law International, 2001, p. 189.

23 An-Na'im, *Islamic Family Law*, p. 108.

24 An-Na'im, *Islamic Family Law*, pp. 136–7.

25 J. L. Esposito (ed.), *Islam and Development: Religion and Sociopolitical Change*, Contemporary Issues in the Middle East, Syracuse: Syracuse University Press, 1980, p. 129.

26 Esposito, *Islam and Development*, p. 129.

27 J. L. Esposito and N. J. DeLong-Bas, *Women in Muslim Family Law*, 2nd ed., Contemporary Issues in the Middle East, Syracuse: Syracuse University Press, 2001, p. xiv.

28 Y. Y. Haddad and J. L. Esposito (eds), *Islam, Gender and Social Change*, New York: Oxford University Press, 1998, p. 15.

29 Haddad and Esposito, *Islam, Gender and Social Change*, p. 17.

30 M. Badran, 'Feminisms and Islamisms', *Journal of Women's History*, 10(4) 1999: 196–205.

31 D. Pearl and W. Menski, *Muslim Family Law*, 3rd ed., London: Sweet and Maxwell, 1998, p. 72.
32 Pearl and Menski, *Muslim Family Law*, p. 72.
33 An-Na'im, *Islamic Family Law*, p. 18.
34 Pearl and Menski, *Muslim Family Law*, p. 51.
35 Pearl and Menski, *Muslim Family Law*, p. 64.
36 Pearl and Menski, *Muslim Family Law*, p. 67.
37 Pearl and Menski, *Muslim Family Law*, p. 67.
38 Pearl and Menski, *Muslim Family Law*, p. 68.
39 Pearl and Menski, *Muslim Family Law*, p. 69.
40 J. Hussain, 'Family Law and Muslim Communities', in A. Saeed and S. Akbarzadeh (eds), *Muslim Communities in Australia*, Sydney: University of New South Wales Press, 2001, p. 184.
41 An-Na'im, *Islamic Family Law*, p. 1.
42 An-Na'im, *Islamic Family Law*, p. 2.
43 M. H. Kamali, *Islamic Law in Malaysia: Issues and Developments*, Kuala Lumpur: Ilmiah, 2000, p. 62.
44 Kamali, *Islamic Law*, p. 63.
45 Abou El Fadl, *Speaking in God's Name*, p. 171.

5 Theological thought

* I am grateful for Redha Ameur who helped me in utilising the following sources in French in several sections of this chapter.

Abdurrahmân Badawi. *Histoire de la Philosophy en Islam*. 2 vols. Etudes de Philosophie Médiévale 60. Paris, Vrin, 1972; L. Gardet and M.M. Anawati. *Introduction à la Théologie Musulmane. Essai de Théologie Comparée*. Etudes de philosophie médiévale, xxxvii. Paris 1948.

1 Traditions expressing these sentiments can be found in collections by Tirmidhi, Ibn Maja and Abu Da'ud.
2 H. Corbin, *History of Islamic Philosophy*, trans. L. Sherrard and P. Sherrard, London: Kegan Paul, 1993, pp. 108–9.
3 H. Laoust, 'Ahmad b. Hanbal', in P. J. Bearman et al. (eds), *Encyclopaedia of Islam Online*, 12 vols, Leiden: Brill, 2004 <http://www.encislam.brill.nl>; A. Rippin, *Muslims: Their Religious Beliefs and Practices, Library of Religious Beliefs and Practices*, London: Routledge, 1990, vol. 1, p. 63.
4 Laoust, 'Ahmad b. Hanbal'.
5 M. Abdul Hye, 'Ash'arism', in M. M. Sharif (ed.), *A History of Muslim Philosophy: With Short Accounts of Other Disciplines and the Modern Renaissance in Muslim Lands*, 2 vols, Wiesbaden: Harrassowitz, 1963–6, vol. 1, pp. 222–3.
6 A. S. Tritton, *Muslim Theology*, James G. Forlong Fund 23, [London]: Luzac for Royal Asiatic Society, 1947, pp. 169, 178–9; M. Abdul Hye, 'Ash'arism', in M. M. Sharif (ed.), *A History of Muslim Philosophy*, vol. 1, pp. 230–2.
7 Paraphrase of argument made in Ash'ari's *Al-Luma'*, Badawi, *Histoire de la Philosophie en Islam*, 2 vols, Études de Philosophie Médiévale 60, Paris: Vrin, 1972, pp. 281–3.
8 Hye, 'Ash'arism', pp. 226–8; Tritton, *Muslim Theology*, pp. 167–9.
9 Hye, 'Ash'arism', pp. 234–5; Tritton, *Muslim Theology*, p 173.
10 Tritton, *Muslim Theology*, p. 172; Hye, 'Ash'arism', pp. 235–7.
11 Hye, 'Ash'arism', pp. 229–30; C. L. Cahen and L. Gardet, 'Kasb', in P. J. Bearman et al. (eds). *Encyclopaedia of Islam Online*, 12 vols, Leiden: Brill, 2004 <http://www.encislam.brill.nl>

12 W. Montgomery Watt (trans.), *Islamic Creeds: A Selection*, Edinburgh: Edinburgh University Press, 1994, pp. 86–9.
13 A. K. M. Ayyub Ali, 'Maturidism', in Sharif, *A History of Muslim Philosophy*, vol. 1, pp. 269–71.
14 A. K. M. Ayyub Ali, 'Maturidism', pp. 271–2.
15 W. M. Watt, *The Formative Period of Islamic Thought*, Oxford: Oneworld, 1998, pp. 314–15.
16 Watt, *Formative Period*, pp. 315–16.
17 Ayyub Ali, 'Maturidism', pp. 262–4.
18 Ayyub Ali, 'Maturidism', pp. 267–9.
19 Watt, *Formative Period*, pp. 122–4.
20 W. M. Watt, *Islamic Philosophy and Theology: An Extended Survey*, 2nd ed., Edinburgh: Edinburgh University Press, 1985.
21 M. Abduh, *The Theology of Unity (Risalat al-Tauhid)*, trans. I. Musa'ad and K. Cragg (1966), Kuala Lumpur: Islamic Book Trust, 2004, p. 132.
22 Redha Ameur, *The Concept of Tajdid in Nursi's Thought* (Ph.D. thesis in progress)
23 Abduh, *Risalat al-Tawhid*, p. 167.
24 Redha Ameur, *The Concept of Tajdid in Nursi's Thought* (Ph.D. thesis in progress)
25 Abduh, *Theology*, pp. 63–4.
26 Abduh, *Theology*, p. 129.

6 Mystical thought: Sufism

1 J. Spencer Trimingham, *The Sufi Orders in Islam*, 1971, Oxford: Oxford University Press, 1998, p. 1.
2 Sufis often call God *haqiqah* ('Reality' or 'the Real').
3 Trimingham, *Sufi Orders*, p. 1.
4 Trimingham, *Sufi Orders*, p. 2.
5 Margaret Smith, *Studies in Early Mysticism in the Near and Middle East*, Amsterdam: Philo Press, 1973, p. 155.
6 Smith, *Studies in Early Mysticism*, p. 158.
7 Smith, *Studies in Early Mysticism*, p. 161.
8 Smith, *Studies in Early Mysticism*, p. 161.
9 Smith, *Studies in Early Mysticism*, p. 162.
10 A. Harvey and E. Hanut, *Perfume of the Desert: Inspirations from Sufi Wisdom*, 1st Quest ed., Wheaton, IL: Quest, 1999, p. 79.
11 Smith, *Studies in Early Mysticism*, p. 165.
12 Smith, *Studies in Early Mysticism*, p. 165.
13 Smith, *Studies in Early Mysticism*, p. 166.
14 Trimingham, *Sufi Orders*, p. 3.
15 Trimingham, *Sufi Orders*, p. 4.
16 Trimingham, *Sufi Orders*, p. 10.
17 Trimingham, *Sufi Orders*, p. 9.
18 Trimingham, *Sufi Orders*, p. 9.
19 Trimingham, *Sufi Orders*, p. 9.
20 Trimingham, *Sufi Orders*, p. 5.
21 Trimingham, *Sufi Orders*, p. 9.
22 Trimingham, *Sufi Orders*, p. 5.
23 Trimingham, *Sufi Orders*, p. 9.
24 Trimingham, *Sufi Orders*, p. 10.
25 Smith, *Studies in Early Mysticism*, p. 170.

26 A. J. Arberry, *Sufism: An Account of the Mystics of Islam*, London: Allen & Unwin, 1950, p. 79.
27 M. Sells (trans.), *Approaching the Qur'an: The Early Revelations*, Ashland: White Cloud Press, 1999, p. 197.
28 Smith, *Studies in Early Mysticism*, p. 171.
29 Smith, *Studies in Early Mysticism*, p. 171.
30 Smith, *Studies in Early Mysticism*, p. 174.
31 S. H. Nasr (ed.), *Islamic Spirituality Manifestations*, New York: SCM, 1991.
32 S. H. Nasr, 'Prelude: The Spiritual Significance of the Rise and Growth of the *Sufi Orders*', in S. H. Nasr, *Islamic Spirituality Manifestations*, p. 3.
33 Sufi orders are many and varied and often divided into several sub-orders.
34 K. A. Nizami, 'The Qadiriyyah Order', in Nasr, *Islamic Spirituality Manifestations*, p. 13.
35 Nizami, 'Qadiriyyah', p. 6.
36 Nizami, 'Qadiriyyah', pp. 6–7.
37 Nizami, 'Qadiriyyah', pp. 8–9.
38 J. Van Ess, 'Kadiriyya', in P. J. Bearman et al. (eds), *Encyclopaedia of Islam Online*, 12 vols, Leiden: Brill, 2004 <http://www.encislam.brill.nl>.
39 Al-Jilani, Abd al-Qadir, *The Sublime Revelation (Al-Fath ar-Rabbani): A Collection of Sixty-Two Discourses*, trans. Muhtar Holland (Fort Lauderdale, FL: Al-Baz, 1993), 17 June 2005 <http://web.archive.org/web/20040408000517/http://www.al-baz.com/shaikhabdalqadir/Books_and_Text_of_Wisdom/Al-Fath_ar-Rabbani/Al-Fath_ar-Rabbani_-_15/al-fath_ar-rabbani_-_15.htm>. The words in square brackets are added by the translator.
40 V. Danner, 'The Shadiliyyah and North African Sufism', in Nasr, *Islamic Spirituality Manifestations*, p. 26.
41 Danner, 'Shadhiliyyah', p. 27; P. Lory, 'Shadhiliyya', in P. J. Bearman et al. (eds), *Encyclopaedia of Islam Online* 12 vols, Leiden: Brill, 2004 <http://www.encislam.brill.nl>.
42 Danner, 'Shadhiliyyah', p. 30.
43 Lory, 'Shadhiliyya'.
44 Lory, 'Shadhiliyya'.
45 S. M. Al-Busiri, 'Al-Burda: The Prophet's Mantle', trans. T. M. Allam, *Iqra Islamic Publications*, 7 September 2005 <http://www.iqra.net/qasaaid1/burda>.
46 K. A. Nizami, 'The Naqshbandiyyah Order', in Nasr, *Islamic Spirituality Manifestations*, p. 163.
47 H. Algar and K.A. Nizami, 'Nakshbandiyya'. in P. J. Bearman et al. (eds), *Encyclopaedia of Islam Online*, 12 vols, Leiden: Brill, 2004 <http://www.encislam. brill.nl>.
48 Hülya Yilmaz, *Ahmed Ziyauddin Gumush-khanewi*, 18 June 2005 <http://web.archive.org/web/20041009180913/http://gumushkhanawidargah.8m.com/silsile32.html>, trans. from *Dünden Bugüne Gümüshànevî Mektebi*, Istanbul: Seha Yayinevi, 1997.
49 Algar and Nizami, 'Nakshbandiyya', in P. J. Bearman et al.
50 D. Damrel, 'The Religious Roots of Conflict: Russia and Chechnya', *Religious Studies News*, 10.3, September 1995, 10, 18 June 2005 <http://web.archive.org/web/20041009221321/http://www.iol.ie/~afifi/Articles/chechnya.htm>.
51 *Shaykh Muhammad Hisham Kabbani*, 18 June 2005 <http://web.archive.org/web/20041123083937/http://www.naqshbandi.org/about/Sh_Kabbani_bio.htm>.
52 *Practices in the Naqshbandi Sufi Way*, 18 June 2005 <http://web.archive.org/web/20011116051523/http://naqshbandi.org/dhikr/frmdawra.htm>.

53 William C. Chittick, 'Ibn 'Arabi and His School', in Nasr, *Islamic Spirituality Manifestations*, p. 49.
54 A. Ates, 'Ibn al-'Arabi', in P. J. Bearman et al. (eds), *Encyclopaedia of Islam Online*, 12 vols, Leiden: Brill, 2004 <http://www.encislam.brill.nl>.
55 Chittick, 'Ibn 'Arabi', p. 49.
56 Chittick, 'Ibn 'Arabi' pp. 52–4.
57 Chittick, 'Ibn 'Arabi', p. 60.
58 R. Arnaldez, 'Al-Insan al-Kamil', in Bearman, *Encyclopaedia of Islam Online*, 12 vols, Leiden: Brill, 2004 <http://www.encislam.brill.nl>.
59 Muhyi al-Din Ibn al-'Arabi, *Fusus al-Hikam*, Algiers: Mufam li al-Nashr, 1990, pp. 157–61, 163–70.
60 Quoted in J. G. J. ter Haar, *Follower and Heir of the Prophet: Shaykh Ahmad Sirhindi (1564–1624) as Mystic*, Leiden: Het Oosters Instituut, 1992, p. 128.
61 For a detailed discussion of *wahdat al-wujud* and *wahdat al-shuhud* see Burhan Ahmad Faruqi, *The Mujaddid's Conception of Tawhid*, Lahore: n.p., 1940.
62 See M. A. H. Ansari, *Sufism and Shari'ah: A Study of Shaykh Ahmad Sirhindi's Effort to Reform Sufism*, Leicester: Islamic Foundation, 1986, pp. 101–39.
63 See Yohanan Friedmann, *Shaykh Ahmad Sirhindi: An Outline of His Thought and a Study of His Image in the Eye of Posterity*, Montreal: McGill University, Institute of Islamic Studies, 1971, pp. 59–68.
64 Haar, *Follower*, pp. 130–1.
65 Haar, *Follower*, p. 133.
66 C. W. Ernst, *Words of Ecstasy in Sufism*, SUNY Series in Islam, Albany: State University of New York Press, 1985.
67 Ernst, *Words*, p. 117.
68 Ernst, *Words*, p. 117.
69 Ernst, *Words*, p. 118.
70 Ernst, *Words*, pp. 117–25.
71 Ernst, *Words*, p. 118.
72 Ernst, *Words*, p. 119.
73 Ernst, *Words*, p. 121.
74 Ernst, *Words*, p. 120.
75 Ernst, *Words*, p. 122.
76 Ernst, *Words*, pp. 125–6.
77 Ernst, *Words*, p. 3.
78 Ernst, *Words*, p. 128.
79 Ernst, *Words*, p. 128.
80 J. Hunwick, 'Africa and Islamic Revival: Historical and Contemporary Perspectives', online posting, 14 June 1996, MSA News, Department of Religion, University of Georgia, 19 June 2005 <http://web.archive.org/web/2004102303 4851/http://www.uga.edu/islam/hunwick.html>.
81 *Annemarie Schimmel*, The Institute of Ismaili Studies, 19 June 2005 <http:// web.archive.org/web/20041025091657/http://www.iis.ac.uk/research/academic_ publications/schimmel.htm>.
82 Alan Godlas, 'Sufism, the West, and Modernity', in *Sufism, Sufis, and Sufi Orders: Sufism's Many Paths*, Department of Religion, University of Georgia, 19 June 2005 <http://web.archive.org/web/20041128092207/http://www.uga.edu/islam/ sufismwest.html>.

7 Artistic expression

1 'Islamic Art', def., *WorldImages.com: Glossary of Art Terms and Definitions*, 10 September 2005 <http://www.worldimages.com/art_glossary.php>.

2 *Islamic Art*, March 2002, Sala@m, 10 September 2005 <http://www.salaam. co.uk/themeofthemonth/march02_index.php?l=0>.
3 'The Book Pertaining to Clothes and Decoration (*Kitab al-Libas wa al-Zinah*)', *Sahih Muslim Book Twenty Four*, trans. A. H. Siddiqui, MSA-USC, 31 October 2005 <http://www.usc.edu/dept/MSA/fundamentals/hadithsunnah/muslim/024. smt.html>.
4 'The Book Pertaining to Clothes', Sahih Muslim.
5 S. J. Abas and A. S. Salman, *Symmetries of Islamic Geometrical Patterns*, Singapore: World Scientific, 1995, p. 9.
6 The script of Baghdad differs from *kufic* in that letters are fully formed and presented in an elegant style. The difference increased under the vizier Abu Ali b. Muqla and his secretary Ali b. Hilal, known as Ibn al-Baghdad. Ibn Muqla is considered to have codified calligraphy. A. Khatibi and M. Sijelmassi, *The Splendour of Islamic Calligraphy*, London: Thames and Hudson, 2001, p. 97.
7 Khatibi and Sijelmassi, *The Splendour*, pp. 78–9.
8 Khatibi and Sijelmassi, *The Splendour*, p. 79.
9 Khatibi and Sijelmassi, *The Splendour*, p. 81.
10 M. Sabri, 'A Topic of Dispute in Islam: Music', 1910, trans. Muaz Özyigit, *Anadolu*, 5.4, 1995, 16 June 2005 <http://www.wakeup.org/anadolu/05/4/ mustafa_sabri_en.html>.
11 A. J. Racy and J. Logan, 'Arab Music: Part One', *Music in Our World*, San Diego State University, 16 July 2005 <http://trumpet.sdsu.edu/M345/Arab_Music1. html>.
12 Racy and Logan, 'Arab Music'.
13 Racy and Logan, 'Arab Music'.
14 Racy and Logan, 'Arab Music'.
15 Racy and Logan, 'Arab Music'.
16 Racy and Logan, 'Arab Music'.
17 Q.31: 6.
18 Quoted in M. S. Al-Munajjid, 'Ruling on Music, Singing and Dancing', fatwa, ref. no. 5000, *Islam Q&A*, 12 September 2005.
19 Q.17: 64.
20 Quoted in Al-Munajjid, 'Ruling on Music'.
21 Quoted in Al-Munajjid, 'Ruling on Music'.
22 Quoted in Al-Munajjid, 'Ruling on Music'.
23 Al-Munajjid, 'Ruling on Music'.
24 'Music Art Sciences', *Sufi Order-Tariqat Gul Nur Jihaniyya Radiant Valley Association*, 1998, 16 June 2005 <http://www.angelfire.com/ca2/mysticalpathway nurhu/MusicArtSciences.html>.
25 'Music Art Sciences'.
26 M. H. Siddiqi, 'Songs and Music', fatwa, *Pakistan Link*, 1997, 12 September 2005 <http://pakistanlink.com/religion/97/re02-21-97.html>.
27 'The Two Festivals (Eids)', in *Sahih Bukhari Book Fifteen*, trans. M. M. Khan, MSA-USC, 20 September 2005 <http://www.usc.edu/dept/MSA/fundamentals/ hadithsunnah/bukhari/015.sbt.html>.
28 See 'Singing & Music: Islamic View', fatwa, *IslamOnline.net*, 13 January 2004, 12 September 2005 <http://www.islamonline.net/servlet/Satellite?pagename =IslamOnline-English-Ask_Scholar/FatwaE/FatwaE&cid=1119503544202>.
29 Q. 31: 6.
30 Ibn Hazm, 'Risala fi al-Ghina', In Muhammad Amara, *al-Islam wa al-Funun al-Jamila*, Cairo: Dar al-Shuruq, 1991, pp. 155–60.
31 Ibn Hazm, 'Risala fi al-Ghina', pp. 155–60.
32 Ibn Hazm, 'Risala fi al-Ghina', pp. 160–3.
33 'Singing & Music'.

34 Islamic Arts and Architecture Organization, <http://www.islamicart.com/main/architecture/index.html>.

8 Philosophical thought

*I am grateful for Redha Ameur who helped me in utilising the following sources in French in several sections of this chapter.

Abdurrahmân Badawi. *Histoire de la Philosophy en Islam*. 2 vols. Etudes de Philosophie Médiévale 60. Paris, Vrin, 1972; L. Gardet and M.M. Anawati. *Introduction à la Théologie Musulmane. Essai de Théologie Comparée*. Etudes de philosophie médiévale, xxxvii. Paris 1948.

1 The five main areas of philosophy are: metaphysics (theories of reality); epistemology (theories of knowledge); ethics (moral values); logic (principles of good, valid and sound reasoning); aesthetics (theories of art and beauty). J. J. Gusmano, *Thinking Philosophically: An Introduction to Philosophy with Readings*, Lanham, MD: University Press of America, 1990, pp. 13–16.
2 Quoted in Gusmano, *Thinking Philosophically*, p. 3.
3 Gusmano, *Thinking Philosophically*, pp. 28–30.
4 A. W. Levi, 'Nature of Philosophy and the Writing of Its History (from Philosophy, History of)', in M. R. McCudden (ed.), *Encyclopaedia Britannica Deluxe Edition 2004*, CD-ROM, Disc 2, Ver. 2004, Chicago, IL: Encyclopaedia Britannica, 2004.
5 A. W. Levi, 'The Pre-Socratic Philosophers (from Philosophy, History of)', in McCudden, *Encyclopaedia Britannica*.
6 A. W. Levi, 'The Seminal Thinkers of Greek Philosophy (from Philosophy, History of)', in McCudden, *Encyclopaedia Britannica*.
7 A. W. Levi, 'Hellenistic and Roman Philosophy (from Philosophy, History of)', in McCudden, *Encyclopaedia Britannica*.
8 Levi, 'Hellenistic and Roman Philosophy'.
9 M. Fakhry, *A History of Islamic Philosophy*, 3rd ed., New York: Columbia University Press, 2004, pp. 2–3.
10 Fakhry, *History*, pp. 2–4.
11 Fakhry, *History*, pp. 33–7.
12 Fakhry, *History*, p. 5.
13 See 'A. Badawi, *Histoire de la Philosophie en Islam*, 2 vols, Études de Philosophie Médiévale 60, Paris: Vrin, 1972, vol. 1, p. 386.
14 Fakhry, *History*, p. xxv.
15 Fakhry, *History*, pp. 21–2.
16 F. E. Peters, *Aristotle and the Arabs: The Aristotelian Tradition in Islam*, New York University Studies in Near Eastern Civilization 1, New York: New York University Press, 1968, p. 88.
17 Fakhry, *History*, pp. 39–43.
18 Fakhry, *History*, pp. 43–4.
19 Fakhry, *History*, pp. 44–5.
20 Peters, *Aristotle*, pp. 73–4.
21 M. S. Mahdi, 'The Western Philosophers (from Islam)', in McCudden, *Encyclopaedia Britannica*.
22 B. H. Siddiqi, 'Ibn Tufail', in M. M. Sharif (ed.), *A History of Muslim Philosophy: With Short Accounts of Other Disciplines and the Modern Renaissance in Muslim Lands*, 2 vols, Wiesbaden: Harrassowitz, 1963–6, vol. 1, pp. 526–8.
23 M. S. Mahdi, 'The New Wisdom: Synthesis of Philosophy and Mysticism (from Islam)', in McCudden, *Encyclopaedia Britannica*.
24 S. H. Nasr, 'Mystical Philosophy in Islam', in E. Craig (ed.), *Routledge*

Encyclopedia of Philosophy Online, ver. 2.0, 2005, London: Routledge <http://222.rep.routledge.com>. <http://www.rep.routledge.com/article/H004>; S. H. Nasr, 'The School of Ispahan', in Sharif, *A History of Muslim Philosophy*, vol. 2, p. 914.

25 G. N. Atiyeh, *Al-Kindi: The Philosopher of the Arabs*, Publications of the Islamic Research Institute (Pakistan) 6, Rawalpindi: Islamic Research Institute, 1966, p. 34; A. F. El-Ehwany, 'Al-Kindi', in Sharif, *A History of Muslim Philosophy*, vol. 1, pp. 421–3; Fakhry, *History*, p. 69.

26 Atiyeh, *Al-Kindi*, pp. 26, 44; El-Ehwany, 'Al-Kindi' 429.

27 El-Ehwany, 'Al-Kindi', 423–8; Atiyeh, *Al-Kindi*, pp. 17–18, 22–5, 29–32; Fakhry, *History*, pp. 69–70.

28 Atiyeh, *Al-Kindi*, pp. 57–69; El-Ehwany, 'Al-Kindi', p. 428; Fakhry, *History*, pp. 74–5.

29 Atiyeh, *Al-Kindi*, pp. 45–9; El-Ehwany, 'Al-Kindi', p. 428.

30 Atiyeh, *Al-Kindi*, pp. 49–57; El-Ehwany, 'Al-Kindi', p. 430; Fakhry, *History*, pp. 75–9.

31 El-Ehwany, 'Al-Kindi', pp. 430–1; Fakhry, *History*, pp. 75–7.

32 Atiyeh, *Al-Kindi*, pp. 69–82; Fakhry, *History*, p. 84.

33 El-Ehwany, 'Al-Kindi', pp. 432–4; Fakhry, *History*, pp. 85–7.

34 S. H. Nasr, *Three Muslim Sages: Avicenna, Suhrawardi, Ibn 'Arabi*, Cambridge, MA: Harvard University Press, 1964, p. 17.

35 I. Madkour, 'Al-Farabi', in Sharif, *A History of Muslim Philosophy*, vol. 1, pp. 457–60.

36 Fakhry, *History*, pp. 122–8.

37 Madkour, 'Al-Farabi', in Sharif, *A History of Muslim Philosophy*, vol. 1, pp. 457–8.

38 Madkour, 'Al-Farabi', p. 459.

39 Madkour, 'Al-Farabi', pp. 460–3; Fakhry, *History*, pp. 115–16.

40 Madkour, 'Al-Farabi', pp. 463–7; Fakhry, *History*, pp. 128–32.

41 Madkour, 'Al-Farabi', p. 465.

42 Madkour, 'Al-Farabi', pp. 466–7.

43 Daniel Brown, *A New Introduction to Islam*, Malden, MA: Blackwell, 2004, pp. 150–1.

44 From al-Farabi's *Maqala fi ma'ani al-'aql* (*On Meanings of 'Intellect'*), quoted in Badawi, *Histoire*, p. 553.

45 For a discussion of Farabi's concept of perceptive faculties see Daniel Brown, *A New Introduction to Islam*, Malden, MA: Blackwell, 2004, pp. 150–1.

46 Nasr, *Three Muslim Sages*, pp. 20–2; Fakhry, *History*, pp. 132–4.

47 Fakhry, *History*, pp. 135–7; Nasr, *Three Muslim Sages*, p. 24.

48 Nasr, *Three Muslim Sages*, pp. 27–8; S. M. Afnan, *Avicenna: His Life and Works*, London: Allen & Unwin, 1958, pp. 115–19; Fazlur Rahman, 'Ibn Sina', in Sharif, *A History of Muslim Philosophy*, vol. 1, pp. 482–6.

49 Badawi, *Histoire*, p. 656.

50 Nasr, *Three Muslim Sages*, pp. 28–30; M. S. Mahdi, 'The Teachings of Avicenna (from Islam)', in McCudden; Rahman, 'Ibn Sina' p. 481.

51 Badawi, *Histoire*, p. 718.

52 Siddiqi, 'Ibn Tufail', pp. 526–7; Fakhry, *History*, pp. 273–4; L. E. Goodman, 'Ibn Tufayl', in S. H. Nasr and O. Leaman (eds), *History of Islamic Philosophy*, Routledge History of World Philosophies 1, London: Routledge, 1996, pp. 314–5, 318.

53 Fakhry, *History*, pp. 274–80; Siddiqi, 'Ibn Tufail', pp. 528–9; Goodman, 'Ibn Tufayl', pp. 315–28.

54 Badawi, *Histoire*, p. 735.
55 Siddiqi, 'Ibn Tufail', pp. 533–4.
56 Siddiqi, 'Ibn Tufail', pp. 534–5.
57 K. Nakamura, 'Al-Ghazali, Abu Hamid (1058–1111)', in Craig, *Routledge Encyclopedia of Philosophy Online* <http://www.rep.routledge.com/article/H028>; M. S. Sheikh, 'Al-Ghazali: Metaphysics', in Sharif, *History of Muslim Philosophy*, vol. 1, pp. 581–5.
58 Nakamura, 'Al-Ghazali'; Sheikh, 'Al-Ghazali', pp. 585–7.
59 Sheikh, 'Al-Ghazali, pp. 594–616; I. A. Bello, *The Medieval Islamic Controversy Between Philosophy and Orthodoxy: Ijma' and Ta'wil in the Conflict Between Al-Ghazali and Ibn Rushd*, Islamic Philosophy and Theology 3, Leiden: Brill, 1989, p. 83.
60 Sheikh, 'Al-Ghazali', pp. 599, 607; Bello, *Medieval*, pp. 91–3.
61 Sheikh, 'Al-Ghazali', p. 613.
62 Sheikh, 'Al-Ghazali', pp. 615–16; Bello, *Medieval*, pp. 131–2.
63 Sheikh, 'Al-Ghazali', pp. 615–16.
64 See Gardet and Anawati, *Introduction*, pp. 268–73.
65 Badawi, *Histoire*, p. 742.
66 Fakhry, *History*, pp. 280–2; A. F. El-Ehwany, 'Ibn Rushd', in Sharif, *History of Muslim Philosophy*, vol. 1, p. 544.
67 Q.3: 7. The original Arabic does not have punctuation marks as such, and the verse can be read in two ways: (1) No one knows its explanation but God and those deeply rooted in knowledge. Say: 'We believe in it. It is all from our Lord' or (2) No one knows its explanation but God. And those deeply rooted in knowledge say: 'We believe in it. It is all from our Lord.' Here, Ibn Rushd has chosen the former reading.
68 El-Ehwany, 'Ibn Rushd', pp. 544–7; Fakhry, *History*, pp. 287–90.
69 O. Leaman, *Averroes and His Philosophy*, Oxford: Clarendon, 1988, pp. 42–81; El-Ehwany, 'Ibn Rushd', pp. 547–64.
70 Leaman, *Averroes*, pp. 42–5, 64–8; Bello, *Medieval*, p. 103.
71 BID, pp. 811–12.
72 El-Ehwany, 'Ibn Rushd', p. 545.
73 El-Ehwany, 'Ibn Rushd', p. 546.
74 Fakhry, *History*, pp. 292–3; El-Ehwany, 'Ibn Rushd', pp. 546–7.
75 Fakhry, *History*, pp. 291–2.
76 Leaman, *Averroes*, pp. 71–81.
77 Quoted in Leaman, *Averroes*, pp. 56–7.
78 Leaman, *Averroes*, pp. 52–5.
79 S. H. Nasr, 'Sadr al-Din Shirazi (Mulla Sadra)', in Sharif, *History of Muslim Philosophy*, vol. 2, pp. 932–5, 937–40; Fakhry, *History*, p. 315.
80 Nasr, 'Sadr al-Din', p. 938.
81 Nasr, 'Sadr al-Din', pp. 942–6.
82 Nasr, 'Sadr al-Din', pp. 948–51.
83 Nasr, 'Sadr al-Din', pp. 951–3.
84 Nasr, 'Sadr al-Din', p. 952.
85 Nasr, 'Sadr al-Din', pp. 953–8.
86 M. Abed al-Jabri, *Arab-Islamic Philosophy: A Contemporary Critique*, trans. Aziz Abbassi, Middle East Monograph Series 12, Austin, TX: Center for Middle Eastern Studies, University of Texas at Austin, 1999, p. 2.
87 Al-Jabri, *Arab-Islamic*, p. 3.
88 Al-Jabri, *Arab-Islamic*, p. 125.
89 Al-Jabri, *Arab-Islamic*, p. 86.
90 Al-Jabri, *Arab-Islamic*, p. 102.

91 See the final chapter of S. M. al-Naquib al-Attas, *Islam and Secularism*, Kuala Lumpur: Muslim Youth Movement of Malaysia, 1978.
92 Al-Attas, *Islam and Secularism*, p. 36.
93 S. M. N. al-Attas, *Prolegomena to the Metaphysics of Islam: An Exposition of the Fundamental Elements of the Worldview of Islam*, Kuala Lumpur: International Institute of Islamic Thought and Civilization, 1995, p. 38.
94 Al-Attas, *Prolegomena*, p. 114.
95 S. H. Nasr, *Traditional Islam in the Modern World*, London: Kegan Paul, 1987, p. 12.
96 Nasr, *Traditional Islam*, p. 13.

9 Political thought

1 K. A. El Fadl, *Islam and the Challenge of Democracy*, ed. J. Cohen and D. Chasman, Princeton, NJ: Princeton University Press, 2004, p. 5.
2 F. M. Donner, 'Muhammad and the Caliphate: Political History of the Islamic Empire up to the Mongol Conquest', in J. L. Esposito (ed.), *The Oxford History of Islam*, Oxford: Oxford University Press, 1999, p. 11.
3 A. Saeed and H. Saeed, *Freedom of Religion, Apostasy and Islam*, Aldershot: Ashgate, 2004, pp. 65–6.
4 Saeed and Saeed, *Freedom of Religion*, pp. 65–6.
5 Taken from a phrase in the Qur'an, e.g. Q.22: 41.
6 G. Levi Della Vida, 'Kharidjites', in P. J. Bearman et al. (eds), *Encyclopaedia of Islam Online*, 12 vols, Leiden: Brill, 2004 <http://www.encislam.brill.nl>.
7 A. K. S. Lambton, *State and Government in Medieval Islam: An Introduction to the Study of Islamic Political Theory: The Jurists*, London Oriental Series 36, Oxford: Oxford University Press, 1981.
8 V. J. Hoffman, '*Ibadi* Islam: An Introduction', in *Sufism, Sufis, and Sufi Orders: Sufism's Many Paths*, Department of Religion, University of Georgia, 15 September 2005 <http://www.uga.edu/islam/ibadis.html>.
9 Q.5: 55.
10 M. H. Tabatabai, *Shi'a*, trans. S. H. Nasr, Qum: Ansarian, circa 1971, p.177, 30 October 2005 <http://www.balagh.net/english/shia/shia/09.htm>.
11 This includes a tradition in which the severely ill Prophet had asked for pen and paper presumably in order to give instructions about who was to succeed him. However, before the pen and paper could be brought, the Prophet was forced to ask for privacy because of the Companions' arguing. See Tabatabai, *Shi'a*, pp. 178–82.
12 Quoted in Tabatabai, *Shi'a*, p. 178.
13 Tabatabai, *Shi'a*, pp. 185–6; W. Madelung, 'Imama', in P. J. Bearman et al. (eds), *Encyclopaedia of Islam Online*.
14 I. Amini, *Al-Imam al-Mahdi: The Just Leader of Humanity*, trans. A. Sachedina, Ahlul Bayt Digital Islamic Library Project, 1 November 2005 <http://al-islam.org/mahdi/nontl/>.
15 H. Halm, *Shiism*, trans. J. Watson, Islamic Surveys 18, Edinburgh: Edinburgh University Press, 1991, p. 57.
16 Lambton, *State and Government*, p. 252.
17 Lambton, *State and Government*, p. 252.
18 Lambton, *State and Government*, p. 252.
19 Halm, *Shiism*, p. 57.
20 A. Black, *The History of Islamic Political Thought: From the Prophet to the Present*, New York: Routledge, 2001, p. 22.
21 Black, *History of Islamic Political Thought*, pp. 22–3.

22 Black, *History of Islamic Political Thought*, p. 23.
23 Lambton, *State and Government*, p. 85.
24 Mawardi in Lambton, *State and Government*, p. 85.
25 A. Saeed, 'The Official Ulema and Religious Legitimacy of the Modern Nation State', in *Islamic and Political Legitimacy*, ed. S. Akbarzadeh and A. Saeed, London: RoutledgeCurzon, 2003, p.18.
26 Saeed, 'Official Ulama', pp. 14–28.
27 B. Lewis, *The Middle East*, p. 81.
28 Lewis, *Middle East*, p. 148.
29 Black, *History of Islamic Political Thought*, p. 111.
30 Lambton, *State and Government*, pp. 128–9.
31 Black, *History of Islamic Political Thought*, p. 113.
32 Black, *History of Islamic Political Thought*, p. 113.
33 Black, *History of Islamic Political Thought*, p. 113.
34 Lambton, *State and Government*, p. 128.
35 For a brief discussion on the topic see J. Zaydan, *History of Islamic Civilization: Umayyads and 'Abbasids*, trans. D. S. Margoliouth, 1907, New Delhi: Kitab Bhavan, 1981, pp. 248–50.
36 With their coming to power, the Abbasids effectively changed the caliphate to one in which a caliph officially became the Imam, head of Muslims by *religious* sanction, an emphasis that had not existed before in that form. They took upon themselves titles such as 'Ruler in the Name of God', 'Shadow of God on Earth', 'the Caliph of God', 'One Who Rules in the Name of God', or the 'Representative of God'. (See Saeed, 'Official Ulama' p.17.)
37 Al-Sayyid Abi al-Hasan Ali al-Husni al-Nadwi, *Madha Khasira al-Alam bi-Inhitat al-Muslimin*, 2nd ed., Cairo: Maktabat Dar al-Uruba, 1379 (1959), p. 133.
38 A. Saeed, 'Rethinking Citizenship Rights of Non-Muslims in an Islamic State: Rashid al-Ghannushi's Contribution to the Evolving Debate', *Journal of Islam and Christian–Muslim Relations*, 10(3), 1999, pp. 307–23.
39 I. Ahmed, *The Concept of an Islamic State: An Analysis of the Ideological Controversy in Pakistan*, London: Pinter, 1987, p. 87; Saeed, 'Rethinking Citizenship', pp. 307–323.
40 Ahmed, *Concept of an Islamic State*, pp. 101–2.
41 M. Asad, *The Principles of State and Government in Islam*, Berkeley, CA: University of California Press, 1961, pp. 74–5; Saeed, 'Rethinking Citizenship' pp. 307–23.
42 'A. 'A. al-Raziq, *Al-Islam wa Usul al-Hukm*, Tunis: Dar al-Janub li al-Nashr, 1996.
43 Saeed, 'Rethinking Citizenship', pp. 307–23.
44 Ahmed, *Concept of an Islamic State*, p. 79.
45 Saeed, 'Rethinking Citizenship', pp. 307–23.
46 A. A. An-Na'im, *Toward an Islamic Reformation: Civil Liberties, Human Rights, and International Law*, Contemporary Issues in the Middle East, 1990; New York: Syracuse University Press, 1996, p. 84.
47 Quoted in L. C. Brown, *Religion and State: The Muslim Approach to Politics*, New York: Columbia University Press, 2000, p. 172.
48 Brown, *Religion and State*, p. 172.
49 *Hizb al-Nahdah* was formerly known as *Harakat al-Ittijah al-Islami*, or Islamic Tendency Movement.
50 R. Ghannouchi, 'The Conflict Between the West and Islam, the Tunisian Case: Reality and Prospects: Chatham House', Royal Institute of International Affairs, Chatham House, London, 9 May 1995, trans. A. Tamimi, 15 September 2005 <http://www.ghannouchi.net/chatham.htm>.

51 Ghannouchi, 'Conflict'.
52 Ghannushi, *Huquq al-Muwatanah*, p. 49
53 Q.2: 256.
54 R. Ghannushi, 'Tunisia's Islamists are Different from Those in Algeria', *Al-Shira*, Beirut, October 1994.
55 'IntraView: With Tunisian Sheikh Rached Ghannoushi', 10 February 1998, 12 September 2005 <http://msanews.mynet.net/intra2.html>.
56 Ghannushi, 'Tunisia's Islamists'.

10 Renewal, reform and Muslim modernism

1 Rudolf Peters 'Idjtihad and Taqlid in 18th and 19th Century Islam', *Die Welt des Islams*, NS 20 (3–4), 1980, pp. 131–45.
2 For further details, see Muhammad al-Ghazali, *The Socio-Political Thought of Shah Wali Allah*, Islamabad: The International Institute of Islamic Thought, 2001; Shah Wali Allah, *Hujjat Allah al-baligha*, trans. Marcia Hermansen, *The Conclusive Argument from God*, Leiden: E. J. Brill, 1996; Sayyid Abul A'la Maududi, *A Short History of the Revivalist Movements in Islam*, Lahore: n.p., 1963; Allah Ditta Muztar, *Shah Wali Allah: A Saint Scholar of Muslim India*, Islamabad: n.p., 1979.
3 'Deoband School', *Encyclopaedia Britannica*, 2006, Encyclopaedia Britannica Premium Service, 24 February 2006 <http://www.britannica.com/eb/article-9029970>.
4 For example, Maududi simply cuts out the Sufism of Shah Wali Allah from other aspects of his thought and activities. (See Maududi, *Short History*).
5 E. Peskes and W. Ende, 'Wahhabiyya', in P. J. Bearman et al. (eds), *Encyclopaedia of Islam Online*, 12 vols, Leiden: Brill, 2004 <http://www.encislam.brill.nl>.
6 Muhammad bin Abdul-Wahhab, *Kitab at-tauhid*, trans. by Compilation and Research Department, Dar-us-Salam, New York, NY: Dar-us-Salam Publications, 1996; Abd al-Halim al-Jindi, *al-Imam Muhammad ibn Abd al-Wahhab*, Cairo: Dar al-Ma'arif, 1986.
7 Peskes, 'Wahhabiyya'.
8 Peskes, 'Wahhabiyya'.
9 Sharif, M.M. (ed.), 'Renaissance in North Africa: the Sanusiyyah Movement' in Sharif, *A History of Muslim Philosophy*, vol. 2, pp. 1456–80.
10 D. M. Last, ''Uthman b. Fudi', in P. J. Bearman et al. (eds), *Encyclopaedia of Islam Online*.
11 J. Boyd, 'Distance Learning from Purdah in Nineteenth-Century Northern Nigeria: the Work of Asma'u Fodiyo', *Journal of African Cultural Studies*, 14.1, June 2001, pp. 7–22.
12 I am grateful for Redha Ameur for providing information on several points in this section.
13 Hafeez Malik, *Sir Sayyid Ahmad Khan and the Muslim Modernization of India*. New York: Columbia University Press, 1980; Christian W. Troll, *Sayyid Ahmad Khan: A Reinterpretation of Muslim Theology*, New Delhi: Vikas Publishing House, 1978.
14 H. Malik, *Sir Sayyid Ahmad Khan*, p. 13.
15 *Aligarh Muslim University*. 29 October 2005 <http://web.archive.org/web/2004 1106044551/http://www.amu.ac.in/>.
16 Muhammad 'Abduh, *Al-Islam wa al-Nasraniyyah*, Cairo: Matba'at al-Manar, 1954; Muhammad Abduh, *Risalat al-tawhid*, Cairo: Dar-al-Ma'arif, 1977; Zaki Badawi, *The Reformers of Egypt*, London: Croom Helm, 1978.
17 Fazlur Rahman, 'The Impact of Modernity on Islam', *Islamic Studies*, 5 (2), June

1966, pp. 112–28; Fazlur Rahman, 'My Belief in Action', in Phillip L. Berman (ed.) *The Courage of Conviction*, New York: Dodd, Mead, 1985; Fazlur Rahman, 'Social Change and Early Sunnah', *Islamic Studies* 2 (2), June 1963, p. 206; Fazlur Rahman, 'Towards Reformulating the Methodology of Islamic Law', *Journal of International Law and Politics*, 12 (2), 1979, pp. 205–22, p. 221; Fazlur Rahman, *Islam and Modernity: Transformation of an Intellectual Tradition*, Chicago: University of Chicago Press, 1982; Fazlur Rahman, *Islam*, Chicago: University of Chicago Press, 1966, 1979; Fazlur Rahman, *Major Themes of the Qur'an*, Minneapolis: Bibliotheca Islamica, 1980; Fazlur Rahman, *Revival and Reform in Islam: A Study of Islamic Fundamentalism*, ed. Ebrahim Moosa, Oxford: Oneworld, 2000; Fazlur Rahman, 'Islamic Modernism: Its Scope, Method and Alternatives', *International Journal of Middle East Studies* 1 (1970), pp. 317–33; Fazlur Rahman, 'Towards Reformulating the Methodology of Islamic Law', *New York University Journal of International Law and Politics*, 12 (2), Fall 1979, pp. 205–22.
18 Rahman, *Revival and Reform in Islam*, p. 1. The biographical section relies heavily on this work, as well as Rahman's own statements about his life and work. For example see Rahman, 'My Belief in Action'.
19 Rahman, *Revival and Reform in Islam*, pp. 1–2.
20 Earle H. Waugh, 'The Legacies of Fazlur Rahman for Islam in America', *The American Journal of Islamic Social Sciences*, 16 (3), Fall 1999, p. 31.
21 See bibliography for details.
22 Waugh, 'The Legacies of Fazlur Rahman for Islam in America', p. 31.

Epilogue

1 <http://www.islamfortoday.com/qaradawi.htm>.
2 <http://www.islamonline.net/servlet/Satellite?cid=1119503549588&pagename =IslamOnline-English-Ask_Scholar/FatwaE/FatwaEAskTheScholar>.
3 <http://www.jamaat.org/overview/founder.html>.
4 Mawdudi 'The Process of Islamic Revolution' from a speech delivered at Muslim University, Aligarh (India) on 12 September 1940 <http://www.witness-pioneer. org/vil/Books/M_PIR/part1.htm>. Accessed 11 December 2005.
5 'A Secular Muslim Manifesto' by Tewfik Allal and Brigitte Bardet. The Manifesto attracted several hundred signatories and a list of 'Les Amis du Manifeste' (Friends of the Manifesto) composed of non-Muslim intellectuals expressing their solidarity (<http://www.manifeste.org>). Tewfik Allal, a French union activist, who was born in Morocco of Algerian parents, and his wife Brigitte Bardet, a teacher and feminist activist, are the authors of this Manifesto.
6 Muhammad b. Salih al-Uthaymin was born in the city of Unayzah, Saudi Arabia, in 1929 into a famous religious family. He studied with many prominent scholars including Shaykh Muhammad Amin al-Shanqiti and Shaykh Abd al-Aziz ibn Baz. Ibn al-Uthaymin has issued over fifty religious verdicts (fatwas) and he bases these on evidence from the Qur'an and Sunna. Among his appointments are faculty member at the Faculty of Shari'a at Imam Muhammad ibn Sa'ud University and member of the Senior Scholars Committee of Saudi Arabia. He is considered to be among the leading Salafi scholars of today. His fatwas on the issue of residing in the land of the 'unbelievers' indicate some aspects of his approach to questions of law. 'Shaikh Muhammad Ibn Saalih al-Uthaymeen', Allaahuakbar.net, 14 July 2005 <http://www.allaahuakbar.net/scholars/uthaymeen/>.
7 'Residing in the Land of Unbelievers', Allaahuakbar.net, 14 July 2005 <http:// www.allaahuakbar.net/scholars/uthaymeen/residing_in_land_of_unbelievers. htm>.

8 Text of fatwa urging jihad against Americans. Published in *Al-Quds al-Arabi* on 23 February 1998. Statement signed by Usamah bin Muhammad bin Ladin; Ayman al-Zawahiri, leader of the Jihad Group in Egypt; Abu Yasir Rifa'i Ahmad Taha, a leader of the Islamic Group; Mir Hamzah, secretary of the Jamiat-ul-Ulema-e-Pakistan; and Fazlul Rahman, leader of the Jihad Movement in Bangladesh.

9 Omid Safi, 'Introduction' in Omid Safi (ed.), *Progressive Muslims on Justice, Gender, and Pluralism*, Oxford: Oneworld, 2003.

10 Safi, 'Introduction', p. 18.

11 K. Ali, 'Progressive Muslims and Islamic Jurisprudence: The Necessity for Critical Engagement with Marriage and Divorce Law', in Safi (ed.), *Progressive Muslims*, p. 183.

12 Amina Wadud, *Quran and Woman: Rereading the Sacred Text from a Woman's Perspective*, 2nd ed., New York: Oxford University Press, 1999, p. 95, *Questia*, 23 Feb. 2006 <http://www.questia.com/PM.qst?a=o&d=55490439>.

13 T. Ramadan, *To Be a European Muslim*, Leicester: Islamic Foundation, 1999, p. 114.

14 Ramadan, *To Be a European Muslim*, p. 114.

15 Muqtedar Khan, 'Constructing the American Muslim Community', in J. Esposito, Y. Haddad and J. Smith (eds), *Becoming American*, Oxford University Press, 2001, p. 193.

16 Ramadan, *To Be A European Muslim*, pp. 197–8.

Bibliography

Printed resources

Abas, Syed Jan and Amer Shaker Salaman. *Symmetries of Islamic Geometrical Patterns*. Singapore: World Scientific, 1995.

Abd al-Qadir, al-Jilani. *The Sublime Revelation (Al-Fath ar-Rabbani): A Collection of Sixty-Two Discourses*. Trans. Muhtar Holland. Fort Lauderdale, FL: Al-Baz, 1993.

Abd al-Raziq, Ali. *al-Islam wa Usul al-Hukm*. Tunis: Dar al-Janub li al-Nashr, 1996.

Abduh al-Masri, Muhammad. *Risalat al-Tawhid*. 5th ed. Cairo: Dar al-Ma'arif, 1977.

Abduh, Muhammad. *al-Islam wa al-Nasraniyya ma'a al-Ilm wa-al-Madaniyya*. Cairo: Matba'at Ali Subayh, 1954.

Abduh, Muhammad. *Tarikh al-Ustad al-Imam*. Vol. 1. Cairo: Mataba'at al-Manar, 1324 [1906].

Abduh, Muhammad. *The Theology of Unity (Risalat al-Tauhid)*. Trans. Ishaq Musa'ad and Kenneth Cragg. 1966. Kuala Lumpur: Islamic Book Trust, 2004.

Abdul Hye, M. 'Ash'arism'. In *A History of Muslim Philosophy: With Short Accounts of Other Disciplines and the Modern Renaissance in Muslim Lands*, ed. M. M. Sharif. Wiesbaden: Harrassowitz, 1963–6, pp. 220–43.

Abu Nu'aym al-Isbahani, Ahmad ibn Abd Allah. *Hilyat al-Awliya' wa Tabaqat al-Assfiya'*. Vol. 2. Beirut: Dar al-Kutub al-Ilmiyya, 1418 [1997].

Abou El Fadl, Khaled. *Islam and the Challenge of Democracy*, ed. Joshua Cohen and Deborah Chasman. Princeton, NJ: Princeton University Press, 2004.

Abou El Fadl, Khaled. *Speaking in God's Name: Islamic Law, Authority and Women*. Oxford: Oneworld, 2001.

Afnan, Soheil Muhsin. *Avicenna: His Life and Works*. London: Allen & Unwin, 1958.

Ahmed, Ishtiaq. *The Concept of an Islamic State: An Analysis of the Ideological Controversy in Pakistan*. London: Pinter, 1987.

Al-Attas, Syed Muhammad Naquib. *Islam and Secularism*. Kuala Lumpur: Muslim Youth Movement of Malaysia, 1978.

Al-Attas, Syed Muhammad Naquib. *Prolegomena to the Metaphysics of Islam: An Exposition of the Fundamental Elements of the Worldview of Islam*. Kuala Lumpur: International Institute of Islamic Thought and Civilization, 1995.

Al-Fadli, Abd al-Hadi. *Introduction to Hadith*. Trans. Nazmina Virjee. London: ICAS, 2002.

Ali, A. K. M. Ayyub. 'Maturidism'. In *A History of Muslim Philosophy: With Short Accounts of Other Disciplines and the Modern Renaissance in Muslim Lands*, ed. M. M. Sharif. Wiesbaden: Harrassowitz, 1963–6, vol. 1, pp. 259–74.

Ali, Abdullah Yusuf, trans., *The Meaning of the Holy Qur'an*. New rev. 9th ed. Beltsville, MD: Amana, 1999, reprint of *The Holy Qur'an*, 1989.

Ali, K. 'Progressive Muslims and Islamic Jurisprudence: The Necessity for Critical Engagement with Marriage and Divorce Law'. In *Progressive Muslims*, ed. Omid Safi. Oxford: Oneworld, 2003.

Ali, Muhammad. 'Collection and Preservation of Hadith'. In *Hadith and Sunnah: Ideals and Realities*. ed. P. K. Koya. Kuala Lumpur: Islamic Book Trust, 1996, pp. 23–57.

Allah Ditta Muztar. *Shah Wali Allah: A Saint Scholar of Muslim India*. Islamabad: n.p., 1979.

Amin, Ahmad. *Fajr al-Islam*. Cairo: Maktabat al-Nahda al-Misriyya, 1975.

An-Na'im, Abdullahi A., ed. *Islamic Family Law in a Changing World: A Global Resource Book*. London: Zed; New York: Palgrave, 2002.

An-Na'im, Abdullahi Ahmed. *Toward an Islamic Reformation: Civil Liberties, Human Rights, and International Law*. New York: Syracuse University Press, 1996.

Ansari, Muhammad Abdul Haq. *Sufism and Shari'ah: A Study of Shaykh Ahmad Sirhindi's Effort to Reform Sufism*. Leicester: Islamic Foundation, 1986.

Arabi, Oussama. *Studies in Modern Islamic Law and Jurisprudence*. The Hague: Kluwer Law International, 2001.

Arberry, A. J. *Sufism: An Account of the Mystics of Islam*. London: Allen & Unwin, 1950.

Asad, Muhammad. *The Principles of State and Government in Islam*. Berkeley, CA: University of California Press, 1961.

Asad, Muhammad. *The Message of the Qur'an*. Trans. Muhammad Asad. Gibraltar: Dar-al-Andalus, 1980.

Atiyeh, George N. *Al-Kindi: The Philosopher of the Arabs*. Publications of the Islamic Research Institute (Pakistan) 6. Rawalpindi: Islamic Research Institute, 1966.

Azami, Muhammad Mustafa. *Studies in Early Hadith Literature*. Indianapolis: American Trust, 1978.

Azami, Muhammad Mustafa. *Studies in Hadith Methodology and Literature*. Kuala Lumpur: Islamic Book Trust, n.d.

Badawi, Abd al-Rahman. *Tarikh al-Tasawwuf al-Islami*. Kuwait: Wikalat al-Maṭbu'at, 1978.

Badawi, Abdurrahman. *Histoire de la Philosophie en Islam*. 2 vols. Etudes de Philosophie Médiévale 60. Paris: Vrin, 1972.

Badawi, M. A. Zaki. *The Reformers of Egypt*. London: Croom Helm, 1978.

Badawi, Zaki. *The Reformers of Egypt*. London: Croom Helm, 1978.

Badran, Margot. 'Feminisms and Islamisms', *Journal of Women's History*, 10 (4) (1999): 196–205.

Bakar, Osman. *Classification of Knowledge in Islam*. Cambridge: Islamic Texts Society, 1998.

Bar-Asher, Meir M. *Scripture and Exegesis in Early Imami Shiism*. Islamic Philosophy, Theology and Science: Texts and Studies, 37. Leiden: Brill, 1999.

Barlas, Asma. *'Believing Women' in Islam: Unreading Patriarchal Interpretations of the Qur'an*. Austin, TX: University of Texas Press, 2002.

Bello, Iysa A. *The Medieval Islamic Controversy Between Philosophy and Orthodoxy: Ijma' and Ta'wil in the Conflict Between Al-Ghazali and Ibn Rushd*. Islamic Philosophy and Theology 3. Leiden: Brill, 1989.

Black, Antony. *The History of Islamic Political Thought: From the Prophet to the Present*. New York: Routledge, 2001.

Boyd, Jean. 'Distance Learning from Purdah in Nineteenth-Century Northern Nigeria: The Work of Asma'u Fodiyo', *Journal of African Cultural Studies*, 14 (1) (June 2001): 7–22.

Brown, Daniel. *A New Introduction to Islam*. Malden, MA: Blackwell, 2004.

Brown, L. Carl. *Religion and State: The Muslim Approach to Politics*. New York: Columbia University Press, 2000.

Burton, John. *An Introduction to the Hadith*. Edinburgh: Edinburgh University Press, 1994.

Calder, Norman. *Studies in Early Muslim Jurisprudence*. Oxford: Oxford University Press, 1993.

Chamberlain, Michael. *Knowledge and Social Practice in Medieval Damascus, 1190–1350*. Cambridge: Cambridge University Press, 1994.

Chittick, William C. 'Ibn 'Arabi and His School'. In *Islamic Spirituality Manifestations*, ed. S. H. Nasr. World Spirituality 20. New York: SCM, 1991, pp. 49–79.

Cleary, Thomas. *The Qur'an: A New Translation*. Trans. Thomas Cleary. Chicago: Starlatch Press, 2004.

Corbin, Henry. *History of Islamic Philosophy*. Trans. Liadain Sherrard and Philip Sherrard. London: Kegan Paul, 1993.

Coulson, N. J. *A History of Islamic Law*. Islamic Surveys 2. Edinburgh: Edinburgh University Press, 1964.

Danner, Victor. 'The Shadiliyyah and North African Sufism'. In *Islamic Spirituality Manifestations*, ed. S. H. Nasr. World Spirituality 20. New York: SCM, 1991, 26–49.

Donner, Fred M. 'Muhammad and the Caliphate: Political History of the Islamic Empire up to the Mongol Conquest'. In *The Oxford History of Islam*, ed. John L. Esposito. Oxford: Oxford University Press, 1999.

El-Ehwany, Ahmed Fouad. 'Al-Kindi'. In *A History of Muslim Philosophy: With Short Accounts of Other Disciplines and the Modern Renaissance in Muslim Lands*. 2 vols, ed. M. M. Sharif. Wiesbaden: Harrassowitz, 1963–6, vol. 1, pp. 421–34.

El-Ehwany, Ahmed Fouad. 'Ibn Rushd'. In *A History of Muslim Philosophy: With Short Accounts of Other Disciplines and the Modern Renaissance in Muslim Lands*. 2 vols, ed. M. M. Sharif. Wiesbaden: Harrassowitz, 1963–6, vol. 1, pp. 540–64.

Ernst, Carl W. *Words of Ecstasy in Sufism*. Albany: State University of New York Press, 1985.

Esposito, John L., ed. *Islam and Development: Religion and Sociopolitical Change*. Contemporary Issues in the Middle East. Syracuse: Syracuse University Press, 1980.

Esposito, John L. and Natana J. DeLong-Bas. *Women in Muslim Family Law*.

2nd ed. *Contemporary Issues in the Middle East*. Syracuse: Syracuse University Press, 2001.

Al-Fadli, A. H. *Introduction to Hadith*, trans. Nazmina Virjee. London: ICAS, 2002.

Fakhry, Majid. *A History of Islamic Philosophy*. 3rd ed. New York: Columbia University Press, 2004.

Faridi, Shah Shahidullah. 'The Fallacies of Anti-Hadith Arguments'. In *Hadith and Sunnah: Ideals and Realities*, ed. P. K. Koya. Kuala Lumpur: Islamic Book Trust, 1996, pp. 190–209.

Faruqi, Burhan Ahmad. *The Mujaddid's Conception of Tawhid*. Lahore: n.p., 1940.

Friedmann, Yohanan. *Shaykh Ahmad Sirhindi: An Outline of His Thought and a Study of His Image in the Eye of Posterity*. Montreal: McGill University, Institute of Islamic Studies, 1971.

Gardet, Louis and M. M. Anawati. *Introduction à la Théologie Musulmane: Essai de Théologie Comparée*. Etudes de Philosophie Médiévale 37. Paris: Vrin, 1948.

Ghannushi, Rashid. 'Tunisia's Islamists are Different from Those in Algeria', *Al-Shira*. Beirut. October 1994.

Ghazali, Muhammad al-. *The Socio-Political Thought of Shah Wali Allah*. Islamabad: The International Institute of Islamic Thought, 2001.

Goldziher, Ignaz. *Muslim Studies*, ed. S. M. Stern. Trans. C. R. Barber and S. M. Stern. Trans. of *Muhammedanische Studien*. London: Allen & Unwin, 1971.

Goodman, Lenn E. 'Ibn Tufayl'. In *History of Islamic Philosophy*, ed. Seyyed Hossein Nasr and Oliver Leaman. Routledge History of World Philosophies 1. London: Routledge, 1996.

Gusmano, Joseph J. *Thinking Philosophically: An Introduction to Philosophy with Readings*. Lanham, MD: University Press of America, 1990.

Haar, J. G. J. ter. *Follower and Heir of the Prophet: Shaykh Ahmad Sirhindi (1564–1624) as Mystic*. Leiden: Het Oosters Instituut, 1992.

Haddad, Yvonne Yazbeck and John L. Esposito, eds. *Islam, Gender and Social Change*. New York: Oxford University Press, 1998.

Hallaq, Wael B. *A History of Islamic Legal Theories: An Introduction to Sunni Usul al-Fiqh*. Cambridge: Cambridge University Press, 1997.

Halm, Heinz. *Shiism*. Trans. Janet Watson. Islamic Surveys 18. Edinburgh: Edinburgh University Press, 1991.

Harvey, Andrew and Eryk Hanut. *Perfume of the Desert: Inspirations from Sufi Wisdom*. 1st Quest ed. Wheaton, IL: Quest, 1999.

Hasan, Ahmad. *The Early Development of Islamic Jurisprudence*. Islamabad: Islamic Research Institute, 1970.

Haykel, Bernard. *Revival and Reform in Islam: The Legacy of Muhammad al-Shawkani*. Cambridge: Cambridge University Press, 2003.

Hermansen, Marcia K. 'Translator's Introduction'. *The Conclusive Argument from God: Shah Wali Allah of Delhi's Hujjat Allah al-Baligha*. Trans. Marcia K. Hermansen. Islamic Philosophy, Theology, and Science 25. Leiden: Brill, 1996, pp. xv–xl.

Hourani, Albert. *Arabic Thought in the Liberal Age, 1798–1939*. London: Oxford University Press, 1962.

Husaini, S. Waqar Ahmed. *Islamic Environmental Systems Engineering*. London: Macmillan; Indianapolis: American Trust, 1980.

Hussain, Jamila. 'Family Law and Muslim Communities'. In *Muslim Communities in Australia*, ed. A. Saeed and S. Akbarzadeh. Sydney: University of New South Wales Press, 2001, pp. 161–87.

Ibn al-Arabi, Muhyi al-Din. *Fusus al-Hikam*. Algiers: Mufam li al-Nashr, 1990.

Ibn Asakir, Ali ibn al-Ḥasan. *Tabyin Kadhib al-Muftari fi-ma Nusiba ila al-Imam Abi al-Hasan al-Ashʿari*. 2nd ed. Damascus: Dar al-Fikr, 1399 [1979].

Ibrahim, Ezzeddin and Denys Johnson-Davies. 'Introduction'. In *Forty Hadith Qudsi*. Selected and trans. Ezzeddin Ibrahim and Denys Johnson-Davies. N.p.: Millat Book Center, n.d.

Iqbal, Muhammad. *The Reconstruction of Religious Thought in Islam*. Lahore: Bazar, 1958.

Jabri, Mohammed Abed al-. *Arab-Islamic Philosophy: A Contemporary Critique*. Trans. Aziz Abbassi. Middle East Monograph Series 12. Austin, TX: Center for Middle Eastern Studies, University of Texas at Austin, 1999.

Jindi, Abd al-Halim al-. *al-Imam Muhammad ibn Abd al-Wahhab*. Cairo: Dar al-Maʿarif, 1986

Johns, A. H. and A. Saeed. 'The Muslim Communities in Australia: The Building of a Community'. In *Muslim Minorities in the West: Visible and Invisible*, ed. Yvonne Yazbeck Haddad and Jane I. Smith. Lanham, MD: Altamira Press, 2002.

Johns, A. H. and A. Saeed. 'Nurcholish Madjid and the Interpretation of the Qurʾan: Religious Pluralism and Tolerance'. In *Modern Muslim Intellectuals & the Qurʾan*, ed. Suha Taji-Farouki. Oxford: Oxford University Press, 2004.

Juynboll, G. H. A. *Muslim Tradition: Studies in Chronology, Provenance, and Authorship of Early* Hadith. Cambridge: Cambridge University Press, 1983.

Juynboll, G. H. A. 'Some *Isnad* – Analytical Methods Illustrated on the Basis of Several Women-Demeaning Sayings from *Hadith* Literature', *Al-Qantara: Revista de Estudos Árabes*, 10 (2) (1989): 343–84. Reprinted in *Studies on the Origins and Uses of Islamic Hadith*. Aldershot: Variorum-Ashgate, 1996.

Kamali, Mohammad Hashim. *Islamic Law in Malaysia: Issues and Developments*. Kuala Lumpur: Ilmiah, 2000.

Kazi, Mazhar U. *A Treasury of Ahadith*. Jeddah: Abul-Qasim, 1992.

Khan, Muqtedar. 'Constructing the American Muslim Community.' In *Becoming American*, ed. J. Esposito, Y. Haddad and J. Smith. Oxford: Oxford University Press, 2001.

Khatibi, Abdelkebir and Mohamed Sijelmassi. *The Splendour of Islamic Calligraphy*. London: Thames and Hudson, 2001.

Khuri, Richard K. *Freedom, Modernity, and Islam: Toward a Creative Synthesis*. Modern Intellectual and Political History of the Middle East. Syracuse: Syracuse University Press, 1998.

Klein, Walter C. *Abuʾl-Hasan ʿAli ibn Ismaʿil al-Ashʿariʾs al-Ibanah ʿan Usul ad-Diyanah (The Elucidation of Islamʾs Foundation): A Translation with Introduction and Notes*. American Oriental Series 19. 1940. New York: Kraus, 1967.

Koya, P. K. 'Introduction'. In *Hadith and Sunnah: Ideals and Realities*, ed. P. K. Koya. Kuala Lumpur: Islamic Book Trust, 1996, pp. xi–xxii.

Koya, P. K., ed. *Hadith and Sunnah: Ideals and Realities*. Kuala Lumpur: Islamic Book Trust, 1996.

Lambton, Ann K. S. *State and Government in Medieval Islam: An Introduction to the Study of Islamic Political Theory: The Jurists*. London Oriental Series 36. Oxford: Oxford University Press, 1981.

Leaman, Oliver. *Averroes and His Philosophy*. Oxford: Clarendon, 1988.

Lewis, Bernard, *The Middle East*, London: Weidenfeld, 1995.

McAuliffe, Jane Dammen et al., eds. *Encyclopaedia of the Qur'an*. Leiden: Brill, 2002.

Madkour, Ibrahim. 'Al-Farabi'. In *A History of Muslim Philosophy: With Short Accounts of Other Disciplines and the Modern Renaissance in Muslim Lands*. 2 vols, ed. M. M. Sharif. Wiesbaden: Harrassowitz, 1963–6, vol. 1, pp. 450–68.

Mahmasani, Subhi Rajab. *Falsafat al-Tashri fi al-Islam: The Philosophy of Jurisprudence in Islam*. Trans. Farhat J. Ziadeh. Leiden: Brill, 1961.

Mahmasani, Subhi Rajab. *Turath al-Khulafa' al-Rashidin fi al-Fiqh wa-al-Qada'*. Beirut: Dar al-Ilm lil-Malayin, 1984.

Makki, Abu Talib Muhammad al-. *Qut al-Qulub*. Vol. 1. Cairo: Azhar University Press, 1932.

Malik ibn Anas, *Al-Muwatta of Imam Malik ibn Anas: The First Formulation of Islamic Law*. Rev. and trans. Aisha Abdurrahman Bewley. Islamic Classical Library Edition, 1991. Inverness: Madinah, 2001.

Malik, Hafeez. *Sir Sayyid Ahmad Khan and Muslim Modernization in India and Pakistan*. Studies in Oriental Culture 15. New York: Columbia University Press, 1980.

Maududi, Sayyid Abul A'la. *A Short History of the Revivalist Movements in Islam*. Lahore: n.p., 1963.

Mawdudi, Abul A'la. *Towards Understanding the Qur'an*. Trans. and ed. Zafar Ishaq Ansari. 7 vols. Trans. of *Tafhim al-Qur'an*. Leicester: Islamic Foundation, 1988–2001.

Mernissi, Fatima. *The Veil and the Male Elite: A Feminist Interpretation of Women's Rights in Islam*. Trans. Mary Jo Lakeland. New York: Perseus, 1991.

Nadwi, al-Sayyid Abi al-Hasan Ali al-. *Madha Khasira al-Alam bi-Inhitat al-Muslimin*. 2nd ed. Cairo: Maktabat Dar al-Uruba, 1379 [1959].

Nasr, Seyyed Hossein. 'Sadr al-Din Shirazi (Mulla Sadra)'. In *A History of Muslim Philosophy: With Short Accounts of Other Disciplines and the Modern Renaissance in Muslim Lands*. 2 vols, ed. M. M. Sharif. Wiesbaden: Harrassowitz, 1963–6, vol. 2, pp. 932–61.

Nasr, Seyyed Hossein. 'The School of Ispahan'. In *A History of Muslim Philosophy: With Short Accounts of Other Disciplines and the Modern Renaissance in Muslim Lands*. 2 vols, ed. M. M. Sharif. Wiesbaden: Harrassowitz, 1963–6, vol. 2, pp. 904–32.

Nasr, Seyyed Hossein. *Three Muslim Sages: Avicenna, Suhrawardi, Ibn 'Arabi*. Cambridge, MA: Harvard University Press, 1964.

Nasr, Seyyed Hossein. *Ideals and Realities of Islam*. London: Allen & Unwin, 1966.

Nasr, Seyyed Hossein. *Traditional Islam in the Modern World*. London: Kegan Paul, 1987.

Nasr, Seyyed Hossein, ed. *Islamic Spirituality Manifestations*. World Spirituality 20. New York: SCM, 1991.

Nasr, Seyyed Hossein. 'Prelude: The Spiritual Significance of the Rise and Growth of the Sufi Orders'. In *Islamic Spirituality Manifestations*, ed. S. H. Nasr. World Spirituality 20. New York: SCM, 1991–5.

Al-Nawawi. *Forty Hadith Qudsi*. Selected and trans. Ezzeddin Ibrahim and Denys Johnson-Davies. N.p.: Millat Book Center, n.d.

Nizami, K. A. 'The Naqshbandiyyah Order'. In *Islamic Spirituality Manifestations*, ed. S. H. Nasr. World Spirituality 20. New York: SCM, 1991, pp. 162–93.

Nizami, K. A. 'The Qadiriyyah Order'. In *Islamic Spirituality Manifestations*, ed. S. H. Nasr. World Spirituality 20. New York: SCM, 1991, pp. 6–25.

Pearl, David and Werner Menski. *Muslim Family Law*. 3rd ed. London: Sweet and Maxwell, 1998.

Peters, F. E. *Aristotle and the Arabs: The Aristotelian Tradition in Islam*. New York University Studies in Near Eastern Civilization 1. New York: New York University Press, 1968.

Peters, F. E. *Judaism, Christianity, and Islam: The Classical Texts and Their Interpretation*. Vol. 2. Princeton: Princeton University Press, 1990.

Peters, Rudolf. 'Idjtihad and Taqlid in 18th and 19th Century Islam', *Die Welt des Islams*, NS 20 (3–4) (1980): 131–45.

Philips, Abu Ameenah Bilal. *The Evolution of Fiqh: Islamic Law & the Madh-habs*. Riyadh: Tawheed, 1988.

Qurtubi, Abu al-Abbas Ahmad ibn Umar al-. *Talkhis Sahih al-Imam Muslim ibn Hajjaj al-Qushayri al-Naysaburi*. Vol. 1. Cairo: Dar al-Salam, 1414 [1993].

Rahman, Fazlur. 'Social Change and Early Sunnah', *Islamic Studies*, 2 (2) (June 1963): 206.

Rahman, Fazlur. 'Ibn Sina'. In *A History of Muslim Philosophy: With Short Accounts of Other Disciplines and the Modern Renaissance in Muslim Lands*. 2 vols, ed. M. M. Sharif. Wiesbaden: Harrassowitz, 1963–6, vol. 1, pp. 480–506.

Rahman, Fazlur. 'The Impact of Modernity on Islam', *Islamic Studies*, 5 (2) (June 1966): 112–28.

Rahman, Fazlur. *Islam*. Chicago: University of Chicago Press, 1966, 1979.

Rahman, Fazlur. 'Islamic Modernism: Its Scope, Method and Alternatives', *International Journal of Middle East Studies*, 1 (1970): 317–33.

Rahman, Fazlur. 'Shah Waliyullah and Iqbal: The Philosophers of the Modern Age', *Islamic Studies*, 13 (1974): 225–34.

Rahman, Fazlur. 'Towards Reformulating the Methodology of Islamic Law', *New York University Journal of International Law and Politics*, 12 (2) (Fall 1979): 205–22.

Rahman, Fazlur. *Major Themes of the Qur'an*. Minneapolis: Bibliotheca Islamica, 1980.

Rahman, Fazlur. *Islam and Modernity: Transformation of an Intellectual Tradition*. Publications of the Center for Middle Eastern Studies 15. Chicago: University of Chicago Press, 1982.

Rahman, Fazlur. 'My Belief in Action'. In *The Courage of Conviction*, ed. Phillip L. Berman. New York: Dodd, 1985.

Rahman, Fazlur. 'The Living Sunnah and *Al-Sunnah wa'l Jama'ah*'. In *Hadith and Sunnah: Ideals and Realities*, ed. P. K. Koya. Kuala Lumpur: Islamic Book Trust, 1996, pp. 129–89.

Rahman, Fazlur. *Major Themes of the Qur'an*. 2nd ed. 1989. Kuala Lumpur: Islamic Book Trust, 1999.

Rahman, Fazlur. *Revival and Reform in Islam: A Study of Islamic Fundamentalism*, ed. Ebrahim Moosa. Oxford: Oneworld, 2000.

Ramadan, Said. *Islamic Law: Its Scope and Equity*. London: Macmillan, 1961.

Ramadan, Tariq. *To Be a European Muslim*. Leicester: Islamic Foundation, 1999.

Rida, Muhammad Rashid. *Tafsir al-Qur'an al-Hakim, al-Shahir bi-Tafsir al-Manar*. 2nd ed. 12 vols. Beirut: Dar al-Ma'rifa, 1973.

Rippin, Andrew, ed. *Approaches to the History of the Interpretation of the Qur'an*. Oxford: Clarendon; New York: Oxford University Press, 1988.

Rippin, Andrew. *Muslims: Their Religious Beliefs and Practices*. Vol. I. London: Routledge, 1990.

Robinson, Francis, ed. *The Cambridge Illustrated History of the Islamic World*. New York: Cambridge University Press, 1996.

Saeed, Abdullah. 'Rethinking Citizenship Rights of Non-Muslims in an Islamic State: Rashid al-Ghannushi's Contribution to the Evolving Debate', *Journal of Islam and Christian–Muslim Relations*, 10 (3) (1999): 307–23.

Saeed, Abdullah. 'Jihad and Violence: Changing Understanding of Jihad among Muslims'. In *Terrorism and Violence*, ed. Tony Coady and Michael O'Keefe. Melbourne: Melbourne University Press, 2002, pp. 72–86.

Saeed, Abdullah. 'The Charge of Distortion of Jewish and Christian Scriptures: Tension between the Popular Muslim View and the Qur'anic/Tafsir View', *The Muslim World*, 92 (3&4) (Fall 2002): 419–36.

Saeed, Abdullah. 'The Official Ulema and Religious Legitimacy of the Modern Nation State'. In *Islamic and Political Legitimacy*, ed. Shahram Akbarzadeh and Abdullah Saeed. London: RoutledgeCurzon, 2003, pp. 14–28.

Saeed, Abdullah. 'Fazlur Rahman: A Framework for Interpreting the Ethico-Legal Content of the Qur'an'. In *Modern Muslim Intellectuals & the Qur'an*, ed. Suha Taji-Farouki. Oxford: Oxford University Press, 2004.

Saeed, Abdullah. 'Islamic Banking and Finance: In Search of an Islamic but Pragmatic Model'. In *Islamic Perspectives on the New Millenium*, ed. Virginia Hooker and Amin Saikal. Singapore: Institute of Southeast Asian Studies, 2004.

Saeed, Abdullah. 'Qur'an: Tradition of Scholarship and Interpretation', 'Qur'an: Tradition of Scholarship and Interpretation'. In *Encyclopedia of Religion*. Farmington, MI: Thomson Gale, 2005.

Saeed, Abdullah (ed.). *Approaches to the Qur'an in Contemporary Indonesia*. Oxford: Oxford University Press, 2005.

Saeed, Abdullah. *Interpreting the Qur'an: Towards a Contemporary Approach*. London and New York: Routledge, 2006.

Saeed, Abdullah. 'Contextualizing'. In *The Blackwell Companion to the Qur'an*, ed. A. Rippin. Oxford: Blackwell, 2006, pp. 36–50.

Saeed, Abdullah and Hassan Saeed. *Freedom of Religion, Apostasy and Islam*. Aldershot: Ashgate, 2004.

Safi, Omid, 'Introduction'. In *Progressive Muslims on Justice, Gender, and Pluralism*, ed. Omid Safi. Oxford: Oneworld, 2003.

Schacht, Joseph. *An Introduction to Islamic Law*. Oxford: Clarendon, 1964.

Schwarz, Adam. *A Nation in Waiting: Indonesia's Search for Stability*. Sydney: Allen and Unwin, 1994.

Sells, Michael, trans. *Approaching the Qur'an: The Early Revelations*. Ashland: White Cloud, 1999.

Sharif, M. M., ed. *A History of Muslim Philosophy: With Short Accounts of Other Disciplines and the Modern Renaissance in Muslim Lands*. 2 vols. Wiesbaden: Harrassowitz, 1963–6.

Sheikh, M. Saeed. 'Al-Ghazali: Metaphysics'. In *A History of Muslim Philosophy:*

With Short Accounts of Other Disciplines and the Modern Renaissance in Muslim Lands. 2 vols, ed. M. M. Sharif. Wiesbaden: Harrassowitz, 1963–6, vol. 1, pp. 581–616.

Siddiqi, Bakhtyar Husain. 'Ibn Tufail'. In *A History of Muslim Philosophy: With Short Accounts of Other Disciplines and the Modern Renaissance in Muslim Lands.* 2 vols, ed. M. M. Sharif. Wiesbaden: Harrassowitz, 1963–6, vol. 1, pp. 526–40.

Siddiqi, Muhammad Zubayr. *Hadith Literature: Its Origin, Development & Special Features.* Ed. and rev. Abdal-Hakim Murad. Rev. ed. Cambridge: Islamic Texts Society, 1993.

Siddiqi, Muhammad Zubayr. 'Hadith – A Subject of Keen Interest'. In *Hadith and Sunnah: Ideals and Realities,* ed. P. K. Koya. Kuala Lumpur: Islamic Book Trust, 1996, pp. 3–22.

Siddiqi, Muhammad Zubayr. 'The Sciences and Critique of Hadith (*'Ulum al-Hadith*)'. In *Hadith and Sunnah: Ideals and Realities,* ed. P. K. Koya. Kuala Lumpur: Islamic Book Trust, 1996, pp. 72–102.

Siddiqi, Muhammad Zubayr. *The Hadith for Beginners: An Introduction to Major Hadith Works and Their Compilers.* New Delhi: Goodword, 2001.

Tabari, Abu Ja'far Muhammad b. Jarir al-. *The Commentary on the Qur'an,* ed. W. F. Madelung and A. Jones. Oxford: Oxford University Press, 1987.

Tabataba'i, Muhammad Husayn. *The Qur'an in Islam: Its Impact and Influence on the Life of Muslims.* London: Zahra, 1987.

Trimingham, J. Spencer. *The Sufi Orders in Islam.* Oxford: Oxford University Press, 1998.

Tritton, A. S. *Muslim Theology.* James G. Forlong Fund 23. [London]: Luzac for Royal Asiatic Society, 1947.

Troll, Christian W. *Sayyid Ahmad Khan: A Reinterpretation of Muslim Theology.* New Delhi: Vikas, 1978.

Tufi, Najm al-Din al-. *Risalat al-Imam al-Tufi fi Taqdim al-Maslaha fi'l-Mu'amalat ala al-Nass.* Annotated by Jamal Din al-Qasimi al-Dimashqi. Ed. Mahmud Abu Rayya. Cairo: n.p., 1966.

Vikor, Knut S. *Sufi and Scholar on the Desert Edge: Muhammad b. Ali al-Sanusi and His Brotherhood.* Series in Islam and Society in Africa. London: Hurst, 1995.

Von Denffer, Ahmad. *'Ulum al-Qur'an: An Introduction to the Sciences of the Qur'an.* Rev. ed. Markfield: Islamic Foundation, 2000.

Wadud-Muhsin, Amina. *Qur'an and Woman.* Kuala Lumpur: Fajar Bakti, 1988.

Wahhab, Muhammad bin Abd al. *Kitab at-Tauhid.* Trans. by Compilation and Research Department, Dar-us-Salam. New York, NY: Dar-us-Salam Publications, 1996.

Wali Allah, Shah, *The Conclusive Argument from God: Shah Wali Allah of Delhi's Hujjat Allah al-Baligha.* Trans. Marcia K. Hermansen. Islamic Philosophy, Theology, and Science 25. Leiden: Brill, 1996.

Watt, W. Montgomery. *Islamic Philosophy and Theology: An Extended Survey.* 2nd ed. Edinburgh: Edinburgh University Press, 1985.

Watt, W. Montgomery. *The Majesty that Was Islam: The Islamic World 661–1100.* 1974. London: Sidgwick; New York: St Martin's, 1990.

Watt, W. Montgomery, trans. *Islamic Creeds: A Selection.* Edinburgh: Edinburgh University Press, 1994.

Watt, W. Montgomery. *The Formative Period of Islamic Thought*. Oxford: Oneworld, 1998.

Waugh, Earle H. 'The Legacies of Fazlur Rahman for Islam in America', *The American Journal of Islamic Social Sciences*, 16 (3) (Fall 1999).

Zayadan, Jurji. *History of Islamic Civilization: Umayyads and 'Abbasids*. Trans. D. S. Margoliouth. 1907. New Delhi: Kitab Bhavan, 1981.

Zuhayli, Wahba al-. *Usul al-Fiqh al-Islami*. Damascus: Dar al-Fikr, 1417 [1996].

Web-based resources

Aga Khan University, *The Future of the Aga Khan University: Evolution of a Vision: Report of the Chancellor's Commission*, Aga Khan University, 4 July 2005 <http://www.aku.edu/creport/>.

Al-Akiti, M. Afifi. 'Kissing the Thumbs, etc. during Adhan?' Fatwa. *Living Islam: Islamic Tradition*. 22 June 2005 <http://www.livingislam.org/maa/ktda_e.html>.

Al-Busiri, Sharafuddin Muhammad. 'Al-Burda: The Prophet's Mantle'. Trans. Thoraya Mahdi Allam. Iqra Islamic Publications. 7 September 2005 <http://www.iqra.net/qasaaid1/burda>.

Algar, Hamid and K. A. Nizami. 'Nakshbandiyya'. In *Encyclopaedia of Islam Online*. 12 vols, ed. P. J. Bearman et al. Leiden: Brill, 2004. 17 June 2005. <http://www.encislam.brill.nl>.

Al-Munajjid, Muhammad Salih. 'Ruling on Music, Singing and Dancing'. Fatwa. Ref. no. 5000. *Islam Q&A*. 12 September 2005

Amini, Ibrahim. *Al-Imam al-Mahdi: The Just Leader of Humanity*. Trans. Abdulaziz Sachedina. Ahlul Bayt Digital Islamic Library Project. 1 November 2005 <http://al-islam.org/mahdi/nontl/>.

Annemarie Schimmel. The Institute of Ismaili Studies. 19 June 2005 <http://www.iis.ac.uk/research/academic_publications/schimmel.htm>.

Arnaldez, R. 'Al-Insan al-Kamil'. In *Encyclopaedia of Islam Online*. 12 vols, ed. P. J. Bearman et al. Leiden: Brill, 2004. 17 June 2005 <http://www.encislam.brill.nl/>.

Arnaldez, R. 'Falsafa'. In *Encyclopaedia of Islam Online*. 12 vols, ed. P. J. Bearman et al. Leiden: Brill, 2004. 17 June 2005 <http://www.encislam.brill.nl/>.

Ates, A. 'Ibn al-'Arabi'. In *Encyclopaedia of Islam Online*. 12 vols, ed. P. J. Bearman et al. Leiden: Brill, 2004. 17 June 2005 <http://www.encislam.brill.nl/>.

Bearman, P. J. et al., eds. *Encyclopaedia of Islam Online*. 12 vols. Leiden: Brill, 2004. 17 June 2005 <http://www.encislam.brill.nl/>.

Blois, F. C. de. 'Zindik'. In *Encyclopaedia of Islam Online*. 12 vols, ed. P. J. Bearman et al. Leiden: Brill, 2004. 17 June 2005 <http://www.encislam.brill.nl/>.

Cahen, C. L. and L. Gardet. 'Kasb'. In *Encyclopaedia of Islam Online*. 12 vols, ed. P. J. Bearman et al. Leiden: Brill, 2004. 17 June 2005 <http://www.encislam.brill.nl/>.

Cobb, P. M. ''Umar (II) b. 'Abd al-'Aziz'. In *Encyclopaedia of Islam Online*. 12 vols, ed. P. J. Bearman et al. Leiden: Brill, 2004. 17 June 2005 <http://www.encislam.brill.nl/>.

Craig, Edward, ed. *Routledge Encyclopedia of Philosophy Online*. Ver. 2.0. 2005. London: Routledge. 12 September 2005 <http://www.rep.routledge.com>.

Damrel, David. 'The Religious Roots of Conflict: Russia and Chechnya', *Religious Studies News*, 10 (3) (September 1995): 10. 18 June 2005 <http://www.iol.ie/~afifi/Articles/chechnya.htm>.

Encyclopaedia Britannica. 'Deoband School'. In *Encyclopaedia Britannica*, 2006. Encyclopaedia Britannica Premium Service. 24 Feb. 2006 <http://www.britannica.com/eb/article-9029970>.

Ess, J. Van, 'Kadiriyya'. In *Encyclopaedia of Islam Online*. 12 vols, ed. P. J. Bearman et al. Leiden: Brill, 2004. 17 June 2005. <http://www.encislam.brill.nl>.

Ghannouchi, Rachid. 'The Conflict Between the West and Islam, the Tunisian Case: Reality and Prospects: Chatham House'. Royal Institute of International Affairs. Chatham House, London. 9 May 1995. Trans. Azzam Tamimi. 15 September 2005 <http://www.ghannouchi.net/chatham.htm>.

Ghannoushi, Rached. 'IntraView: With Tunisian Sheikh Rached Ghannoushi'. 10 February 1998. 12 September 2005 <http://msanews.mynet.net/intra2.html>.

Godlas, Alan. 'Sufism, the West, and Modernity'. In *Sufism, Sufis, and Sufi Orders: Sufism's Many Paths*. Department of Religion, University of Georgia. 19 June 2005 <http://www.uga.edu/islam/sufismwest.html>.

Hoffman, Valerie J. 'Ibadi Islam: An Introduction'. In *Sufism, Sufis, and Sufi Orders: Sufism's Many Paths*. Department of Religion, University of Georgia. 15 September 2005 <http://www.uga.edu/islam/ibadis.html>.

Humphreys, R. S. et al. 'Tarika'. In *Encyclopaedia of Islam Online*. 12 vols, ed. P. J. Bearman et al. Leiden: Brill, 2004. 17 June 2005 <http://www.encislam.brill.nl/>.

Hunwick, John. 'Africa and Islamic Revival: Historical and Contemporary Perspectives'. Online posting. 14 June 1996. MSA News. Department of Religion, University of Georgia. 19 June 2005 <http://www.uga.edu/islam/hunwick.html>.

'Islamic Art'. Def. *WorldImages.com: Glossary of Art Terms and Definitions*. 10 September 2005 <http://www.worldimages.com/art_glossary.php>.

Islamic Art. March 2002. Sala@m. 10 September 2005 <http://www.salaam.co.uk/themeofthemonth/march02_index.php?l=0>.

Laoust, H. 'Ahmad b. Hanbal'. In *Encyclopaedia of Islam Online*. 12 vols, ed. P. J. Bearman et al. Leiden: Brill, 2004. 17 June 2005. <http://www.encislam.brill.nl>.

Last, D. M. 'Uthman b. Fudi'. In *Encyclopaedia of Islam Online*. 12 vols, ed. P. J. Bearman et al. Leiden: Brill, 2004. 17 June 2005. <http://www.encislam.brill.nl>.

Levi Della Vida, G. 'Kharidjites'. In *Encyclopaedia of Islam Online*. 12 vols, ed. P. J. Bearman et al. Leiden: Brill, 2004. 17 June 2005. <http://www.encislam.brill.nl>.

Levi, Albert William. 'Hellenistic and Roman Philosophy (from Philosophy, History of'. In *Encyclopaedia Britannica Deluxe Edition 2004 CD-ROM*, ed. McCudden. CD-ROM. Disc 2. Ver. 2004. Chicago, IL: Encyclopaedia Britannica, 2004.

Levi, Albert William. 'Nature of Philosophy and the Writing of Its History (from Philosophy, History of)'. In *Encyclopaedia Britannica Deluxe Edition 2004 CD-ROM*, ed. McCudden. CD-ROM. Disc 2. Ver. 2004. Chicago, IL: Encyclopaedia Britannica, 2004.

Levi, Albert William. 'The Pre-Socratic Philosophers (from Philosophy, History of)'. In *Encyclopaedia Britannica Deluxe Edition 2004 CD-ROM*, ed. McCudden. CD-ROM. Disc 2. Ver. 2004. Chicago, IL: Encyclopaedia Britannica, 2004.

Levi, Albert William. 'The Seminal Thinkers of Greek Philosophy (from Philosophy, History of)'. In *Encyclopaedia Britannica Deluxe Edition 2004 CD-ROM*, ed. McCudden. CD-ROM. Disc 2. Ver. 2004. Chicago, IL: Encyclopaedia Britannica, 2004.

Lory, P. 'Shadhiliyya'. In *Encyclopaedia of Islam Online*. 12 vols, ed. P. J. Bearman et al. Leiden: Brill, 2004. 17 June 2005 <http://www.encislam.brill.nl>.

McCudden, Mary Rose, ed. *Encyclopaedia Britannica Deluxe Edition 2004 CD-ROM*. CD-ROM. Disc 2. Ver. 2004. Chicago, IL: Encyclopaedia Britannica, 2004.

Madelung, W. 'Imama'. In *Encyclopaedia of Islam Online*. 12 vols, ed. P.J. Bearman et al. Leiden: Brill, 2004. 17 June 2005. <http://www.encislam.brill.nl>.

Mahdi, Muhsin S. 'The New Wisdom: Synthesis of Philosophy and Mysticism (from Islam)'. In *Encyclopaedia Britannica Deluxe Edition 2004 CD-ROM*, ed. McCudden. CD-ROM Disc 2. Ver. 2004. Chicago, IL: Encyclopaedia Britannica, 2004.

Mahdi, Muhsin S. 'The Teachings of Avicenna (from Islam)'. In *Encyclopaedia Britannica Deluxe Edition 2004 CD-ROM*, ed. McCudden. CD-ROM. Disc 2. Ver. 2004. Chicago, IL: Encyclopaedia Britannica, 2004.

Mahdi, Muhsin S. 'The Western Philosophers (from Islam)'. In *Encyclopaedia Britannica Deluxe Edition 2004 CD-ROM*, ed. McCudden. CD-ROM. Disc 2. Ver. 2004. Chicago, IL: Encyclopaedia Britannica, 2004.

'Music Art Sciences'. *Sufi Order-Tariqat Gul Nur Jihaniyya Radiant Valley Association*. 1998. 16 June 2005 <http://www.angelfire.com/ca2/mysticalpathway nurhu/MusicArtSciences.html>.

Nakamura, Kojiro. 'Al-Ghazali, Abu Hamid (1058–1111)'. In *Routledge Encyclopedia of Philosophy Online*. Ver. 2.0. 2005 ed. E. Craig London: Routledge. 12 September 2005. <http://www.rep. routledge.com/article/H028>.

Nasr, Seyyed Hossein. 'Mystical Philosophy in Islam'. In *Routledge Encyclopedia of Philosophy Online*. Ver. 2.0. 2005 ed. E. Craig London: Routledge. 12 September 2005. <http://www.rep. routledge.com/article/H004>.

Peace X Peace, 4 July 2005 <https://www.peacexpeace.org/bookrecs.htm>.

Peskes, Esther and W. Ende. 'Wahhabiyya'. In *Encyclopaedia of Islam Online*. 12 vols, ed. P. J. Bearman et al. Leiden: Brill, 2004. 17 June 2005. <http://www.encislam.brill.nl>.

Practices in the Naqshbandi Sufi Way. 18 June 2005 <http://naqshbandi.org/dhikr/frmdawra.htm>.

Racy, Ali Jihad and Jack Logan. 'Arab Music: Part One'. *Music in Our World*. San Diego State University. 16 July 2005 <http://trumpet.sdsu.edu/M345/Arab_Music1.html>.

Reda, Nevin. 'What Would the Prophet Do? The Islamic Basis for Female-Led Prayer'. *Muslim Wakeup!* 10 March 2005. 24 June 2005 <http://www.muslimwakeup.com/main/archives/2005/03/women_imamat.php>.

'Residing in the Land of Unbelievers', *Allaahuakbar.net*. 14 July 2005 <http://www.allaahuakbar.net/scholars/uthaymeen/residing_in_land_of_unbelievers.htm>.

Robson, J. 'Bukhari, Muhammad b. Isma'il'. In *Encyclopaedia of Islam Online*.

12 vols, ed. P. J. Bearman et al. Leiden: Brill, 2004. 17 June 2005. <http://www.encislam.brill.nl>.

Sabri, Mustafa. 'A Topic of Dispute in Islam: Music'. 1910. Trans. Muaz Özyigit. *Anadolu* 5(4) (1995). 16 June 2005 <http://www.wakeup.org/anadolu/05/4/mustafa_sabri_en.html>.

'Shaikh Muhammad Ibn Saalih al-Uthaymeen', *Allaahuakbar.net*. 14 July 2005 <http://www.allaahuakbar.net/scholars/uthaymeen/>.

Shakir, Zaid. 'An Examination of the Issue of Female Prayer Leadership'. *Progressive Muslim Union of North America*. 23 March 2005. 24 June 2005 <http://www.pmuna.org/archives/female_imam-3.pdf>.

Shaykh Muhammad Hisham Kabbani. 18 June 2005 <http://www.naqshbandi.org/about/Sh_Kabbani_bio.htm>.

Siddiqi, Muzammil H. 'Songs and Music'. Fatwa. *Pakistan Link*. 1997. 12 September 2005 <http://pakistanlink.com/religion/97/re02-21-97.html>.

'Singing & Music: Islamic View'. Fatwa. *IslamOnline.net*. 13 January 2004. 12 September 2005 <http://www.islamonline.net>.

Tabatabai, Muhammad Husayn. *Shi'a*. Trans. Sayyid Husayn Nasr. Qum: Ansarian, circa 1971. 30 October 2005 <http://www.balagh.net/english/shia/shia/>.

'The Two Festivals (Eids)'. *Sahih Bukhari Book Fifteen*. Trans. M. Muhsin Khan. MSA-USC. 20 September 2005 <http://www.usc.edu/dept/MSA/fundamentals/hadithsunnah/bukhari/015.sbt.html>.

Van Ess, J. 'Kadiriyya'. In *Encyclopaedia of Islam Online*. 12 vols, ed. P. J. Bearman et al. Leiden: Brill, 2004. 17 June 2005. <http://www.encislam.brill.nl>.

Watt, W. Montgomery. 'Ash'ariyya'. In *Encyclopaedia of Islam Online*. 12 vols, ed. P. J. Bearman et al. Leiden: Brill, 2004 <http://www.encislam.brill.nl>.

Yilmaz, Hülya. *Ahmed Ziyauddin Gumush-khanewi*. 18 June 2005 <http://gumushkhanawidargah.8m.com/silsile32.html>. Trans. from *Dünden Bugüne Gümüshànevî Mektebi*. Istanbul: Seha Yayinevi, 1997.

Index

Fifty Key Figures in Islam
Roy Jackson

If you would like to learn more about the Muslim culture, people and its teachings, then this is the perfect resource for you. Roy Jackson explores the lives and thoughts of fifty influential figures in Islam and surveys a heritage which spans 1500 years. *Fifty Key Figures in Islam* could not have come at a more interesting time in history.

Fully cross referenced, for each figure the book provides:

- Biographical details
- A presentation and analysis of their main ideas
- An account of their impact and influence within and, if appropriate, beyond the Islamic tradition
- List of major works and additional reading.

0–415–35468–4

Available at all good bookshops
For ordering and further information please visit www.routledge.com

Islam: The Basics

Colin Turner

With nearly 1500 rich years of history and culture to its name, Islam is one of the world's great faiths and, in modern times, the subject of increasingly passionate debate by believers and non-believers alike. *Islam: The Basics* is a concise and timely introduction to all aspects of Muslim belief and practice. Topics covered include:

- The Koran and its teachings
- The life of the Prophet Muhammad
- Women in Islam
- Sufism and Shi'ism
- Islam and the modern world
- Non-Muslim approaches to Islam

Complete with a glossary of terms, pointers to further reading and a chronology of key dates, *Islam: The Basics* provides an invaluable overview of the history and the contemporary relevance of this always fascinating and important subject.

0–415–34106–X

Available at all good bookshops
For ordering and further information please visit www.routledge.com

Related titles from Routledge

Classical Islam:
A sourcebook of religious literature

Edited and translated by Norman Calder,
Jawid Mojaddedi and Andrew Rippin

*A substantial and rich selection from key texts, together with clear and
helpful explanations of the literature and subjects discussed.*
**Gerald Hawting, Professor of the History of the Near and Middle East,
School of Oriental and African Studies, University of London**

This definitive sourcebook presents more than fifty authoritative new
translations of key Islamic texts. Edited and translated by three leading
specialists and clearly contextualized for introductory-level students, it
illustrates the growth of Islamic thought from its seventh-century origins,
through to the end of the medieval period. Eight thematically-organized
sections cover the Qur'an and its interpretation, the life of Muhammad,
hadīth, law, ritual, mysticism, and Islamic history. Among the selections
are Ibn 'Abbās's account of the heavenly journey; al-Taftāzānī on the
uncreatedness of the Qur'an as God's speech; al-Fārābī on the faculties of
the soul; and extracts from Rūmī's *Mathnawī*.
   Classical Islam includes a glossary, extensive bibliography and explanatory prefaces for each text. With many extracts translated here for the first
time into English, this is an essential resource for the study of early and
medieval Islam and its legacy.

ISBN10: 0–415–24032–8 (hbk)
ISBN10: 0–415–07693–5 (pbk)

ISBN13: 978–0–415–24032–1 (hbk)
ISBN13: 978–0–415–07693–7 (pbk)

Available at all good bookshops
For ordering and further information please visit:
www.routledge.com

Related titles from Routledge

Buddhist Thought
A Complete Introduction to the Indian Tradition

Paul Williams and Anthony Tribe

Though there is no shortage of introductions to Buddhism on the market, I found this one compelling reading, for the ideas are presented with logical cogency and stylistic clarity. The summary of the Buddha's own views would be hard to better.

Richard Gombrich, Balliol College, Oxford

Buddhist Thought guides the reader towards a richer understanding of the central concepts of classical Indian Buddhist thought, from the time of Buddha, to the latest scholarly perspectives and controversies. Abstract and complex ideas are made understandable by the authors' lucid style. Of particular interest is the up-to-date survey of Buddhist Tantra in India, a branch of Buddhism where strictly controlled sexual activity can play a part in the religious path. Williams' discussion of this controversial practice as well as of many other subjects makes *Buddhist Thought* crucial reading for all interested in Buddhism.

ISBN10: 0–415–20700–2 (hbk)
ISBN10: 0–415–20701–0 (pbk)

ISBN 13: 978–0–415–20700–3 (hbk)
ISBN 13: 978–0–415–20701–0 (pbk)

Available at all good bookshops
For ordering and further information please visit:
www.routledge.com

Related titles from Routledge

Jewish Thought

Oliver Leaman

Committed to the principle that 'There are no principles in Judaism,' Oliver Leaman's **Jewish Thought: An Introduction** *presents a fascinating overview of Jewish thought and sensibility from the organizing perspective that the commonalities of Jewish tradition consist in recurring 'arguments and controversies' that are rearticulated in new historical contexts across the generations. For a late modern audience whose affirmations and doubts are often both equally suspended and situated in such a way as to ironically play off each other, this book serves as a superb introduction to Judaism.*
Aryeh Botwinick, Professor of Political Science, Temple University, USA

This is a fresh and contemporary introduction to the Jewish faith, its philosophies and world views. Written by a leading figure in the field, it explores debates which have preoccupied Jewish thinkers over the centuries and examines their continuing influence in contemporary Judaism.

Jewish Thought surveys the central controversies in Judaism, including the protracted arguments within the religion itself. Topics range from the relations between Judaism and other religions, such as Islam and Christianity, to contemporary issues such as sex and gender and modernity. Central themes such as authority and obedience, the relations between Jewish and Greek thought, and the position and status of the State of Israel are also considered. The debates are further illuminated by reference to the Bible, as a profoundly realistic text in describing the long interaction between the Jews, their ancestors and God, as well as discussions about major thinkers, and passages from the ancient texts: the Mishnah, Talmud and Midrash.

Oliver Leaman's lively approach and light touch makes *Jewish Thought* ideal reading for anyone who wants to understand more about the Jewish faith and its outlook, past and present.

ISBN10: 0–415–37425–1 (hbk)
ISBN10: 0–415–37426–X (pbk)

ISBN13: 978–0–415–37425–5 (hbk)
ISBN13: 978–0–415–37426–2 (pbk)

Available at all good bookshops
For ordering and further information please visit:
www.routledge.com

Related titles from Routledge

Muslims
Their Religious Beliefs and Practices

Third edition

Andrew Rippin

Praise for previous editions:

'Every page of it is a delight. . . . not sacrificing subtlety and historical accuracy and a highly readable style.'
Vera B. Moreen, *Department of Religious Studies, Franklin & Marshall College*

'. . . probably the best general account of what Muslims believe.'
Robert Irwin, *Guardian*

This concise and authoritative guide provides a complete survey of Islamic history and thought from its formative period to the present day. It examines the unique elements which have combined to form Islam, in particular the Qu'ran and the influence of Muhammad, and traces the ways in which these sources have interacted historically to create Muslim theology and law, as well as the alternative visions of Islam found in Shi'ism and Sufism.

Combining core source materials with coverage of current scholarship and of recent events in the Islamic world, Andrew Rippin introduces this hugely diverse and widespread religion in a succinct, challenging and refreshing way. Using a distinctive critical approach which promotes engagement with key issues, from fundamentalism and women's rights to problems of identity and modernity, it is ideal for students seeking to understand Muslims and their faith.

The improved and expanded third edition now contains brand new sections on twenty-first century developments, from the Taliban to Jihad and Al-Qaeda, and includes updated references throughout.

Library of Religious Beliefs and Practices
Series editors: John Hinnells and the late Ninian Smart

ISBN10: 0–415–34882–X (hbk)
ISBN10: 0–415–34888–9 (pbk)

ISBN13: 978–0–415–34882–9 (hbk)
ISBN13: 978–0–415–34888–1 (pbk)

Related titles from Routledge

Interpreting the Qur'an
Towards a contemporary approach
Abdullah Saeed

'Debates among Muslims over the conception of the authority of the Qur'an underlie much of what is read about Islam in the popular media these days. This book by Abdullah Saeed will add a new voice to those debates and, as its impact is felt, broaden the popular conception of what Islam is all about today.' – *Andrew Rippin, University of Victoria, Canada*

How is the Qur'an - central to all Muslims societies - to be understood today in order to meet the needs of these societies? Abdullah Saeed, a distinguished Muslim scholar, explores the interpretation of the ethico-legal content of the Qur'an, whilst taking into consideration the changing nature of the modern world.

Saeed explores the current debates surrounding the interpretation of the Qur'an, and their impact on contemporary understanding of this sacred text. Discussing the text's relevance to modern issues without compromising the overall framework of the Qur'an and its core beliefs and practices, he proposes a fresh approach, which takes into account the historical and contemporary contexts of interpretation.

Inspiring healthy debate, this book is essential reading for students and scholars seeking a contemporary approach to the interpretation of the Qur'anic text.

ISBN10: 0–415–36537–6 (hbk)
ISBN10: 0–415–36538–4 (pbk)

ISBN13: 978–0–415–36537–6 (hbk)
ISBN13: 978–0–415–36538–3 (pbk)

Available at all good bookshops
For ordering and further information please visit:
www.routledge.com

Related titles from Routledge

Religions of South Asia

Edited by Sushil Mittal and Gene R. Thursby

South Asia is home to many of the world's most vibrant religious faiths. It is also one of the most dynamic and historically rich regions on earth, where changing political and social structures have caused religions to interact and hybridise in unique ways. This textbook introduces the contemporary religions of South Asia, from the indigenous religions such as the Hindu, Jain, Buddhist and Sikh traditions, to incoming influences such as Christianity, Judaism and Islam. In ten chapters, it surveys the nine leading belief systems of South Asia and explains their history, practices, values and worldviews. A final chapter helps students relate what they have learnt to religious theory, paving the way for future study.

   Entirely written by leading experts, *Religions of South Asia* combines solid scholarship with clear and lively writing to provide students with an accessible and comprehensive introduction. All chapters are specially designed to aid cross-religious comparison, following a standard format covering set topics and issues; the book reveals to students the core principles of each faith, compares it to neighbouring traditions, and its particular place in South Asian history and society. It is a perfect resource for all students of South Asia's diverse and fascinating faiths.

ISBN10: 0–415–22390–3 (hbk)
ISBN10: 0–415–22391–1 (pbk)

ISBN13: 978–0–415–22390–4 (hbk)
ISBN13: 978–0–415–22391–1 (pbk)

Available at all good bookshops
For ordering and further information please visit:
www.routledge.com